The Virgin Kiss

and Other Adventures

by Frank Scoblete

Research Services Unlimited
6845 Highway 90E, Suite 105
Daphne, Alabama 36526
www.rsucasinobooks.com

The Virgin Kiss and Other Adventures

Copyright © 2007, Frank Scoblete

Address all inquires to the publisher:

Research Services Unlimited
6845 Highway 90E, Suite 105
Daphne, Alabama 36526
1-251-625-6161
Email: **info@rsucasinobooks.com**
Manufactured in the United States of America

ISBN 10: 0-912177-17-9
ISBN 13: 978-0-912177-17-5
Cover design by Ben Jordan
Cover photo by Ted Levin: **www.pbase.com/automat42**

Page layout and typesetting by DeepNet Technologies: **www.DeepNetTech.com**

Publisher's Cataloging-in-Publication
(Provided by Quality Books, Inc.)

Scoblete, Frank.
    The virgin kiss : and other adventures / by Frank Scoblete.
    p. cm.
    LCCN 2007937404
    ISBN-13: 978-0-912177-17-5
    ISBN-10: 0-912177-17-9

    1. Scoblete, Frank. 2. Gamblers--United States--
Biography. 3. Family. 4. Teachers--New York (State)--
Biography. 5. Casinos--Anecdotes. 6. Haunted places--
Anecdotes 7. Kissing. 8. Clairvoyance.   I. Title.

HV6710.3.S36A3 2008   795'.092
                  QBI07-600285

The truth, the whole truth,
and nothing but the truth.

We start in the now
Go back to the then
Try to construct
Our lives again

Table of Contents

- Part One - Adventures in Mortality 1

- Part Two - Adventures in Mississippi 9

- Part Three - Adventure at Dinner 49

- Part Four - Adventure at Craps - July 2005............................71

- Part Five - Adventures in the Weird World - '73 to '84 95

- Part Six - Adventures in Fighting - '63 and Today.................169

- Part Seven - The Virgin Kiss: An Adventure in Love............175

- Part Eight - Adventures in Teaching.......................................211

- Part Nine - Adventures Growing Up in New York 273

- Part Ten - Adventures of Today 291

- Part Eleven - Epilogue...301

- Part One -
Adventures in Mortality

On January 9, 2007 I received the Last Rites at the Robert Wood Johnson University Hospital in New Brunswick, New Jersey. The priest who gave me the last rites was Father Donovan. Strangely enough a priest in my parish on Long Island is also a Father Donovan, although maybe there are many Father Donovans across the country.

I have no memory of the Last Rites. I have no memory of this particular Father Donovan. I have little memory of most of a 48-hour period when I was almost dead to the world.

On the morning of January 9, I had a Grand Mal seizure while visiting my son Greg and my daughter-in-law Dawn in New Jersey. Actually my son Greg was on a business trip to Las Vegas (lucky man!) and we were helping Dawn with our beautiful grandson, John Charles. My seizure happened around 1:45AM. I went to sleep on January 8, feeling just fine – actually feeling happy as could be having played with my grandson for two days – and woke up at noon, actually semi-woke-up, on January 9 in the ICU of the hospital.

Thankfully my wife, the beautiful A.P., woke up while I was having this seizure, saw me thrashing in bed uttering animal sounds and she immediately called the ambulance service when she couldn't rouse me.

One of the members of the ambulance service lives across the street from my son and daughter-in-law. I've been told that I thanked him in a very personal way by throwing up on him in the ambulance. "It was projectile vomit," A.P. later told me. Great, I can be the new secret weapon against the terrorists.

I have no memory of that, thankfully, but we did send a donation to the ambulance corps and a thank you letter to the guy I threw up on.

1

I have no memory of the ambulance ride or of my time in the emergency room or the nurses shoving a catheter into my penis or an air tube down my lungs. I have no memory of the CAT Scan, the MRI or the MRA or the MRV that were done either.

I came swimming up from the elsewhere to hear a doctor, Sotolongo, ask me to blink my eyes, which I did, and wiggle my toes, which I did, and squeeze her hands, which I did. Dr. Sotolongo seemed to be a million miles away in some distant world that my eyes were just barely seeing. I wasn't even quite sure of whom I was – my self-consciousness came back slowly in a world of haze.

The beautiful A.P.'s face floated behind the doctor and I then knew something before I even knew what was going on with me – something I guess I knew all my life – this beautiful person was the little girl in the projects, this was the girl in the school yard, this was the girl of my life, through my schooling, through a disastrous first marriage, through wild journeys into other dimensions, through witnessing murders, through a teaching career, right through to today where I gain great joy beating the casinos at their own games. My God, A.P. had been with me all the time – I knew this without really knowing it and she has no recollection of this at all – until she reads this book.

Floating in the haze behind her was my younger son Michael. A.P. explained to me what was happening, "You've had a seizure. You are going to be all right." I couldn't talk because of the ventilator in my lung. (*It's you; you were the one through it all. I see now, I see everything now. I want to tell you! I've got to talk to you! You've been in other worlds with me! I knew you before I knew you and you knew me!*") This book is going to talk to her because I haven't said anything since I once more became my conscious self. As I swam in semi-conscious waters, I could also feel something in my penis. But my head was swimming far away in the deep waters and I was mostly under those waters. Still it was good to see my wife and son.

And I was under again.

When next I awoke, the air hose and whatever else they had down my throat were out and the catheter was out of my penis. I have a dim recollection of them pulling those things out of me but strong drugs prevented me from feeling any pain – or much of anything. (*Let's hear it for strong life saving drugs!*) I was now in the ICU section of the hospital when I woke up. My nurse was Deborah, a friendly, highly professional nurse. I rewarded her by peeing in the bed three times. I couldn't control it because the catheter made it hard to keep everything back. I also found it impossible to actually keep myself awake for very long periods of time, like more than a minute – or remember much of what was said to me or what I said to others when I was awake. The beautiful A.P. tells me I talked quite a bit in the ICU but I don't remember anything except apologizing for peeing in the bed.

In the past, maybe three times, I had fainted because of dehydration but I had never had a seizure. The initial thought was that I had suffered a stroke. Poor A.P. had to grapple with the idea that I might be seriously impaired because of this stroke/seizure. Thankfully, the CAT scan, the MRI, MRV and MRA showed no new damage to my brain, although I did have evidence of an old injury (this I knew already) – in fact, my brain was in pretty good shape, all things considered.

My neurologist thinks it is possible that my "career" as a boxer in the mid-1960s might be the cause of the brain injury that the CAT scan shows. I put "career" in quotes because while I had 19 fights, largely against really poor amateur boxers, I did not have the will or the skill to become a polished amateur, much less a professional boxer.

I was just a stupid college student looking for the thrill of individual, competitive sport. I've written about some of my athletic experiences in baseball and basketball in other books, but my boxing "career" hasn't touched a page – until now that is.

My last fight, number 19, saw me take on an opponent who was far superior to me. In those days, I used to weigh about 135 pounds and I was in stupendous shape. I would run five days a week – 6 miles, 6 miles, 10 miles, 10 miles, and 12 miles. I could swim two miles at a clip. I could do one thousand sit-ups. I could do 100 pushups, 100 chin ups, 100 pull ups, 100 dips and I could do a pushup almost no one could do – slapping both of my hands behind my back. Those of you young enough to attempt it – give it a try. I could do 25 of them. Those of you who are too old – well, you can pretend that in your prime you might have been able to do one or two of these.

I thought of myself as superman. Yes, hubris reigned supreme in my little brain.

And hubris allowed me to step into the ring with opponent number 19, a Golden Gloves champion, and while I showed him that I did have a good punch and I did have fast hands and fast combinations, I didn't have the skill to really compete with an A-level fighter.

He came out for the first round and immediately ducked into one of my uppercuts. A big mistake some boxers make is ducking into punches before any punches are thrown. He did this. I'm guessing he figured I would not have much of an uppercut since very few amateur fighters have good uppercuts. I fooled him. I did have a good uppercut – with both hands too. He bent down into me and I unleashed a beauty, catching him full in the face. Down he went. I wish the fight had ended there.

It didn't.

He was up quickly, before the ref could even count. That was the big moment of the fight for me because when he got up the rest of round one was *he* whacking *me* around the ring.

After round one my nose bled profusely. In my previous fights I rarely got hit. I was usually too strong and too fast for my opponents, who – please remember this – were not very good. This guy was *very* good. While I was able to land some shots, he countered with better shots of his own. Indeed, in truth, in point of fact, in all honesty – he was beating the crap out of me.

Midway through the second round, I tried another uppercut – and he was ready. I was skidding somewhat along the ropes and I saw him duck low – actually he faked ducking low, figuring I'd figure I'd nail him with my uppercut again, and I dropped my right for the big uppercut. Instead of continuing down, he came up fast and hit me with a left hook before I could bring my right hand back up to protect that side of my face.

I could see all this in slow motion, too, which was really weird because even my memory of this shot to my unprotected face plays itself out in slow motion. I knew as the hook headed for my jaw that I was going to be hit hard. I kept thinking, *I won't be able to get my right hand up to protect my face. I won't be able to get my right hand up to protect my face.*

I was not able to get my right hand up to protect my face.

Then I was at the water cooler, blood pouring out of my nose. I was drinking water. Another boxer was next to me. "What happened?" I asked. "Was I knocked out?"

"No, no," he said. "You did really well in the third round. You battled him like a maniac. You lost a decision."

Third round? Lost a decision? Battled him like a maniac? I have no memory of the rest of that fight from the time the left hook headed for my jaw midway through the second round until I woke up at the water cooler – probably seven minutes of "no time." When I headed back to my fraternity house on campus, I knew I was in bad shape, light headed, nauseous, still bleeding from my nose and aware that I had stupidly been in the ring with someone who made me look like what I was – a total pretender when it came to being a boxer.

I checked myself into the infirmary. I was there for six days – with fever, chills, and the need to sleep. The very first hour they had to cauterize my nose – which entails burning away veins that won't behave themselves because they keep bleeding.

That fight taught me two valuable lessons – keep your right up until the opponent's head actually goes down – and screw fighting again. Having taken such a beating, having lost consciousness for at least seven minutes while my body must have been on automatic pilot, was enough to hammer home that a career in boxing was not for me – I would not become the white Muhammad Ali.

That fight might also be the reason for the signs of an old brain injury that the CAT scans pick up. I can't think of any other serious blows to the head I ever received, except for that wicked left hook, which did leave me unconscious even though my body seems to have worked on its own for those seven minutes of no time. Talk about the will to survival!

I don't relish the thought as I hit the age of 60 that I am going to have to worry about seizures now. I wonder what would have happened had I been in a hotel room, alone, on one of my many trips to the casinos when such a seizure hit. My neurologist thinks that I would probably just wake up about eight hours later, very sore, and somewhat confused but none the worse for wear.

Ironically, I think the reason I took to casino gambling in terms of advantage-play is the same reason I enjoyed being an athlete and a boxer – I like the competition. The fact that the casinos are greedy gargantuan Goliaths makes it that much more fun to slay them in blackjack, craps, video poker, slots, and Pai Gow poker. I teach seminars in all ways to beat the house. Yes, even the lowly slot machines – the very worst bets in the casino – have some machines that on occasion can be positive expectations for savvy players.

Thankfully all my brain tests have come back showing that I am okay. The EEG, which I took a week after my seizure, does not show anything wrong in my gray matter either. Still at 60, the time has come to reveal it all to my readers in order to make some sense of it – talk about my first love, talk about the games I beat, the casinos I play in, my in-laws, the great Captain, my trips into the Weird World of Astral Traveling, the murders I know about, my career as a teacher and some other things as well.

I want you to read this book and tell me, if you can, what it is all about because I just don't know what the theme is. When I was 20 years old, I knew it all. At 60, I haven't a clue. I am basically going backwards from now to when, as that is how our memory works. Travel with me and maybe you can explain my life to me.

- Part Two -
Adventures in Mississippi

Can a venue for casino gambling go from being the best in the country to the worst in a very short period of time? It has happened with Tunica, Mississippi. I used to laud this venue as the town with the best craps games (and tables!), best dealers and pit personnel, best executives, and some of the best blackjack games and the best comps in the country. Sadly none of this is true any longer. Yet even as Tunica started to go downhill I was treated with respect…that is until:

Friday, February 17

I was at LaGuardia Airport in New York for my 11:15AM flight to Memphis, Tennessee on the bankrupt Northwest Airlines. I was already missing my wife, the beautiful A.P., who would not be on this trip with me.

Flying a bankrupt airline can be frightening. What if the company saves money by not having anyone check the engine as often as it needs to be checked? I seem to have made a habit of flying bankrupt airlines as I used America West [now U.S. Airways] to get out to Vegas since the late 1980s. During a lot of that time that airline was bankrupt.

This particular day in this particular February was dreary with intermittent rain and some light winds. I was scheduled to get to Memphis at about 1:15PM, Central Time, and then gambling author and blackjack guru Henry Tamburin, along with Dominator, Stickman and I would set up for the Golden Touch Blackjack class which we were holding in Tunica, Mississippi, near all the casinos but definitely not at one of the casino properties.

Dominator is my partner in most of my business and advantage-play gambling ventures. He is a great dice controller, perhaps the best in the world right now, a strong card counter and an astute businessman with a software company that handles businesses in a half dozen states. He is Italian of the Sicilian variety, which means he can be fiery with a temper that ignites rather quickly. Stickman, who writes for numerous publications, is also a great dice controller and blackjack advantage player.

For those of you not familiar with the concept of casino advantage-play, it's very simple really. The casinos have attempted to set up their games so that these games favor the house. That means the players lose in the long run. However, many games can be beaten if you know how to do it. Most of you have probably heard about card counting at blackjack and perhaps you are familiar with dice control at craps. But even games such as roulette, along with select video poker games, some slot machines, Pai Gow poker and regulation poker can be beaten.

Of course, as a writer I write about all the games – even the ones that can't be beaten – but my casino play tends to center on the games I can beat. And my advantage-play teams strictly concentrate on taking from the casinos what the regular patrons have given them – that is, money.

In the upcoming two weekends in Tunica during this trip, we were doing our advantage-play seminars at blackjack, where we teach the revolutionary Speed Count and the Optimum Basic Strategy, both created by Dan Pronovost, a skinny Canadian, and the next weekend we were doing our Golden Touch dice control seminar, where we teach players how to control the dice at the game of craps. The blackjack method was easy to learn and execute in the casino and could gain a competent player between a one-half and one percent edge over the game. That meant for every $100 wagered, your expectation was to win 50 cents to one dollar. [See Frank's book *Golden Touch Blackjack Revolution* for Speed Count and Optimum Basic Strategy – editors.]

That might not sound like a lot but that is the edge the casino usually has over the players – and over time that edge can win a lot of money. Our Golden Touch Blackjack methods were simplicity themselves.

No so with dice control.

Golden Touch dice control was much harder to master – indeed most students never mastered it – because it took almost daily practice to stay sharp and about six months of such practice to get good enough to get an edge over the casinos. Very few casino gamblers could stay with the program. However, the good news was that your edge with dice control could greatly transcend your edge at blackjack. That was the tradeoff – hard work to become a dice controller, with failure ready to smack you in the face, but with high edges tantalizing you to give it a shot – or ease of learning and use with a small edge in your favor for blackjack.

Dominator and I teach our other advantage techniques in my Casino Killer College courses.

A couple of years before this weekend, we had scheduled a dice control class at Tunica's Grand Casino-Hotel – in fact, the Grand had asked for us to do one of our classes at their property – but when we showed up, all hell broke loose. It seems that a month previously an executive at the Grand had phoned the Mississippi Gaming Control Board and asked if it was all right if we taught students how to play the games.

"The person this executive spoke to," explained Dominator, "was an assistant to an assistant. She wasn't even a lawyer for the board but she started to cause trouble. I think she wanted to make a name for herself. We had to send faxes of our gaming tables so the Board could see that they weren't regulation craps tables because the Grand could not have such tables other than on their gaming floor. When they got the faxes we were okayed. Or so we thought.

"When we showed up on the Friday before class," stated Dominator, "the Control Board announced that Golden Touch couldn't teach anyone the games in Mississippi and our class was summarily cancelled – the day before we were scheduled to hold it! The Control Board went even further and said we would all be arrested if we tried to teach anyone about casino games in Mississippi. We discovered that agents of the Control Board were stationed at all the casinos to make sure we didn't switch properties in order to hold our class. There was security everywhere. Our instructors were even followed by security."

Now think about it. Here we were about to teach students from all over the country who had flown down to out-of-the-way Tunica, Mississippi, about dice control – a legal activity – and a government agency in the land of the free and the home of the brave was stopping us. We had 50 students, 15 highly paid advantage-play dice-control instructors, and no place to go in the land of cotton.

Luckily Dominator set up a phone chain on that Friday night and after dozens of calls we found a hotel at the Memphis Airport (yes, we moved to another state) and the next day we bused everyone to the class there. Then we hired an excellent attorney to petition the Mississippi Gaming Board that our civil right to free speech was being violated because they wouldn't let us teach about the games.

After months and months of hearings and meetings and fees, we won our case. The assistant to the assistant had misread the Mississippi regulations and we were now free to hold classes in Mississippi. The good citizens of Mississippi or elsewhere now had the right to accurate knowledge of the casino games and we had a right to teach them this knowledge.

You can say that weekend was the beginning of the end for me in Tunica.

Still for this current trip I looked forward to getting down there. At that time Tunica had great games, although there were rumblings that Harrah's takeover of the Grand, Sheraton, and the Horseshoe was ruining these previously great properties by making their games far less player friendly. The rumors also stated that the pits, which had been universally friendly to my instructors and me in the past, had undergone a change of heart and now everyone was sweating the money for fear of losing their jobs in the Harrah's takeover.

I'd have to see that for myself. That is if I could see.

I just had a laser procedure on my left eye because of a problem that had developed there after a serious illness to my mother. "This eye thing," said my retina specialist, "is caused by stress over your mother." I was not allowed to have daylight touch my skin for 72 hours so I was completely covered when I entered LaGuardia Airport – the drug they used during the procedure affects the skin's ability to deal with daylight or halogen light. I was wearing an Indiana Jones hat and white gloves so I had almost no skin exposed. People looked at me and then quickly looked away. I wondered if they thought I was a terrorist, or a Michael Jackson impersonator. It must be those white gloves.

I had some real trouble with my vision for several days after that procedure.

The winds in New York that day, what there were of them, delayed the flight for over an hour but once in the air, the flight to Memphis was smooth. Maybe someone had checked the engine after all. I was supposed to meet Dominator at the Memphis Airport but since I was going to be so late, he rented another vehicle and headed to Tunica on his own.

I rented an SUV from Avis. The trip to the Tunica casinos is about a half hour from the Memphis Airport. It's an interesting drive from Memphis to Tunica – cotton fields, shacks, soybean fields, shacks, a strip joint, rice paddies, shacks, billboards, and endless miles of fields in all directions, mud puddles, and then casinos. It's *Viva Las Vegas* meets *Gone with the Wind*.

Once in Tunica, the four of us set up the Golden Touch Blackjack class at the non-casino hotel. We set up blackjack tables, chips, and shoes for cards. It took a couple of hours and then Dominator and I headed over to the Grand so I could check in. He had already checked in.

The Grand was the premier property in Tunica at the time, with three hotels, a golf course, a shooting range, a spa and salon, a Kid's Quest child-care center, and a convention hall. The property was huge with small lakes throughout. The views from the hotel where I stayed, called the Terrace, were beautiful. Supposedly the Terrace is their top hotel on the property. I have to take that on faith since I never stayed at any of the others.

Now when I checked in, I told the desk clerk that the last three nights of my stay were comped with a room comp coupon. The first three nights had also been comped with a different three-night coupon. I had avoided doing the host-RFB thing because I didn't want to have to give any casino four hours of action per day, which is usually what they want to give you everything for free, which I would earn since my average bet is between $300 and $500 per decision. Instead, I wanted to spread my action around all the casinos in Tunica. I was also somewhat concerned by the rumors I had heard about Tunica changing its attitude towards the players. It would be better if I didn't bring too much attention to myself.

That was my thought. Unfortunately for me, everyone in the Tunica casinos knew who I was – whether I told them or not.

I had made an 11-day reservation at the Grand over the Internet, the room rates were ridiculously low, and then I started to get coupon comp offers that didn't require any set time of play. This was my second time staying at Grand's Terrace Hotel. I substituted the free offers for the first three days and now I wanted to substitute another free offer for the last three days of the trip.

"We got you (*we gachew*) for those days already (*aweready*)," said the clerk.

"Yes, I know but I want to use a free coupon for them and not pay for them," I said.

She looked at me as if I were speaking some strange dialect or maybe my New York (*Yawk*) accent was hard to fathom, but I could tell she didn't understand what I was saying as her eyes kind of looked like a deer I once almost hit on the Garden State Parkway in New Jersey on my way to Atlantic City. I figured I would come back once I was registered in the hotel and explain to someone else who could understand me that I wanted to substitute my paid days with the free days.

That night we ate at Murano's, an Italian restaurant, at the Grand Casino. Murano's was the only Italian restaurant in all of the Tunica casinos so we frequented it a lot. Dominator wasn't that hungry so he just had salad. Stickman ate like a horse, and Tamburin and I also ate full meals.

Then we hit the craps tables. Since I couldn't see very well to shoot, I took up the position at the end of the table so that Dominator could throw and not have to worry about hitting another player's chips. I was protecting his landing zone. Dominator was throwing from stick right #1 – which is the position next to the stickman's right – and our GTC instructor Stickman was shooting from stick left #1. Tamburin was all the way on the other side of the table, opposite me, to protect Stickman's landing zone.

Dominator had a decent roll – we made some money on it, which is the definition of decent. Then Stickman had a decent roll. Then the dice made their way from one random roller to another random roller. When we play at crowded tables with random rollers, it doesn't look good not betting on anyone else – so we use the Captain's 5-Count to delay our entrance into the game and reduce the random rolls we wager on by about 57 percent. We also bet very low on random rollers. The amount we lose on these random rollers, also known as "chicken feeders" since many of their throws look as if they are feeding the chickens corn meal – or whatever chickens are fed.

When the dice returned to Dominator, he established a point and then immediately sevened out. Billy the Kid, another one of our Golden Touch instructors, believes that we dice controllers tend to do the point-seven-out more often than normal random rollers because we are trying to protect against the seven and when we are the least off in our throws – bam! Seven-out! He might be right.

Now it was Stickman's turn with the dice. When one of our GTC controlled shooters is rolling we keep a record of the rolls. We use chips. We track the point numbers 4, 5, 6, 8, 9, 10 by putting a chip in the chip rack spot where these numbers would be. Stickman had looked good in his last roll so I went right up on him with $150 on the 6 and 8. Here was Stickman's roll: 4, 6, 6, 6, 6, 6, 6, 4, 6, 6, 9, 6, 6, 6, 10, 6, 6, 8, 6, 6, 6, 6, 6, 8, 6, 6, 6, 6, 6, 7-out. (If you know nothing about craps, a seven-out ends the roll for the shooter and anyone betting with the shooter loses.)

The Grand's boxman would occasionally pick up the dice and look at them, then look suspiciously at Stickman, then put the dice down. That was weird. Usually the Grand's box people are very pleasant. Maybe he thought we had substituted our own dice.

After Stickman's extraordinary hand, hitting 22 sixes in 28 rolls, we colored up and called it a night. One thing I have learned in my casino-playing career is not to be greedy at the casinos where I enjoy playing. I love playing the games but I also know that in many casinos my identity is no secret.

In Tunica I wrote for several magazines and newspapers and I also did a weekly radio show out of Memphis, which was largely sponsored by the casinos. So I tried to keep my winnings within the realm of tolerance. At least I thought that I did that. Even with my advantage-play teams, I usually directed them to casinos that had banned me or had bad reputations or both. Casinos I liked to play in I took it easy in. I liked playing at the Grand.

Foolish me as you will see. The Tunica I was in was not the great player-friendly Tunica of the past, but a new Tunica – a darker place for Dominator and for me.

That night when Dominator got back to his room he called room service. Then he called me.

"Can you believe it?" He was quite agitated.

"What?" I asked.

"The damn room service is closed because of bad weather."

"Bad weather? What bad weather?" I said looking out the picture window at the clear star-studded sky. "It's not bad outside. And how would that affect room service even if it were bad outside?"

"It's supposed to be bad tomorrow," he said.

"Tomorrow? So what?"

"So there's no room service tonight."

Saturday, February 18

So what? Tomorrow was another day and boy was it.

The next morning an ice storm hit Mississippi and Tennessee. It wasn't a particularly bad ice storm and some salt and sand would take care of the roads, making them drivable. I called down for room service and the phone rang interminably and finally someone answered.

"I want to get in touch with room service," I said.

"They ain't no room service. It's closed." She hung up.

I went downstairs to get a newspaper and found that the Gift Shop was also closed. A crudely scrawled sign taped to the front door announced that fact, "We Close." Then I went to get some coffee and a muffin in the Java Grand shop. It was closed.

I went back to my room and drank some water and took my vitamin pills.

An hour later Dominator and I headed for the Golden Touch Blackjack class. We groused about the fact that nothing was open because people hadn't come into work. When we arrived at the hotel where we were holding the class, we asked Stickman, a resident of Tennessee and one of our best instructors, about the fact that no one seems to have come to work at the Grand's Terrace Hotel. He laughed. "People here don't go to work in the bad weather," explained Stickman.

"We drove here and the road was ice. They haven't salted yet," I said. "We could have been killed it was so slippery."

"They don't have salt," said Stickman. "It'll melt on its own. God brought the storm; God will take it away. That's the thinking."

After the class Dominator and I drove back to the hotel, in fear I must say, since the roads were still icy. It was 5 o'clock. We stopped at the valet parking in the front of the Terrace and waited.

And waited.

And waited.

No one came over. Finally we saw a woman who looked like a worker and we called to her.

"Hey, hey!" yelled Dominator, "We want to valet the car!"

She ambled slowly towards us and after a decades long wait she said, "They ain't no valet parking now."

"What?" I asked.

"You're kidding?" Dominator said.

"You got to park yourself," she says.

"You mean we have to go into that icy self-parking lot and park the fucking car ourselves?" said Dominator, his voice rising.

"Yup," she said and started to amble away as if to say, "That's that boys."

"Did the valet parkers come to work?" I asked.

"No, we a different department," she stated.

"What the fuck does that mean?" asked Dominator, really irritated now.

"We a different department," she said gently, ignoring his use of the word "fuck," and speaking to us as if we were lunatics. "You got to park the car. Over there." She pointed to the parking lot about four hundred miles away.

So we drove the car into the icy parking lot – it was a sheet of ice, there were no non-icy spots, and we had to park in the very back of the lot which looked to be about four hundred and ten miles away from our hotel. As I got out of the SUV on the driver's side I slipped, caught myself on the door and luckily didn't fall and kill myself. My Indiana Jones hat fell off my head however. I reached and grabbed it just before it could blow away across the ice flow, and I put it back on.

"God almighty. Be careful, Dom. We can kill ourselves trying to get to the hotel."

So we walked like hockey fans going onto an ice-hockey rink. We slid along the ice. It was scary and dangerous. "You park the car," the woman had said as she walked away from us. You come to a hotel for services and amenities; you don't come to a hotel so that you have to park your own car on an iceberg because the valet attendants don't show up for work on bad days.

Inside the hotel there was no bartender at the bar. I could have used a drink but the bar was closed. Why would that be surprising? No one comes to work in bad weather. Great.

In the elevator, Dominator, a native New Yorker like me, rattled off, "No room service, no gift shop, no coffee shop, no valet, no bar, no salt or sand on the roads. What the hell? Does it get worse than this?"

Sunday, February 19

Today is worse.

I looked out my window and there was ice everywhere. I didn't bother with room service. I drank some water, took my vitamins, showered, dressed, knocked on Dominator's door – we had adjoining rooms – and off we go to the Golden Touch Blackjack class.

Of course, we first had to negotiate our way into the parking lot to get our SUV – it was like walking over the frozen steppes. We needed a Sherpa guide.

As we inched through the Grand's property, the ice glistened everywhere, except on the roads that the shuttles use in order to take the players from the hotels to the Grand Casino; there was plenty of sand on those roads. Trying to exit the Grand property was hair-raising; I drove about 10 miles per hour.

"Do they want their fucking players to die?" screamed Dominator as the SUV did a little skid to the side of the road. Luckily we didn't go into the ditch.

"They are trapped on the property," I said as I righted the SUV. "You have a hard time getting out of here so the players have to play here." The SUV skidded again. "I hope we get out of here alive."

There was no sand, no salt, on any of the exit roads from the Grand. There was no sand, no salt on any of the roads to the other hotel either. Just about all the blackjack students came late to class, as they too had to maneuver the treacherous roads.

The common refrain from the students who flew in from other areas of the country was: "What the hell is wrong with these people? Don't they know how to handle ice?"

The answer to that was, "No."

We taught the class and at 5PM we headed back to the Grand along the same icy roads. We parked in the guest lot, which now seemed about eight million miles from the Terrace Hotel, and walked – no, snowshoed – our way to the hotel. Tonight was worse than yesterday as frozen winds had covered everything in ice – even the sides of the building. Cars that had remained in the parking lot during this storm looked like ice sculptures.

Once safely in, I went to the front desk to explain about my three free room nights the next weekend. Again the desk person, a different person than before, didn't understand what I was saying. I explained it three times, in three different ways, all three ways engendering looks as if I were talking gibberish – "Ugab noto klepto descarties."

"Wha?" asked the desk clerk for the millionth time.

"Mwamba latta dell poo poo tur," I said.

"You nights in already," said the desk clerk, looking at the computer behind the reservation desk.

I gave up. "Never mind, I'll take care of it some other time," I said.

"You haff a good evnin', sir," said the desk clerk.

"Thanks," I said.

The people you meet in Tunica are universally friendly but there's a slowness here that can drive a New Yorker crazy – a slowness, and no sand or salt on the roads; and no one coming to work in bad weather.

We called the restaurant line to make reservations from Dominator's room and finally someone answered. This woman didn't know if any restaurants would be open that night. "Depends if anyone's coming to work," she said.

"If they salt the damn roads people could drive!" shouted Dominator into the phone. Dominator looked at me. "She hung up."

"Crap."

Miracle of miracles that night at the Grand Casino all the restaurants were open. A few people made it to work after all. We ate at the steak house and while service was slow – service is always slow in Tunica but you get used to that after many visits – we had a fine meal.

We went to the craps tables but they were filled and then we checked out the blackjack games but they were not very good. When you use Speed Count, which is the method Dominator and I now use at the game, the most important thing is depth of penetration. We wanted about 60 percent or more.

Tonight the Grand was giving about 50 percent penetration on their double-deck games and while we still had an edge at that level it wasn't big enough to waste our time playing. We were also tired. But we'd have a whole week to play the games starting tomorrow – as long as the forecasted sun came out and melted the snow so we could check out other casinos.

I had in mind hitting Fitzgeralds casino where our team had hammered them last November when Dominator and I put together a five-person team for a magazine spread by another writer who wanted to chronicle how such a team worked and how a young lady card counter he was writing about would play the games in the context of such team play.

Dominator and I were in charge of creating the five-person team and we chose Stickman, an excellent card counter, and Street Dog, another excellent card counter to join us. These two have been on many of my teams. I trust their honesty and their playing skills.

The young woman player was – strangely enough – unable to come up with the $10,000 investment to join the team – but was being heralded by this writer acquaintance as a great card counter and one who had played with the MIT teams that had become quite famous. We had figured on a bankroll of $50,000 for three days of play in Tunica. The betting would be $100 to $500; although we also allowed $50 to $500 – if the player felt he or she could get away with that spread. But $500 was the maximum bet no matter what, although a $100 to $400 spread was also just fine. Betting lower was better than betting higher since we didn't want fluctuations [in English = bad luck] to blow us away.

We also didn't want anyone to get the boot from the casinos. I certainly didn't want to be banned since I loved playing in Tunica. I felt that over the years I had sent tens of thousands of my readers to Tunica's casinos because of Tunica's good games, easy comps, and great atmosphere and I had it in my mind that this was appreciated by the casino executives who would allow me to play as long as I didn't take too much of their casinos' money. A few of them had told me so, in fact.

As to our team, with the four men playing four hours per day, two hands each, that would give us about 7,600 hands. The young woman, let's call her Connie, would play about eight hours each day – dressing up in various guises to make herself appear to be different people, a prostitute, a doctor, a secretary, a bimbo, a drunken whatever. That's what this other writer wanted – a dramatic story of an identity shifting card counter playing as a part of a well-oiled machine. She would play one or two hands at the table and we figured she would be good for about 2,400 hands, which gave us about 10,000 hands of play for the three-day period.

If my guess was correct, and I was guessing since the blackjack playing conditions in the various casinos were somewhat different, although all were favorable, we should make about $10,000 (give or take a couple of thousand) in team winnings. With the swings in such short play (about 72 combined hours) and with an average win of between $50 to $150 per hour of play, it was a pretty good bet that we had going for us. Of course, we could also lose; win much less; win much more. I've been on all ends of the blackjack equation but I liked our chances nevertheless – and I was helping out a writer acquaintance as well.

Also a $10,000 win spread out among Tunica's casinos wouldn't even be noticed.

We were committed to doing this as Connie and the writer had flown down just for this team play piece, which would (and did ultimately) appear in a national magazine.

Actually she flew in from California and he flew in from New York.

Of course, those win rates were for a $50,000 bankroll. But we only had $40,000 now because Connie was investing no money. None of us knew Connie from a hole in the wall but she talked a good game and this writer was vouching for her. But we had to decide what we were going to do with Connie since she wasn't investing.

"Fuck her," said Street Dog. "She gets shit."

"Let her play," said Stickman, "But she doesn't get any of the wins."

"So we get the wins, we absorb the loss, and they get their story," I said.

"Okay, that's how we do it," said Dominator.

So she could play with our money but she got nothing if she won but we would absorb any losses. She was doing this for fame; we were doing it for fortune, a fair trade.

In the three evenings of play, I won $8,800; Dom won, $4,250; Stickman won $1,775; and Street Dog won $1,750; while Connie won $640 and had a grand time changing clothes and personas to impress her personal chronicler. Not a bad weekend of play, averaging about $240 per hour for the team.

While I hadn't played Fitzgeralds, both Stickman and Street Dog had hit the place hard. That game at that time was the best double-deck game in Tunica (perhaps in all of America) with extremely deep penetration. Of course, what one casino gave another would take away and while our two teammates hammered Fitzgeralds, they were themselves hammered at Grand and Sam's Town during their play, whereas Dominator and I hammered those two casinos but were flattened at Horseshoe, which at that time had the second best double-deck games in Tunica.

But the bottom line was a success and we split up the money on Sunday evening when play was finished. The writer got his story; the young lady got her fame (she has since appeared on several television blackjack challenges); and we got the money – a fair outcome all around.

Monday, February 20

I went down to the Bellissimo Spa at 7AM to work out. It was closed. It was supposed to open at 7AM. I went back to my room and came down at 8AM. It was now open; thank the Lord! I worked out for an hour on the treadmill and then did a half hour of weight training. Dominator came down about a half hour into my workout and did his workout as well. Dominator is a very strong guy and lifts monumental weight compared to me.

Today I could jettison the hat and the gloves as 72 hours had passed and I wasn't susceptible to light any more. My eye was also getting a little better. And the sun was out, strong and bright, and melting all the ice. God had brought the storm and God was getting rid of the remnants of the storm.

All was right with the world. Or so I thought.

The ice was melting rapidly and the valet parking was open. After our showers, we took the shuttle to the Grand Casino to eat at the buffet. Of course, the gift shop was still closed as was the Java Grand but it looked as if they would open later that day since the hand-made signs were no longer posted.

At the buffet there was no butter until the waiter found some in the kitchen. That took about five months as the toast turned cold in the wait time.

"They didn't put it out," he said by way of explanation.

"I know that," I said.

Obviously they didn't put it out! That's why I asked you to go find some! But rather than be New-Yawk nasty to him and saying this out loud, I said, "Thank you." I also left him a decent tip for bringing the butter.

We had thus far experienced no room service, no gift shop, no coffee shop, no valet, no bar, no salt or sand on the exit roads, no understanding on the part of the check-in clerks and no butter at the buffet.

But the worst was yet to come.

After breakfast we went into the casino to play craps. That day in four turns with the dice, Dominator and I each had 50+ rolls. Not to put too fine an edge on it, we were spectacular. During our turns with the dice, a huge suit conference was held in the craps pit – with what I took to be floor-people and pit bosses and whoever else wears a suit in the casinos attending the meeting and everyone occasionally glancing at us. The suits were nodding to each other, looking at the computer screens, nodding some more to each other, and then surreptitiously looking over at us.

And they didn't look friendly. We carted a boatload of chips from the craps table that morning.

Tuesday, February 21

The Bellissimo Spa opened at 7AM today and I worked out for an hour, just doing the treadmill. I went back to my room, showered, shaved, and knocked on Dominator's door. We headed to the buffet breakfast.

At the omelet station, the toaster oven deposited the toast in the back on the counter so that you couldn't get to it. You had to call over the worker – who slowly ambled over, letting the toast get chilled – to pick up your toast for you. It was rather weird that the toast came out the back and it was also unsanitary that the toast fell directly onto the counter instead of in a plate or a basket or onto anything but a counter! The butter wouldn't melt on the toast, of course, because the toast was cold by the time you got it back to your table and by the time you got the butter at the Southern Fried Foods station, which was way across the room from where they made the toast.

After breakfast I tried to explain to the new desk person at the Terrace about my three free nights this upcoming weekend.

"Oggle baba woudo mako nugatth," the clerk heard me say. (Actually I said, "I want to exchange three free nights for the three paid nights next weekend.")

"Huh?" she said.

"Macholutajkiuta," she heard. ("I want to speak to the manager.")

The clerk looked at me as if I spoke some space-alien tongue. We stood there and looked at each other. Time passed. Ice flows in Antarctica melted due to global warming. She was silent. I was silent.

"Never mind," I finally said and left.

At noon, Dominator wanted to send out a rush overnight Fed Ex package to one of his clients. But the staff at the desk said that the package couldn't be delivered until tomorrow.

"What are you talking about?" asked Dom, "Fed Ex picks up at 5PM. It's noon now for God's sake." The desk clerk took the Fed Ex package from Dominator.

That afternoon Dominator had to take care of some business and I had to write, so we decided to hold off on the playing of games until after dinner when we would go to Fitzgeralds to play their delicious double-deck blackjack games.

The sign on the elevator wall said Murano's was closed on Wednesdays but open on Tuesdays. I'm not a big steak eater and this was the only Italian restaurant in Tunica. Thankfully it was open tonight. Just about all the other restaurants in Tunica are steak houses or barbeque joints. I prefer pasta. So we headed over to Murano's, which was Tuesday and it was open, right, because the sign said that, right? No, it was closed! So we ate at some café at the Grand where the service was slower than a stop sign.

Back in the elevator going back to our rooms, I showed Dominator the sign on the wall. It said Muranos was open on Tuesdays, closed on Wednesdays. Except it was really closed on Tuesday and actually opened on Wednesday as I later found out. Whoever did the sign did it wrong – it might have been the same guy who was in charge of the butter at the buffet!

Dominator expounded on that, "What the fuck!"

So we each went into our rooms to wash up, get our money, and prepare to tackle Fitzgeralds. In my room I suddenly heard a scream from Dominator's room. "Aaarrrgghhhhh! You STUPID FUCKS!"

I knocked on his door and he opened it. He looked like a madman. The rush Fed Ex package had been returned to his room, while we had dinner – it was sitting right on the bed – because the Terrace staff thought it was addressed to him.

"They delivered the package to me!" he screamed. "They delivered the fucking package back to me!"

At Fitzgeralds, Dominator went into the high roller room first – and about 15 minutes later I went in. We played at the same table but we bet different ways since we were playing as a team. However we pretended not to know each other. However, within 10 minutes of my entrance to the game a stern-looking woman executive came over to me and tapped me on the shoulder.

All card counters reading this book know about "the Tap."

"Frank," she said, "we don't want you playing at Fitzgeralds anymore. Not craps, not blackjack. I am trespassing you." Any more? Any more? I had played at Fitzgeralds maybe three times in all of my Tunica trips over the last ten years. But I had done remote control radio shows from that casino more often than that. I was stunned that they were banning me and I was even more stunned they were trespassing me, which meant if I returned I could be arrested.

Then she turned to Dominator. "You too," she said. "You understand that if either of you come back to this casino, you will be arrested for trespassing? You can take your chips to the cage and they..." she indicated two security guards, "will escort you to the cage and out the door."

A woman at our table said, "What did they do wrong?"

"It is all taken care of," said the Fitzgeralds executive.

"They didn't do anything wrong? I've been playing here with them. Why can't they play?" asked the woman at the table.

"Everything is fine," said the Fitzgeralds executive.

So we went to the cage, cashed our chips, and left. The security guards followed us to valet parking, waited with us as we waited (forever) for our van, and watched us as we drove off.

"Those fucks!" said Dominator in the van. "Those fucks!"

So we headed over to Horseshoe to check out the craps and blackjack games. Horseshoe was crowded. In those days the Horseshoe was always crowded. But something had changed – the craps tables were like trampolines and the dice would often bounce off the tables. These tables reminded me of the tables at the Flamingo Hilton in Vegas. Why had they messed with their tables? The Horseshoe had made the most money from the table games of any casino in Tunica – why screw around with what worked?

Dominator went to the high roller room to play blackjack and I would follow in a few minutes. Except that I didn't have to follow because he came walking back over to me and whispered, "Let's get out of here." So we went to valet, silently got the van, and then, "They stopped me from playing," said Dominator. "They knew who I was and they mentioned you too. Just like that."

"This place used to be the friendliest casino on earth," said Dominator.

"It was the best casino in the country," I said.

"Harrah's fucked this place good," reflected Dominator.

"So we are out at Fitzgeralds and Horseshoe," I mused. "I never expected anything like this."

"Fuck," said Dominator, who then lit a cigarette.

"I thought you were cutting down on the smoking?"

"Fuck," said Dominator.

Wednesday, February 22

I had a great workout in the spa. That wound up being the highlight of my day.

We went over to the buffet after my workout and now the toast popped out of the front of the toaster onto the counter top – unless you could catch it in time. You still had to hunt around for the butter, which seemed to change its location on a daily basis. Why didn't they keep the butter where they made the toast? Why didn't they come to work in bad weather? Why didn't they have the right information on the Murano's poster?

"Shouldn't you have a basket or something to catch the toast?" I asked the woman who worked at this station. She was engaged in a heated discussion with a co-worker over the fact that the Grand didn't pay them some money they felt they were owed. They talked very loud even though they were inches apart and face-to-face.

She ignored me and continued her conversation. I asked my question again and she showed her annoyance, "What? What?"

"Shouldn't you have a basket or something to catch the toast?" I repeated for a third time.

"You just catch it with (*witch*) your hand, sir," and she turned back to her conversation.

We went down to play some craps and we were the only two at the craps table. Dominator would roll first from stick right #1 and I would roll from stick left #1 and we had our Pass Line bets up and Dom established his point as 6 and we placed our numbers and then a loud holler came from across the casino.

"Stop! Stop!" yelled a voice. At first I thought it was a player wanting to get into the game – sometimes the players don't know the rules of how and when to enter a craps game. But it was a Grand executive. "Frank, I am really sorry," he said a little out of breath, "but we don't want you to play blackjack or craps in our casino anymore. You too," he said to Dominator.

"What the fuck?" said Dominator. "Do you think we are going to break you? What the fuck is this?"

"It isn't me," said the executive, "and I am sorry but that's how it is." Then he turned to the dealers, "Give them all their bets back."

"You can keep your tips," I said to them.

The dealers pushed all of our bets back to us but deposited their tips in the toke box.

"This is really fucking stupid," said Dominator, his face red, the veins in his neck bulging.

"We're leaving," I said. "We're not going to give you any trouble."

"Fuck!" said Dominator.

"Hey, it wasn't me guys, it wasn't," said the Grand executive.

Several days later a friendly executive in the Harrah's empire who shall remain nameless forevermore called me and said, "Frank, you just won too much money and you teach those classes. No one wants you to play in Tunica anymore. That's coming from above." I asked him about the countless thousands of people I have sent to Tunica but all he could say was, "That's the way it is for now."

After getting the boot at the Grand, we went over to Sam's Town. I had been invited to speak at Sam's Town twice in the past by their executives and I was very friendly with some of the suits there.

The one opened craps table was crowded so we went over to a Pai Gow poker table to play while waiting for our spots to open at the craps table. Pai Gow Poker is a great game and there is a way to get an edge at it if you can structure your betting properly. When the house is the bank at the game, you bet low – table minimum. However, you ask to bank every other hand as many casinos allow the players to bank 50 percent of the time. You just have to have enough money on the table to cover everyone else's bets. You want the other players at the table, the players you are banking against, to be big bettors because when you bank you have a small edge over all those players at the game because you win certain tied hands. That small edge against all the other players compensates for the 2.5 percent house edge on your small bet against the house when the casino banks and you wind up with a tiny edge over the house overall.

Sam's Town did not let you bank 50 percent of the time so it was not even theoretically a beatable game we were playing. That didn't matter. Dominator and I were just wasting time with five-dollar bets. There were only two other people at the table – both five-dollar bettors – so even if this had been a good game; it could not be a moneymaker for us.

Except.

That didn't matter because we got tapped. Tapped at Pai Gow Poker! That had to be a first.

The executive who tapped us out was one of the guys who had hired me to speak to his players several years before. He had been very friendly then. Today he said coldly, "We don't want you playing in our casino, Frank. Take your chips and cash them."

It looked to me as if Dominator was ready to take his chips and shove them down this executive's throat. But after saying a few "fucks," he picked up his chips and we left.

That night we had dinner at the Chicago Steakhouse at Gold Strike, a casino that had become insane about players shooting the dice and allowing their arms to extend past the stickman. Many of the Golden Touch dice control instructors were coming in that night and we arranged to have a meal for all of us. At dinner Howard "Rock 'n Roller," one of our instructors, said, "It was weird at the table tonight. I was rolling the dice, was at 21 rolls, and the pit boss comes over and says, 'You know that's all bullshit about being able to control the dice. That Scoblete is full of shit.'"

"I ignored him and rolled," said Rock 'n Roller, "but then he said, 'And Scoblete is banned from every casino in Mississippi, you know, he can't play here anymore. He's been banned everywhere.'"

"One of the players at the table," continued Rock 'n Roller, "said 'Well if it doesn't work, why is he banned?' And the pit boss walked away saying something like, 'Scoblete gives players crazy ideas that they can beat the house.'"

I looked at Dominator and Dominator looked at me. Then we told our tales of being asked to leave the casinos and being trespassed at Fitzgeralds. Evidently we were banned from every casino in Tunica if that casino guy was correct – maybe every casino in Mississippi.

Just to keep you savvy about advantage-play back offs and bannings, the casino has two ways to stop a player who has an edge. The first is to simply tell him not to play certain games but that means the player can come back to the casino to play other games. The other, more drastic way was to trespass the player, which was to tell that player the next time he came on the property he would be arrested for trespassing.

There was a third, illegal and immoral way, too. And that was to backroom the advantage-player and seriously abuse his civil rights by holding him against his will, filing false charges, and sometimes beating him up. I had never been beaten up but I did have a gun put into my back in a downtown Las Vegas casino by a steroidal muscle bound security guard. I walked right out the front door, praying that my wife and playing partner, the beautiful A.P., and I were not shot down in the casino.

Since I never cheated at games and since my partners and team players never cheated at games, we were not doing anything illegal. But the whole thing is still unpleasant. Unfortunately, the casinos' executives had the right to stop you from playing their games because casinos are private property. They could ask anyone to leave for any reason. The trespassing was a serious abuse of power but even the polite, "Go away," was an abuse as well. You could be a war hero, and an American casino could stop you from playing their games. Your buddies could have died fighting for America, or you could have run into the World Trade Center to save people, or you were a police officer, or fireman, or teacher, or doctor, or an average law-abiding American citizen, or someone on a pension – and an American casino could ban you! How un-American was that? How disgusting!

But that was, as they say, that. The very people our fellow American citizens defended with their lives could turn around and tell them to get their worthless butts out of a multi-million-dollar casino.

The Tunica casinos were dead to me. Which really didn't matter ultimately because in the time between the now as I write this and the then when it happened, the games have deteriorated to such an extent that even Atlantic City has become a much preferred destination over Tunica. Tunica has, sadly, become a third-world gaming venue that sweats the action but wants to soak the players. Eight-deck games with dealers hitting soft 17s have come into the mix and those horrid 6-to-5 blackjack games are rearing their ugly heads too. The craps games are still okay, except that Horseshoe, once the greatest place to play craps in America, has become one of the worst due to its trampoline tables. They must lose a lot of money with the dice flying off the tables all the time.

The Tunica I used to love, that I used to write so glowingly about, that I used to advertise any chance I got because of its great games and friendly attitude, has dimmed to the point of being a dump.

But I still had five more days there as we were giving our Golden Touch dice control classes that weekend. What was I going to do in those five days?

Thursday, February 23

Great workout in the spa today.

Then I went over to the front desk afterwards to see if I could get someone to understand about my free rooms. The supervisor at the front desk understood that I wanted to substitute the three free room nights that I have with the three paid ones that I had booked over the Internet. He says, "It's all taken care of sir." I was at last happy. I thanked him.

There was no whole wheat bread at the buffet. "There's just white," said the girl working behind the counter as the toast rocketed out onto the floor. Someone must have increased the toast's exit speed because you could hear sonic booms as the toast left the machine,

Today I went to Elvis Presley's Graceland mansion in Tennessee. Spent the entire day there.

Friday, February 24

I walked 3.5 miles on the treadmill and I lifted weights. These are little 10-pound weights and an old lady, an ancient lady, was lifting 20 pounders – the show off!

Dominator was really frustrated by his stay at the Grand's Terrace Hotel too – today neither of us got wash cloths from housekeeping – so we both decided to talk to the manager of the hotel this morning. The time had come to complain. I wrote a list of what had happened this week that I would read to him.

Dom explained all about how his Fed Ex package wound up back in his room.

"Ah heard about it," says the manager.

I then read my list: "No room service during storm, no gift shop during storm, no coffee shop during storm, no valet during storm, no bar during storm, no salt or sand on the exit roads, no understanding on the part of the check-in clerks about my rooms, no wash cloths, restaurant was closed when it was supposed to be open and no butter at the buffet and no wheat toast either and the damn toaster puts the bread on the counter and today it shot the bread onto the floor."

"Ah am not responsible for the buffet," said the manager.

I looked at the manager. Dom looked at the manager. Is this it? I mean, okay, he's not responsible for the buffet but what about his hotel?

"You come to a hotel," I said calmly, "To enjoy amenities like room service and the other things. That's why we are here. And we didn't get any of the amenities."

"There was a storm," he said.

"So what? So fucking what?" screamed Dom.

"People don't come to work in storms," said the manager.

We all stood there silently.

"How about you pick up the rooms we have paid for to make up for the lousy service?" asked Dom. "A sign of good faith."

"I'd have to talk to the president," stated the manager.

"Great, talk to him," I said.

Dom and I walked away. In the elevator, Dom shouted, "Motherfucker!"

We drove over to the hotel where we were holding our Golden Touch Craps dice control class. We were renting two rooms there and we had a lot of setting up to do – two full size casino craps tables, eight practice tables, in addition to all sorts of dice paraphernalia. The moving of all this stuff to the hotel took a lot of time.

"Let's relax," I said to Dom as we pulled up to the hotel. "We relax and set up the banquet rooms. You did call to remind them to clean the rooms?"

"No, they know they have to do that. They can't be that stupid not to clean the fucking meeting rooms," said Dom.

Both rooms were filthy. There was garbage all over the big banquet room. The smaller room, where we do the lecture part of the class, was being painted by two scrawny guys who looked as if they smoked five packs a day since they were toddlers.

We talked to the manager of the hotel and informed him we had to have both rooms set up today for tomorrow's class. We need that second room now.

"Ah didn't think you needed it," explained the manager slowly, "so we went ahead to paint the molding."

He assured us that he would personally set up the room for tomorrow.

Dominator offered to pay for the meeting rooms in advance. The manager explained we can pay on Sunday, "There ain't no rush. I trust you guys."

"How many students should we set the room for?" asked the manager.

"Set it up for 32 students," said Dom.

Saturday, February 25

The room was set up for 62 students. We had to quickly remove chairs and rearrange things. The front part of the room's wallpaper was starting to peel onto the new paint.

The class went well and we headed back to the Grand's Terrace Hotel. In my room the phone rang. It's the manager of the hotel where we did the Golden Touch Dice Control class.

"We want payment for the banquet rooms right now!" he screamed.

"Didn't you say Sunday was fine?" I asked.

"My boss wants it now!" he screamed.

We drove back and paid him for the two banquet rooms. Dom reminded him to clean up so that when we start tomorrow the rooms were ready to use.

That night Stickman, Mrs. Stickman, Rock 'n Roller, Dominator and I ate at Sheraton's steakhouse. Stickman ordered a Belvedere martini, dry, straight up, no vermouth, and Dom ordered Kettle One on the rocks with an olive. About ten hours later, long after we ordered our meal (which hadn't yet arrived either), the waiter brings over one of those round glasses you get in hotel rooms with some vodka in it and puts it in front of Stickman.

"What's this?" asked Stickman.

"That's (*dats*) your (*yo*) drink," said the waiter.

"I ordered a Martini," said Stickman.

"That bartender he says that this is what it is and he must be kidding me because..." and the waiter goes on and on and on as to why Stickman's drink wasn't his drink. Maybe the bartender was playing a joke? Maybe aliens from another planet had kidnapped his drink? Maybe I couldn't understand what he was saying half the time but it was the longest excuse I have heard in my life.

"Please go back and get me what I ordered," said Stickman.

"Bring my drink too," added Dom, looking disgusted. "How hard is it to get a drink order right?"

The waiter finally brought over our dinners with Stickman's drink, this time made properly, but he didn't have Dom's drink.

"Where's my drink?" asked Dominator.

"Yo drink?"

"Jesus Christ. Forget my drink. I don't want it now," said Dom.

"Ah'll get your drink right away, sir," said the waiter.

"Forget my drink."

"What did yo order?" asked the waiter.

"Forget my drink."

The waiter walked away, checking his notepad.

"You know I think they are trained in school to make excuses," I said. "They are always polite but when they screw up, they just make excuses."

"Even if the excuses make no sense," said Dominator.

Sunday, February 26

I called room service at 6:30AM and ordered some eggs and whole-wheat toast with a small pot of coffee.

"It will be right up, sir," said the woman on the phone. I called down at 7AM to check to see if my order is ready.

"It will be right up sir," said the woman on the phone.

I called down at 7:30AM to see what was taking so long.

"The cook didn't come in. We got no cook," said the woman on the phone.

At 8AM, five minutes before I leave for class, my cold, card-boardy eggs and cold white toast arrived. I wolfed everything down and headed out the door.

At the hotel where we were holding our class, the rooms had not been cleaned – so we cleaned them up.

"I told the fucking guy to clean the damn room," shouted Dominator into the air.

That night we ate at the Grand's Murano's and Rock 'n Roller ordered some penne pasta to go with his meal. After the table was cleared of our desserts and our coffees, the pasta was brought to him.

"What's this?" asked Rock 'n Roller.

"Pasta," said the waiter.

"We had our meal, we had our coffee, we had our desert," said Rock 'n Roller.

"You ordered pasta," said the waiter.

"As a part of my meal," said Rock 'n Roller.

The waiter just stood there. "All right," said Rock 'n Roller, "I'll eat it now."

So with the table cleared; with Stickman, Dominator and I totally finished with our evening of dining, poor Rock 'n Roller ate his pasta. "It's good," he said, "at least the pasta is good."

Dominator, angry as all hell over the week, over the service, over every damn thing, said as we left the Grand, "I want to play one more time."

"You're out of your mind," I said. "You don't want to get arrested do you? You saw *My Cousin Vinny* right?"

"Marisa Tomei was beautiful, a real Brooklyn girl," said Rock 'n Roller.

"Look, I think it's a big mistake," I said.

"If you play, I'll go with you," said Stickman.

"Great, you are going to get poor Dominator arrested," I said.

"I'll go too," said Rock 'n Roller. "I really liked Marisa Tomei."

"I'm not going; I'm going back to my room, watch a movie and go to sleep," I said. "You will be sleeping with big Bubba in a Mississippi jail."

"Frank, I'm telling you, we were hotter than hell last weekend. We hammered them until they kicked our asses out. I feel it tonight my friend. I am ready to bust them wide open," said Dominator.

"I think you just want to gamble," I said. That's one of the ways I get Dominator to see that I am right. I call him a gambler – and he now hates to be called a gambler because before I met him he had more gambler in him than was good for him.

"I didn't gamble all week. I visited the museum, I saw Elvis's house, you know, I held back, but this is the last night and I know I am going to be hot. I can feel it. I won't be gambling," he said.

"I'm going back to my room," I said.

"You don't understand," explained Dominator, "I made myself a costume. Nobody will recognize me. We'll go to a casino that we haven't been to very much and I won't be recognized. I'll take the dice once and that's it. I'll hammer the bastards and leave. I want one more shot at these fucks."

"I did the costume thing in Vegas for a whole summer. It could work but if it doesn't there's a big Bubba in your future," I said.

"Wasn't President Clinton called Bubba?" asked Rock 'n Roller.

"What are you going to be?" asked Stickman.

"I got it in the trunk of the SUV," Dominator said.

"Good luck," I said. "I'm going back to my room."

"You know, Frank, you're smart," said Stickman, "because your face is really well known down here. But Dom might be able to get away with it. I think you have more of a chance to be identified."

"I'll get away with it," said Dominator. "I know I will get away with it."

When I got back to my room I called the airlines and changed my flight back home from Tuesday to Monday afternoon. I was anxious to get home to my beautiful A.P. after having the worst week I ever spent in a casino hotel and a casino town.

About two hours later, I heard a knock on my door between our rooms. I was just falling asleep and I was a little foggy. I opened the door. I wish I could tell you that Dominator had a good roll and won a little money; I can't tell you that, unfortunately.

Instead, he had a MONSTROUS hand that was over the 50-roll mark! He hit so many numbers that the casino suits held a convention behind the table. Except for Rock 'n Roller, Stickman and some of the GTC instructors, no one knew it was the remarkable Dominator "kicking ass" as he said he would on his final night in Tunica, Mississippi.

He pulled out a pile of one hundred dollar bills and laid them on the table. He pointed to them dramatically. "I'm adding this to the pile we already have."

"We? You're letting me share in your winnings?" I asked

"Hey, we were partners on this trip, and we're partners now. In our last playing trip to Tunica, we beat the crap out of them," he said.

"That we did," I agreed. "And tonight I didn't even have to do anything."

Monday, February 27

At the breakfast buffet there was no bread to make toast.

"Where's the bread?" asked Dominator.

"No bread," said the woman behind the counter.

"Why isn't there any bread?" I asked.

"The toaster exploded," she said. Sure enough, no toaster either.

The buffet's waitress took our order as soon as we came in and when we got back to our table we expected our coffees and Dom's orange juice to be waiting for us. Why did we expect that? I don't know. They were not on the table.

Three-quarters through the meal, the waitress came over with our drinks. She placed them down, and walked away. Dom and I were talking. Several moments later Dom reached for his orange juice.

"What happened to my orange juice?" he said. "It was right here." He pointed to the spot where the orange juice had been – I saw it there too. But it wasn't there anymore

Dom called over the waitress. "Where's my orange juice?"

"Your orange juice?"

"Yes, you put my orange juice down here and now it isn't there," said Dom.

"I picked it up and gave it to him," she pointed to a man at a table next to us drinking the orange juice.

"Why did you give my orange juice to him?"

The waitress smiled a big smile but she didn't say anything. She had a very pretty smile. She also could give no reason why she gave Dom's orange juice away. After smiling into our stunned faces, she walked away. That's that.

"The toaster exploded," I said.

"She took my orange juice," Dom said. "Fuck this town."

It's time to leave the Grand and boy am I glad to be going home to my beautiful wife A.P. At the front desk I checked out my bill and there it was in black and white – they charged me for the three free nights. I told the woman at the desk that the last three nights were supposed to be free. She was in the process of training a man to be a reservation agent.

He looked dumbfounded as I spoke. She looked dumbfounded when I spoke too. Her training regimen was obviously going quite well because there were two dumbfounded people looking at me as if there were something wrong with me.

I repeated the fact that my last three nights were free. She looked me up on the computer. "You didn't use them nights. You stayed in the room you was in."

I had a choice to argue or to just sign the bill and get the hell away. I signed the bill.

It was a beautiful day in Tunica. The air was crisp and clean and Dominator, Street Dog and I headed to the airport. I just kept thinking I will get on the plane and head back to New York and home, and I would put this rotten week behind me.

Unfortunately Northwest Airlines was delayed on this beautiful day. My flight took off an hour and twenty minutes late.

I was seated in the aisle seat and next to me was an elderly woman who fell asleep as soon as the plane lifted off. While she slept she snored really loud and then she started to rip the most wicked sounding and horrendously smelling farts. She farted and snored; snored and farted. Oh, God.

When the stewardess came by for drinks, the woman woke up and ordered orange juice. The stewardess handed it to her but the old woman dropped the glass and all the orange juice in my lap.

"Give me another, this one spilled on this man."

This man asked for some napkins to wipe himself off.

"I live in Connecticut," said the old woman and, finishing her orange juice, she promptly fell back asleep, again snoring and farting.

About 50 miles from New York's LaGuardia Airport, the pilot said over the intercom, "You probably noticed that we just made a 180 degree turn. The tower has told us it will be another twenty minutes for us to land. So we've been delayed again. I'll keep you posted."

We finally landed in New York.

Of course, my limo service wasn't there at the airport. I stood outside and there was no one to pick me up. I called my wife and she called the limo service.

Five minutes later my limo arrived. I had been waiting on the departure level of the airport – where I always wait – and he had been waiting for me on the arrival level. He was a new driver.

And we took off for Long Island and home.

Except there were three accidents on New York's busy highways, which stalled me getting home. It took another hour and when I finally arrived home I felt like kissing the ground. Instead I kissed A.P., my beautiful wife. When we disengaged she said, "You smell like oranges."

Sometime in March

I'd been doing a radio show from Memphis, Tennessee for about a dozen years. The Tunica casinos and some other non-casino advertisers supported it. A few weeks after my disastrous trip to Tunica I got a phone call from the owner/host of the show.

"Hey, hey, Frank, my boy," he started.

"What's up?" I asked.

"Frank we got some bad problems on the show. You see some of the casinos are pulling back their advertising and I am just not going to be able to pay you to do your segment of the show any more. We had a pretty good run, ha, ha."

"Twelve years," I said. I had been with this show almost twelve years and he was cutting me loose just like that? Of course, this situation didn't surprise me – it seemed that Tunica's casinos had gone to war against me because they thought I was winning too much money and teaching people advantage play in my Golden Touch classes. These were no-no's. The fact that tens of thousands of non-advantage players had discovered Tunica thanks to my writing was never a factor. Suits are suits. The next logical step would be for them to put pressure on the radio show to dump me. I was a bad boy and I had to be spanked. So I was being spanked.

"Good luck in the future," I said to the radio show's owner. But I felt betrayed. In my casino gambling life, there have been three people that I feel betrayed me – this radio show owner/host is one of them.

"If things get better, I'll let you know," he said.

"Sure," I said, "Are you keeping John on the show?"

"Yeah, yeah, I can still afford to pay him," laughed the owner.

Years ago I had made a deal with this radio show owner that I would never ask for a raise if he started to pay John, the show's slot expert, because up to that time, John was working gratis. The owner and I agreed to this and John received a small stipend from that point on to do his weekly stint on the show. And I never asked for another raise.

Now I was out and John was still in. I guess that's the way of the world. No good deed goes unpunished. To make this even more ridiculous, months after my exit from the show, this owner/host wrote to me and asked if he could put his name to a book I wrote, publish it under his name, and not pay me!

Yes, it is possible that those of you reading this in the future are discovering that Tunica has returned to being the best gaming destination in America. It's also possible that the Tunica casino executives, some of whom had been very friendly to me over the years, have called me and welcomed me back to what had been my favorite place to play in the entire country.

I'm not betting any of that will happen. No, I am betting the games continue to get worse and Tunica will continue becoming the laugh track of casino venues.

Sadly, the great Tunica, Mississippi that I loved is now gone with the wind.

- Part Three -
Adventure at Dinner

I have a little problem with my father-in-law Don Paone. As I write this, he is 85 years old and still going. The problem is – he is going *slowly*. This is not due to his age but rather his temperament. The guy is a slow walker, a slow talker, and a maddeningly slow eater. He has genetic slowness. His wife, my mother-in-law Peg, is just the opposite. She is a fast talker, walker, and eater. But she is a young chick, really, only 84.

Don Paone is a published writer, his concentration philosophy, with an intense concentration in Catholic theology and politics. God created the world in six days but it takes Don Paone 60 days to write a thousand to two thousand word article – if he hurries. I write 30 of such articles in that time. Okay, so I am generally writing about the trivia of gambling, of which I am an unparalleled expert, and Don is writing about heaven, hell, and priests who should know better. There is no comparison in the seriousness of the issues we tackle.

Even for simple articles, Don Paone has to do massive research. His research is endless, which is fine if you are writing about things that aren't timely, but half the time he is sending his articles to the *New York Times* whose editor invariably tells him that what he wrote about, while well written and intelligent, was no longer hot. It was hot about a month or two or three ago. It took Don that long to get his ideas down on the page and by that time nobody cared about the issue at the *New York Times* anymore, or at any newspaper or magazine in America or the world. "Okay, so the world is oval, Don, we already knew that!"

Let me measure his slowness for you. He awakes at 7:30 AM. By 9:30 AM, he has finished his slow shower, his slow shaving (he must shave in two directions, so that's *two* slow shavings) and his slow dressing. He then eats breakfast. *Slowly.*

At 11 o'clock, he is finished with breakfast. The problem is he hasn't finished reading the *New York Times*. He is always behind in his *New York Times* reading. Now, most of you would jump to the conclusion that he is reading the *New York Times* for the news or the editorials. But that is not so. He reads the *New York Times* to *parse* it. Yes, parse it; as in enjoy the structures of the sentences and how the writers go about creating a story. His only real book reading is style and grammar books. These he reads slowly. He never reads a normal fiction or non-fiction book because there "just isn't enough time."

So he is always behind in his *New York Times* reading, day after day after day after day. And he must read the *New York Times* in chronological order so that he always has six or seven papers piled up from days past to read. This is another reason why he is behind when he writes about contemporary things – when he read about them; they aren't contemporary anymore. They are last week's news, which he has just gotten to.

Okay, after breakfast, he must get right to work. To do that, though, he must *slowly* organize what he is going to do for the day. If it's a research day, he gets the computer ready to use the Internet, where he does most of his research. In the old days, when he was younger and slower, he had to plan which library he was going to for his research. That was truly endless – the planning. He'd make a list of which libraries he was going to and it took forever to compile the list as he writes slowly. In those days he was a relatively fast writer; he was banging out an article every six months or so.

But now he gets the computer ready by turning it on. Unfortunately, there's usually some problem with the computer so he has to call his eldest son, Donald, to find out what's wrong. So those days Don just kind of mopes around waiting for Donald to come home and figure out what is wrong with the computer.

Now Don's eldest son Donald, a desired day laborer on Long Island because he can speak both Spanish and English, so the gardeners and home repairmen who need help always pick him up on the designated day-laborer street corners and parking lots so he can help them translate for all the illegal aliens that are also being hired. Suffice it to say that Donald knows computers and not just how to hack into them, but also how to fix them.

When I was away in Vegas for a 12-day trip, Donald decided to fix my computer because we hired him to redo my office. The computer wasn't broken and I am sure you know the old saying about fixing something that isn't broken. My computer has not worked well since then and I no longer have any sound.

Back to Don Paone.

If Don Paone is just going to write, meaning the computer is actually working, then he readies himself at the dining room table where he has his notes written in longhand. With the computer fired up, Don is now ready to blast off. The research is at his fingertips. The Internet is humming. His yellow legal pad is ready to be ripped into. His fully loaded inkwell pen is bursting.

The man is ready to write and his notes are spread out on the dining room table. He is poised over the legal pad. He is clean. He is shaven in two directions. He is fed. He is ready to do the writer's rumble.

Then the interruptions begin.

My mother-in-law Peg usually has something to do in the community that requires Don to come along. This is usually around noon, just as Don hovers over his legal pads, prepared to write about his great ideas about the universe, God and man.

Peg is very big in community activities, both church and state. She is the president of this, of that and of other things in our village on Long Island: If I can remember some of them – the Rosary Society, the Women's Club, the Historical Society to name a few. If she were President of the United States, we'd have a much better country, I can tell you that. Peg could make a teenager tired – her energy is boundless. But she likes Don to be with her when she does some of her community or church work – which is almost every day of the week, including Sundays, as she is the altar chairlady of the local Roman Catholic Church, Our Lady of Lourdes.

Most days, therefore, Don doesn't get to actually write, poised though he might be, which is a shame because he is a good writer. Most days he doesn't get to do his research, either. And all those copies of the *New York Times* pile up waiting for him as well. So he is behind in everything always and from the split second he wakes up.

Now, how do I know all this? Because when I am not gallivanting around the country doing *my* research in casinos, my wife, the beautiful A.P., and I have dinner with Don and Peg on Friday evenings at the Cork 'n Board restaurant. That's how I know Don's behind on everything every week because that's what he says.

I once tried to help Don with his writing. He had asked me how I had written 20 books, three plays, a DVD, six television scripts, three movie scripts, edited and wrote forwards for a dozen more books, and also wrote thousands of articles for the 50 or more magazines and newspapers I write for regularly; all of this in a mere 16 years. He seemed genuinely interested in figuring out how to increase his writing production, which had seen him write about 20 articles in that same 16-year period – a dozen of which were published.

So I told him, pleasantly, that he was nuts to take two or more hours every day getting ready to go downstairs just to have breakfast. Shower in the evening, not in the morning, and shave every other day, not every day – and just do it one way one day! Go up the beard one day, then down the beard on the day after tomorrow. Also, don't get fully dressed (Don has a hard time coordinating his colors so that takes endless amounts of time and ultimately the help of Peg). Just go downstairs in your pajamas or put on a sweat suit and eat breakfast, read a little, and get to work. If you don't finish the paper, recycle it because a new one will be arriving tomorrow. Never waste a morning because that is prime writing time – you are awake, refreshed, and crisp. The afternoon is better for editing and polishing. Use those mornings because you are fully ready to write new material.

That was damn good advice, I must say. That works for me.

But it didn't work for him, even though he never even tried to speed up the writing process. He just couldn't change his habits. Or maybe he is changing them but he is doing so *sooooo* slowly that no one has noticed yet.

Okay, fine, you know we all have different rhythms. Don has a rhythm too, much like a bear in hibernation. I live in my sweats. In fact, I have very few clothes. I don't need them; I don't want them. I'm never behind in my newspapers and I read three a day. I usually read a book or two a week. I read magazines. I watch movies. I write for eight hours every day seven days a week and I am even now writing on my gambling jaunts to the casinos around the country.

But none of that matters, really. That's how I work. That's not how he works. And that's that. It really isn't any of my business.

But here is where I do come in. Those dinners we have with Peg and Don are very nice occasions – but Don eats so slowly that he's always behind the rest of us. I have finished my salad, my soup, and my main course plus a few drinks – which takes me about an hour – and Don is still on the soup. Then he gets to the main course (thankfully he has no salad) and takes forever. New planets have been discovered; new countries have come and some have gone, animals have gone extinct, other animals have just evolved and Don is slowly eating his meal. And he always orders something that has a lot of food in it; like veal francaise with potato pancakes – a huge pile of potato pancakes. At Cork 'n Board you get large quantities of good food.

He cuts the veal slowly, lifts it to his mouth slowly, he looks at the fork with the veal stabbed on it and ponders – what he's pondering about I have no idea, but he ponders and then he puts the food in his mouth and chews in such a way that it can only be caught on stop-action photography, the kind the Discovery Channel uses to show how plants move in the course of 24 hours. Announcer: "You never thought plants moved, did you? Well, look at this incredible stop-action photography and you'll see that plants move several inches *every* 24 hours!" These plants move faster than Don Paone eats!

Because I don't want to finish my meal so far ahead of Don, I decided that when we have dinners together I would order what he ordered and eat as slowly as he ate. When he cut the meat, I would cut the meat – into the same, small piece. When he took a forkful I would take a forkful. When he lifted it up to his mouth, I would lift mine to my mouth. When he pondered I'd ponder. I thought this would work out just fine. Therefore, I would not eat, finish my dinner, and have to watch Don eat as suns in distant galaxies went super nova. I would match him fork for fork, chew for chew, and swallow for swallow.

That was the plan.

It was Friday evening, the first Friday of my grand design, and our regular waitress Debbie came over. She brought our drinks for us since she knows exactly what we want. At Cork 'n Board we have our own table and our own waitress. I like that. Since I am on the road a lot, when I am home I like a lot of routine. Debbie is an outstanding waitress and a hell of a nice person.

"Have you decided?" she asked us.

"Let the women go first," said Don, which is what he always says. We have a regular ritual at these dinners.

"I'll have onion soup, no bread," said my wife, the beautiful A.P. "I'll have shrimp with garlic and oil. No potatoes but extra vegetables." My wife is on the Specific Carbohydrate Diet to help her avoid a flare up of Ulcerative Colitis – something she has been free of for five years now.

"Peg?" asked Debbie.

"I'll have a fruit cup, salad with Russian on the side..."

"Ha! Ha!" laughed Don. "A Russian on the side. Oh, boy!"

Debbie gave a little chuckle.

Don always makes that same joke when Peg orders "Russian on the side." The first time I heard it, two decades ago, it was pretty funny. Debbie has heard it, maybe, several hundred times, but she always manages a chuckle. She is a truly professional waitress.

"Now, Don, you always say that," says Peg. "I'll have salmon, broiled, with lemon and butter and I'll have a baked potato."

"Frank, you go," said Don. This was the dining habit I had to change; otherwise I wouldn't know what Don ordered in order to make my selection. But I had a foolproof plan.

"No, Don, as the patriarch of the family, you should go," I said.

"Uh, I don't know what I want yet," he said.

"Okay," I said. I had this figured cold. "I'll have the cream of broccoli soup, a salad with honey mustard dressing on the side and..." *Here came my moment of triumph!* "...I'll have as my main course, whatever Don is having!" *Ta! Da!*

"Okay, Don?" asked Debbie.

"Uh, to the Queen!" said Don lifting his wine glass for a toast.

"You have to order before we toast," said Peg.

This toast, "To the Queen!" Don made at every meal. I wasn't quite sure what it meant but I always toasted. I wondered if Peg were the Queen? Maybe it was to the Queen of England.

"Oh, right," said Don. "What are you having Frank?"

"Whatever you're having," I said.

"Hmmm," said Don.

"Should I come back?" asked Debbie.

"No!" said the beautiful A.P., knowing that if Don didn't make his decision now we could be in for a long evening.

"Have the veal francaise," said Peg.

"My mother has spoken," said Don. "With potato pancakes."

"That's not funny," said the beautiful A.P. "You shouldn't be calling Peg your mother. That is just nasty. You should stop that."

"I am just joking," said Don, his whole face and baldhead turning beet red.

"Soup?" asked Debbie.

"Oh, the chicken noodle is fine," said Peg, ordering for Don.

"Okay, I'll be right back with the soups," said Debbie.

The course of conversation at these dinners is usually the same week to week as follows: Peg asks me how my family is, I tell her they are fine but my mother is losing more and more of her memory; how are my sons, they are fine, and my little grandson is beautiful, and when am I traveling next, in a few weeks. Then the beautiful A.P. will tell how much she loves being a librarian, which is her new career, a career she has wanted to be in since she was a little girl and then she'll tell about a few maniacs she served the past week (I'll bet you didn't know that public libraries attract maniacs – harmless ones mostly) and the combined elapsed time of A.P. and my conversation takes a total of, oh, about two minutes, three if A.P. has some really funny stories.

Now it is Peg's turn. Actually, make that big letters: PEG'S TURN.

Peg talks in long but precise and intimate detail about people that A.P. and I don't know (we call all of them *Mr. and Mrs. Obscure*) and they are legion, people that Don has totally forgotten ("Don, you know who I am talking about, come on. She was wearing a pillbox hat with a retro sixty's lime green dress at church four weeks ago and was sitting next to Paulie and Theresa Smithy who are having trouble in their marriage and are seeing a marriage counselor who is related to Peggy Hannon whose hip is really giving her trouble after her last trip to Florida where she fell in a row boat and what she was doing getting into a rowboat is beyond me, she's 87 years old, but her son, a retired school bus driver wanted her to get on the boat.") and about how Mr. and Mrs. Obscures' houses are fixed up, and the vacations they took, and what's happening with their children (*kids Obscure*). She speaks at length about their homes, going from room to room chronicling how the owners made all sorts of design changes and at the end of the story Peg mentions that house no longer exists but was torn down thirty years ago to put a bigger house on the property which she then describes in even greater detail.

Peg informs us of all the politics in church and state in our village, which is just about everything going on everywhere. She was instrumental in running out of town a priest (nicknamed *Adolph* after you know whom) who deserved to be run out of town. This guy closed the house for unmarried mothers – called Momma's House – because he wanted to build a bigger church as an edifice to himself. I think he even wanted to name the extension after himself. Peg was one of the architects of his demise. ("We Catholics believe that abortion is murder but he kicks out the women in crisis who agree to go to term on their pregnancies?" Peg would say to the local papers and radio stations that interviewed her.) You don't tangle with

Peg that's for sure. Unfortunately, all the unwed mothers had to leave our community since their house was torn down. But if you want to know what the inside of the house was like, Peg can take you on an inch-by-inch verbal tour of it.

When you dine with Peg you realize that she is writing a verbal book every time she speaks. She never just says something is this or that – no sir; the adjectives flow in the descriptions and there is almost never a time when one word would suffice when dozens of words could also be used.

Peg loves to discuss her son Lawrence and her daughter-in-law Catherine and their two beautiful daughters, Peg's grandchildren, Anna and Laura, ("Oh, that Anna is such a character!") or she discusses the beautiful A.P. Whenever I bring up A.P., I let Peg know just what a great daughter she has and what a great wife A.P. is – which she is.

According to A.P., "Peg loves to throw herself into community work and to talk about all the things going on around her, all the people she knows and she knows just about everybody. Her community business validates her. Before there were liberated women, Peg found that doing things was more fun than just staying home. She's always on the go."

Peg was discussing the color of someone's living room when Debbie brought over our soups. I didn't have to match Don spoon for spoon on the soup because I would have a salad coming next. But I watched the way he ate it. Don and Peg are expert at manners. Dom tilts the soup bowl away from him when he spoons out the soup. He never even drips a little of the soup on the table or the napkin. Unfortunately, some soup always drips on his shirt. None of us, not Peg, not A.P., not me, has ever seen the soup go from spoon to shirt, but somehow it does at every meal.

Don never notices it but Peg always spots it.

"You spilled soup again," says Peg.

"Acchh," says Don and then we all forget about it and continue dinner.

A.P. and I finished our soup, Peg finished her fruit salad, and then the regular salads were brought. Don ate his soup, with the cup now tilted away from him, and the stain growing on his shirt.

Now I slowed down my gastro ministrations. I tried to time my salad eating to finish when he finished his soup and to do that I started to cut my salad into smaller pieces.

I was keeping pace this way.

"Everything all right with your salad, Frank?" asked Debbie

"What?"

"You're cutting it up. Do you want me to have the chef do that?" asked Debbie.

"Oh, no, no," I said. "I, ah, am trying something new, slow down how fast, uh, how much, you know," I said. "I'm getting fat." I hoped she realized that I was trying something new because I wasn't getting fat; I was already fat from too many gourmet meals in the casinos during the past 20 years.

I don't know if she knew something was up but she nodded and headed to another table.

"Is the salad okay?" asked A.P.

"It's fine," I said.

"You're just picking at it," said A.P.

Don had his soup bowl tilted away from him. I tried to see how much soup he had left. I couldn't get a good glimpse because his hand covered it.

"It's fine," I said.

I was determined to begin my dinner when Don began his dinner. Debbie had learned to bring out our main courses even before she brought his. Tonight would be different. Tonight I would start with Don and end with Don.

The end of world hunger, disease and war, and the second coming of Jesus Christ took place and Don finally finished his soup. I finished my salad then too.

"Ready for our main courses, Debbie" I said, happy to see my plan working perfectly.

A few seconds later Debbie placed my plate in front of me and Don's plate in front of him. Problem! Don had much more food than I! Oh, God, how could I keep pace when Don had what looked like an Everest of veal in front of him.

"Don," I said. "You want to switch plates?"

"Huh?"

"I thought you were going on a diet?" asked Peg.

"Yes, well," I said. "That looks like a lot of food for Don." I know I sounded like an idiot, but it would be very hard to stay on pace with Don since his plate looked like the mountain in *Close Encounters of the Third Kind*.

"Oh, I'm fine," said Don. "I'm really hungry." He started to slowly cut a slice of veal.

I was desperate. "If you need me to eat any of your veal I'd be happy to," I said.

"Scobe, what are you saying?" asked A.P. I looked at A.P. She gave me this look that said, *Have you gone crazy?*

"Oh, well, you know," I said. I grabbed my fork and knife. "Hey, let's eat before everything gets cold." Maybe I could rush Don into eating at something like normal speed. Maybe pigs can fly too.

So we started eating. A.P. still glanced at me. I smiled at her. Peg chewed a mouthful of salmon.

But Don had not yet lifted the small slice of veal to his lips. So I fiddled with my veal. I started to cut it, nano-inch by nano-inch, and when I had finished cutting my slice, Don was only just now lifting his slice to his lips. I had to eat half as much as he did to keep pace with him since he had so much food to eat. Don was about to bite when he thought of something, "You know, ah," he blinked. When Don spoke, he blinked a lot. He put down his fork, blink, blink, blink.

"So I said to Mary Contessa that..." started Peg. Peg can start a conversation about anything at any time if she thinks she can get you hooked with her eyes.

And Peg had me on this one because we caught eyes. When you catch Peg's eyes, "she launches" (which is what the beautiful A.P. and I call it) and you are a squirming fish on a hook. Sometimes she just hones in on one person and grabs him/her with her eyes and then she launches into a long soliloquy. She had me pinned now.

Don was blinking.

I put my forkful of veal down.

"I, ah," said Don blinking.

"Mary Cummins was going to miss the Women's Club Meeting..."

"Ah, uhm," said Don.

"What kind of members are these that they miss all the meetings and don't want to open up the club to people who will actually attend the meetings?" said Peg.

"When Cardinal Ratzinger was in charge of, ah," blinked Don.

He still hadn't picked up his first forkful!

"Don," said Peg, "What are you talking about? We're discussing Mary Cummins and Mary Contessa."

"I ...wanted to... say... something," blinked Don.

Peg dropped my gaze for a second. I was free.

"Okay, what do you want to say?" asked Peg.

"I forgot now," he blinked.

Don has some severe memory problems and he forgets a lot – like how to get to places he's gotten to for 60 years.

"The Women's Club is a hard working group," said Peg but I busied myself with my fork. I had to take a mouthful soon.

Don lifted his fork.

"Is everything okay?" asked Debbie.

"Yes," I said.

"Yes," said Don putting down his fork. He still had not taken his first bite!

"You haven't eaten anything, Frank," said Debbie.

"Are you feeling okay?" asked A.P.

"Is he sick?" asked Peg.

"Fine. I'm fine," I said.

"I want to see you take a big mouthful of your food!" laughed Debbie. "Come on!"

What could I do? I took a mouthful.

"One more," said Debbie.

"Okay," I said. So I took a second mouthful. And, wonder of wonders, Don took *his* first mouthful. But Debbie then made me take a third mouthful.

I was behind him in eating by two mouthsful but I could chew slowly. Except Don was the slowest chewer on earth but I was determined to under-chew him.

"Good boy," said Debbie and she walked to another table.

I chewed in stop-action.

"Is the veal okay?" asked A.P.

"Yes," I said. "I'm just relaxing as I chew."

A.P. gave me that *Are you crazy?* glance but she didn't say anything.

Peg now launched into the history of the Women's Club, founded in 1951, none of whose members I knew or cared to know, and how all these Marys (Cummins, Contessa,

O'Toole, Flaherty, and Rineberg) were stuck in the old ways and didn't want new ideas. The youngest of the Marys was 80. The youngest member of the whole club was 70 – a young sprite! I quarter listened to the avalanche of information about the Ladies Auxiliary although I nodded every so often as Peg continued. I didn't want Peg to think I wasn't interested in her story because I do love Peg. But I intensely watched Don. I was keeping pace with him. So far I had four mouthfuls and he had taken eight. God, my plan felt great! If he had twice as much food as I, this eating pattern would allow me to finish when he finished – some time in the 22nd century.

"Hey, Frank," said Tommy the owner of the restaurant. "Is everything all right with that veal? I notice you haven't eaten much."

"The veal is delicious," said Don, putting down the forkful he was *just about to eat*! My fork was in midair too. I put mine down too. I had to keep pace with Don.

"The veal is great," I told Tommy.

"I hope so," said Tommy. "You don't do restaurant reviews do you?" He laughed.

"Not anymore and I would give your restaurant a great review," I said.

Don picked up his fork. If I kept talking to Tommy I might be able to get Don to take that forkful and maybe even another one without me having to eat a thing.

"So anyway, the Yankees…" I started.

"Tommy, I need a carafe of cabernet," said Debbie.

"Oops, gotta go," said Tommy who was also the bartender.

Don excused himself to go to the bathroom. This was becoming an ordeal. Peg talked about Nanette Ludinski whose husband had left her with five kids, a terrible thing to do to a woman, especially in 1947, when Mr. Ludinski flew the coop with some dancer for Radio City Music Hall. I guess it really got to Mrs. Ludinski too because she just died at age 90. "She was really very healthy until the day she died," according to Peg, snapping her fingers.

"Are you okay?" whispered A.P. as Peg continued to talk.

"Yes, damn it, I am fine," I whispered back.

Peg explained that Mrs. Ludinski never trusted men after 1947.

"Why so angry?" whispered A.P.

"I'm *not* angry. I'm just eating *slowly*," I whispered.

"She had one man that she loved in 1956, Paulie Delano, nicknamed PD, a cop, when she was finishing the basement of her first house on Vincent Avenue, although she never really did the walls there quite right because she painted over cinderblock and it was uneven, but she just couldn't say yes to marriage…"

"Why are you eating slowly?" whispered A.P.

"To stay even with Don," I whispered back.

"Ridiculous!" whispered A.P.

"Why is *that* ridiculous?" asked Peg. "She was very hurt. It wasn't easy raising those five kids all by herself since one of them was deaf, one had a club foot, and one had a very bad temper which got him imprisoned when he was in his early twenties for assault after he hit a cop at Jones Beach who told him he had to leave because there was a curfew."

Don slowly walked back from the bathroom.

Peg discussed the various incidents in the lives of Mrs. Ludinski's children but ultimately all the kids turned out okay and retired from different successful professions.

Don took a small bite of one of his potato pancakes. A.P. finished with her meal. Peg finished with hers as well.

Don still had most of Veal Everest remaining and all the potato pancakes except for one small bite out of one of them.

My veal was cold, maybe colder than Mrs. Ludinski right now, and I decided *fuck it! I quit!* and I resumed my normal way of eating. I finished in a flash.

And so, as usual, we all waited for Don.

Peg was on the story of the living room of Davida Davidson who had just sold her house in a neighboring community without ever having done anything to the house in the 30 years she had lived in it. Peg had visited the house once, in 1960-something, and described everything she could remember in great detail. It was enough to get us through Don's eating.

"That house is going to be torn down," said Peg. "The Amaruso Demolition company run by Danny…. Oh, Alene, you went to school with Danny's sister."

"Who?" asked the beautiful A.P., whose first name is Alene, a name I find beautiful and Alene hates because so many people call her Arlene or Eileen.

My cell phone rang. I had forgotten to shut it off.

"Scobe," said A.P. in the voice that said, *You aren't going to answer that in a restaurant are you?*

"It's Dominator," I said as if that made it okay to answer the phone.

"Tell him you'll call him after dinner," said A.P.

"Hey, Dominator," I said, answering the phone.

"You'll never guess but that stupid fuck was murdered!" said Dom.

"The stupid fuck as in *the* stupid fuck?"

"Yep," said Dom. "He was killed in one of those sleazy motels in Vegas. They burned the body and they identified it with teeth. But the big fat fuck is dead."

"His teeth? Christ!"

I felt a kick under the table. A.P. kicked me under the table. She whispered in my ear, "You said *teeth*, Scobe."

I looked at Don Paone and his face was blown up like a red balloon, veins sticking out of his neck, his baldhead, and his forehead. Damn, I had also said the word "fuck." You can't say those words around Don when you are eating or … well, he might die.

"Listen Dominator I am at dinner, I'll call you back in a half hour, okay?"

"Sorry about that, Don, Peg," I said.

Don's swollen head was receding.

At Peg and Don's house there is a table tent placed on the table at all times that has a list of words that cannot be said during a meal: teeth, spit, mucus, saliva, gums, tongue, scrotum, abscess, fart, fungus, armpit, diarrhea, toes, feet, bunions, nails, eardrum, eyeball, root canal, dentist, toilet, bathroom, bladder, kidney, and choke. If those words are said at the table, Don's face becomes bright red and his head swells up, veins bulging ominously. His eyes get watery and he blinks like crazy. We've never pushed the issue because of the obvious pain he's in when those words are spoken.

Except once. By my mother.

She and my father were at Don and Peg's and we were all having a great dinner, which Peg had prepared. Peg is a wonderful cook. My mother, a lovely, kind and generous woman and one who never wants to hurt anyone, saw the table tent. She picked it up.

"Oh, what's this?" she asked.

"Those are words…" started Peg.

"Teeth, root canal, mucus" said my mother.

"Uh, Mom," I said.

"Diarrhea, dentist, nails," continued my mother who is quite deaf.

"Mom," I said.

Don was swelling up. My mother just kept reading: "Tongue, gums, abscess, saliva, bladder, kidney…"

"Mom!" I yelled.

She looked up.

"You can't say those words at the table because..." and I nodded over at Don who was redder than a red beach ball.

"Don, your head is all red," said my mother. Since Don is almost completely bald, you could see the veins bulging at the top of his head. They looked like they were pulsating. "Don, did you *choke* on something?" asked my mother and Don turned redder.

"You can't read these words," I yelled.

"Oh," said my mother and put down the table tent.

I concluded having witnessed that incident that if you pushed those words on Don for any length of time; he would expire.

I hung up with Dominator. "Some guy who wrote some rotten stuff about Dominator on the Internet was found murdered in a sleazy motel in Vegas, burned to a crisp."

"Dominator takes everything too seriously," said A.P.

"Hey, it's no fun having people attack you," I said. "It's taking Dominator some time to get used to the fact that when you are famous people take shots at you."

"You handle it okay," said A.P.

"Yeah, well, it's still not easy," I said.

"The people who attack usually aren't as successful," said Peg. "Ramona Jorgensen was a past president of the Society for the Prevention of Cruelty to Flowers and she didn't do very much and then Sally Blake took over and created a great newsletter that she published once every two months. Sally did such great work around the village that she received so many awards for her holiday floral arrangements throughout the village. Well, Ramona became an increasing critic of Sally to the point where at board meetings she would stand up and just attack Sally every chance she got..."

"The usual after-dinner drinks?" asked Debbie.

"Yes," I said.

"What do I get?" asked Don, who was beginning to forget what our habits of dining were – other than the habit of eating slowly. Peg ordered for him.

"You know the mayor is having a problem with attacks, too," said Peg. "He has been attacked for going on too many trips."

"What? What are we talking about?" asked Don, who sometimes found it hard to follow the conversation – he was also slightly deaf.

Now when Don asked a question, especially about a political figure or someone of prominence in our village, Peg did not like to talk about it too loudly. So she would then cup her hand over her mouth and talk so low that no one could hear her and even a lip reader couldn't read her lips. That was the opposite of what Don needed, someone who would look him in the eyes and talk normally or even loudly. "Mumble, mumble, mayor, mumble, mumble, mumble," said Peg into her hand.

"What?" said Don leaning in and starting to turn red.

"Mumble, mumble, mayor, mumble, mumble, mumble," said Peg into her hand.

"What?"

"Mumble, mumble, mayor, mumble, mumble, mumble," said Peg into her hand.

"Forget it," said Don. "I can't follow this."

Then Peg took her hand away from her mouth and talked in a normal voice and launched into a discussion of what the Rosary Society was doing for their big party next month.

In another hour we were waiting for Don to finish his coffee and his drink. When he finished I paid the check with my airline-miles credit card and Don gave me his and Peg's half in cash. It took forever for him to count out the money since he did it three times to make sure he had the correct amount.

Now a tricky part occurred – could we get out of the restaurant without Peg meeting someone she knew and launching into an endless story? That happened about half the time. We would stand waiting for Peg, as she talked animatedly with someone none of us recognized.

But, in truth, I would never replace these meals. I like true characters, and Peg and Don are truly characters.

- Part Four -
Adventure at Craps - July 2005

The Captain of Craps called me at 11 last night, which is late for him and late for me, and he wanted to know if I wanted to make a trip with him to Atlantic City very early the next morning. It would just be a single day, to play, to talk, to walk, to reminisce. Of course I said, "Of course!" I never miss an opportunity to meet with the Captain, even if it means a day trip that takes three and a half hours. From Long Island to Atlantic City is a long haul.

I had just gotten back from a graduation party for my niece, Melanie, and I was tired. I had not practiced my dice throw since May when we did *The Frank Scoblete Gamblers Jamboree* in Canada. I'd been working on a new book and I had not planned to play craps until I got to Vegas in mid-September so, sad but true, I got lazy. I decided that a late night's practice would probably not help me much since I had to get up at 4 o'clock the next morning. Better to go to sleep and dream that I don't embarrass myself the next day in Atlantic City.

By now just about all savvy craps players know who the Captain is – aside from being the greatest craps player of all time, the Captain is my mentor; the man who taught me more about proper gambling in practice and in theory than I have learned from all the books and articles I have ever read.

I have met most of the greats of casino gambling but the Captain stands alone. I am reminded of Hemingway's *The Old Man and the Sea,* when the young boy, Manolin, is expressing fear about the Yankees not being able to win the pennant. The old man Santiago states, "There are many good ballplayers and some great ones, but there is only DiMaggio."

DiMaggio wasn't just a great ballplayer; he was *the* ballplayer. "...there is only DiMaggio."

There is only the Captain.

The Captain is the true master of the game of craps. Long before I wrote my first words in the late 1980s about how to beat the modern casino craps game with dice control, the Captain and the Arm were in fact beating Atlantic City casinos steadily from the late 1970s and through the 1980s and into the mid-90s when the Arm had to retire due to severe arthritis. I chronicle much of this in my book *The Craps Underground: The Inside Story of How Dice Controllers are Winning Millions from the Casinos!*

I was happy that the Captain shared his secrets with me, that he allowed me to write about how to succeed at craps, and I was privileged to see him and the Arm shoot countless times over those years. The Captain is a great shooter; but the Arm was the greatest I ever saw and I have seen the great ones, many of whom are my colleagues in Golden Touch Craps.

The Captain, now past the mid-80-year-old mark and heading I hope for 90, has lost just about all of his high-rolling friends, known as "the Crew," whom I wrote about in my first book, *Beat the Craps Out of the Casinos: How to Play Craps and Win!*

Jimmy P., Little Vic, Russ the Breather, Frank the fearful, the Doctor, and the Judge are all playing craps in the heavenly kingdom where dice control isn't necessary since all rolls are perfect. One remaining crew member of the Captain's, known as Satch, is now an instructor in the Golden Touch Craps dice control seminars. He was the youngest of the Captain's crew. I wrote about him in *Beat the Craps Out of the Casinos*, too, using his real name of Dave.

Thankfully, I did not have to drive down to Atlantic City. The Captain had the limo pick me up at 4:30 AM and then we picked him up in New York City. Usually the Captain drives down to AC with his wife, or he takes the high roller bus where all the "old guys" (as he calls them) play poker on their way to the shore. What I find fascinating about him is the fact that despite his staggering wins at the game and his success in his businesses, the Captain doesn't have that high roller "give me, give me" attitude. He is a humble man. Greatness and humility are a rare combination in the gambling world where the biggest morons often have the most bloated egos.

In the limo on the way to Atlantic City, the Captain said, "I'm sad, Frank. The Arm is very sick and it doesn't look as if she is going to improve. Her husband thinks she is preparing to go."

The Arm is also in her mid-80s but the years have not been kind to her. I saw her about a year ago and she was shrunken, bent, and a little distant as if she were having a hard time holding herself together. The Captain can walk 8 miles up and down the Boardwalk in Atlantic City, but the Arm now can barely walk across a room. I don't know if it was my father or the Captain who first said to me, "Getting old is a slow process but one day, you fall off a cliff." The Arm seems to have fallen off the cliff.

"What does she have?" I asked him.

"Age," he said.

The Captain had a wistful look. I changed the subject.

"You've been keeping track of your rolls?" I asked.

"Most times, now, I use chips like you said."

In order to tell how many numbers you've hit during a roll at the craps table, the easiest way is to put chips aside as you roll. You use one-dollar chips (usually white) for one through four, then a red chip for a five, add white for six through nine, then two reds for 10 and so on. When the roll gets to 25, use a green chip. It is an easy way to count your rolls without actually having to count your rolls. If you are playing with a friend at the table, the friend can do the counting. Seeing one or two or three green chips set aside is exhilarating. When I had my 89-roll hand in December 2004, seeing three green chips almost took my breath away. I was hoping to get to a black chip but as the dice gods would have it I sevened out before that happened.

Dominator scolded me when I sevened out: "You couldn't get to a hundred?"

"In the old days," smiled the Captain, "the fun of going to Atlantic City was that I played with a whole bunch of friends and I also was able to win money. I had friendship and a challenge all wrapped together. It went very fast. The time. It flew."

It does fly. I am at the stage in my own life where I see that time has flown. My sons…my *little* boys whose small hands I could consume in mine – are now men. I see pictures of them when they were little and I can still feel the *feel* of them from those times. I can almost go back in time, almost but not quite. I am a grandfather, too.

Time.

"You know," said the Captain, "I live more in the past now than in the present. I watch the old movies. Cary Grant, Ingrid Bergman, Ronald Colman. I don't even know today's stars. My generation merely lingers now. We fought Hitler, the Japanese, and Mussolini. We defeated the great enemies of mankind and now we just linger."

In Atlantic City, the time was only 8:30 AM when we checked in but the casino had a suite ready for us. One of the Captain's good friends is a high ranker at one of the biggest casinos and he made sure that the two-story suite was ready for the Captain's day at the Queen of Resorts.

"Let's put our stuff in the room," said the Captain. Room? It was six rooms! But to the Captain it was a room.

"Then let's take a little walk," said the Captain.

"Fine," I said.

We put our bags in the suite. The Captain took one of the bedrooms; I took the other. Mine was actually the better bedroom as I had my own Jacuzzi in it.

We took a walk along the Boardwalk. The Captain and his departed Crew owned this town. They were thousand dollar and more bettors.

"Atlantic City is actually nicer now than it was in 1978 when it was really a ghetto," said the Captain. "The buildings in those days were falling down all over town. It isn't Vegas but Vegas isn't Vegas anymore either."

We walked for about an hour and a half and the Captain recommended that we go back to the room, rest a little, and then hit the tables. The Captain is a firm believer that you have to play rested and that you must never allow the casino's 24-hour-a-day rhythm overwhelm you. I learned that lesson the hard way when my wife, the beautiful A.P. and I lost all our gambling money on one trip because I had played stupidly – over-betting my bankroll and going on tilt. The Captain taught me then how to keep my normal human rhythm in the face of the 24-hour bam, bam, bam of the casino.

In the suite, the Captain went to his room. I lay down on the bed in my room. The Captain did seem wistful today. His perkiness was not at the usual level. The Arm's deterioration must be weighing heavily on him. He and the Arm had won millions together. They had been on the crest of the first wave of the dice control revolution.

It's funny but I never think of people dying. I never think of myself as dying.

I just counted up the people I have been close to who have died. I number only 20 and that includes my grandparents.

The Captain went to a high school class reunion a few years ago and there were only five of his classmates left alive. *Now we just linger.* The Captain was a part of the greatest generation. He had been in the Army Air Corps in World War II. He had been shot down behind enemy lines in the Philippines and had to survive for more than a week hiding from the Japanese soldiers who scoured the jungle looking for

Americans who had been shot down – he caught malaria to boot. He saw the Enola Gay land at his Army air base. He served in Japan during the occupation. I wrote his biography in *Forever Craps: The Five-Step Advantage-Play Method.* He's a fascinating guy.

Now we just linger.

An hour or so later, we were heading for the casino floor. The Captain said he had actually fallen asleep. I must have too since the time went by in the blink of an eye.

Time.

The casino was crowded but we found our two spots open at a 12-foot table. I was on stick left one and the Captain was on stick right one. Something else I noticed. The Captain had gotten shorter in the past few years. He used to be my height, now he was an inch or two shorter. He was in good shape but time had also diminished him somewhat.

The pit boss came over and said hello to him. The Captain took out a marker. The Captain's betting in the past few years has decreased somewhat from his glory days of the 1980s. I took a marker as well.

In Atlantic City, it usually takes a while for the marker to arrive. Unlike Vegas, you don't get your chips until you actually sign the marker. So we had to wait. While we were waiting two hosts came over to say hello to the Captain. They knew him as "the Captain" too. What interests me all the more is why haven't the people who know who the Captain is tell others? These two hosts, long time Atlantic City people, knew him. Three of the casinos biggest honchos in Atlantic City know who he is, too. Indeed, he has some good friends in Atlantic City who work for the casinos. They were kids when he started his craps career, some of them craps dealers, and now they run places. And they still come to him for advice.

Time.

We waited for our markers as the hosts departed.

No big deal. The dice were two people to my left with a squirrelly fellow. He established the 5 as his point, rolled a couple of times, and sevened out. I wanted the markers to come to us just as the Captain was about to roll. Then we wouldn't be wasting any money on random rollers.

When the shooter just before the Captain got the dice, our markers came.

"Sorry this took so long," said the floorwoman. "We're a little understaffed today."

The Captain signed for his marker. I signed for my marker.

We were playing at a 5X odds table with a $10 minimum bet. Both of us *5-Counted* the shooter next to the Captain. He made it to the 4-count and sevened out.

Now it was the Captain's turn. I placed a $15 Pass Line bet and the Captain placed a $30 Pass Line bet. The Captain rolled a 6 as his point. The Captain sets the 3-V set at all times, even though he keeps his bets off during the Come-Out roll, which is perhaps not the optimal way to play when setting dice that way. However, the Captain thinks of the Come-Out roll as a rest period when he shoots. I studied him a few times during his rolls that day and indeed on the Come-Out roll, his intensity is not as great. He is *resting*.

He put up a $300 bet on the 8 and he bought the 4 for $55, paying a two-dollar vig. He put $250 in odds behind his Pass Line bet of 6. His betting today was more than I had seen him bet in the past few years and I wondered why he had upped his action. I had $125 in odds behind the point and I had $150 on the 8. I also bought the 4 for $55, as I would mirror the Captain's betting. If you are going to imitate, you might as well imitate the best.

By betting $15 or $30 on the Pass/Come at a 5X odds game, the casino we were playing in allowed you to "push the house" up on the odds. So you could take $75 for $15 on the Pass/Come or $150 for $30 on the Pass/Come on the 4 and 10,

$100 or $200 on the 5 and 9, and $125 or $250 on the 6 and 8. The Captain is a master at "pushing the house," as he was the first player to get Atlantic City casinos to allow you to buy the 4 or 10 for $35 paying just a $1 vig. He even pushed some casinos to allow you to buy the 4 or 10 for $39 for the same one-dollar vig.

The Captain rolled a 5, a 10, and then he sevened out.

It was my turn.

"Hey, hey, Frank?" said a voice next to me.

"Yes?" I said.

"Kenneth Frasca," he said. "I went to your Jamboree two years ago."

"Hi," I said.

"Put your Pass Line bet up, sir," said the stickman tapping the Pass Line with the stick.

I placed my $15 on the Pass Line.

"You going to get in?" I asked.

"He's coming to lunch with me," said the woman next to him.

"My wife. Linda this is Frank Scoblete, the writer, you met him at the Jamboree," he said.

"Hi Linda," I said and shook her hand.

"Sir, we're waiting for you," said the stickman.

"Okay," I said. "Sorry."

"Hey, the Captain ain't around is he?" joked Kenneth.

"He's on stick right," I said as I took the dice.

"Let's go to lunch," said his wife.

"Oh, Jesus, oh, Jesus, Linda that's the Captain!"

"I'm starving," said Linda.

Kenneth went over and said hello to the Captain. I forgot about Kenneth and rolled.

I took the dice and set for the 7. I hit 11, then two 7s in a row, then a 5. That was my point. I took $100 in odds on my point of 5. I placed $150 on the 6 and $150 on the 8. I also used the 3-V set. I rolled a 6; was paid $175 for it. I rolled another 6. Then I rolled a third 6. Then I sevened out.

My dice were looking good and I figured I would have a good roll next turn. Little did I know there would be no next turn.

We 5-Counted all the shooters. Four of the eight at the table made it through the 5-Count and we put up $10 Come bets on them with double odds. We lost money on them as they all sevened out soon after we had some bets up.

A lot of players don't realize that the 5-Count really does not reduce the house edge on random rollers. It just reduces by 57 percent what you bet on random rollers, thus saving you money. However, as Dr. Don Catlin showed in a massive study of 200 million simulated shooters, if you are at a table with controlled shooters, even if you don't know they are controlled shooters, the 5-Count gets you on them 11 percent more often than a normal player will be. That's where you can make some money.

We Golden Touch Craps dice controllers use the 5-Count to reduce the number of rolls we bet on, and on random rollers we also bet much lower than we will on controlled shooters. The 5-Count is a wonderful tool in a controlled shooter's arsenal if he has to play at the same table as random rollers, which most of us do. As you can see, my total risk on the random rollers who made it through the 5-Count this day was a mere $30. Odds don't count.

Now the Captain got the dice again. The Captain is a calm shooter, second in calmness to the Arm herself. Nothing gets to him. I have rarely seen him lose his temper at the tables. He doesn't practice Zen but he is very Zen-like.

The Captain set the 3-V and rolled. It was 1:15 in the afternoon. He hit a 2. Then he hit a 3. Then he established his point, a 4. We were going up the number scale! The Captain put up $300 on the 6 and 8 and $150 in odds behind his point. I had $150 placed on my 6 and 8 and $75 behind my point.

The Captain rolled a few numbers we weren't on and then hit a 6. Then he hit the 8. Then the 6 again. Then he made the 4. The table gave polite applause. The Captain now added a $55 buy of the 10 to his bets. I did the same.

In Atlantic City, if you want to buy the 4 or 10 for $55, you pay a $2 vig but if you put up both numbers at the same time, you must pay $5 in total. So, the way to bet to save that $1 is to make a bet of one number, then after a roll, bet the other number. Those dollars add up. Unfortunately in Atlantic City, you must pay the vig upfront, which means you pay that vig on winning and losing rolls. In many casinos around the country, the vig is only extracted on the buy bets after you win but not on any losses. That cuts the house edge down considerably.

The Captain established his point, a 6. We both now bought the 4 for $55. We took our 6 place bets down and took odds behind the Pass Line point of 6.

So we were now up on four numbers, the 4, 6, 8 and 10. And the Captain rolled. Now he was focused because he could seven out. And he started hitting numbers. At a certain point he made his point of 6. He then made several more points and many numbers.

The Captain was hot. Other players joined the table.

At the 25-minute mark, the Captain had rolled 32 numbers – one green chip, one red chip and two white chips – and the Captain was on another Come-Out roll. Then he did something that was unusual for him.

"Frank," he said. "Can you get me a chair?"

Since the mid-1980s when I first started to play craps with the Captain, I don't think I ever saw him sit down. I was startled. But I quickly went over to an empty blackjack table and grabbed a chair. I set it behind the Captain. He sat on it right away.

The floorwoman came over and said, "I'm sorry, you can't sit there." Just as quickly the pit boss came over and touched the floorwoman on the arm and said, "He's the exception. Let him sit if he wants to." The floorwoman looked confused but obeyed her boss. The two of them walked away and when they were on the other end of the pit, they started to talk. I have no idea what they were saying but they both kept shooting glances our way.

On the Come-Out roll, all our bets, except our Pass Line bets obviously, were off. The Captain gently lofted the dice down the table. He rolled a 7, and then established a point of 6.

From here on in, it started to get blurry. The Captain rolled numbers and points. I was counting the rolls, putting white chips down, then reds, and then a second green. We were at 45 minutes and the Captain had rolled 54 numbers. On his Come-Out rolls and when the dealers were paying off the bets, he would sit in the chair and just stare straight ahead. He was locked into some kind of meditative state. I never said a word to him. I had bets on all the numbers now and had pressed them once, twice, or three times depending on how often they had hit.

The third green chip went down. The Captain was at 75 numbers. I looked over at him. He did not look at all tired, just reflective, sedate, as if he were in another world. In January of 2004, the Captain had rolled 100 numbers. I wondered if he could reach that plateau again. One hundred numbers is a magic roll.

76 numbers

The Captain has a very easy throw. There is no strain in him when he shoots. He is focused. He is in total control of himself.

77 numbers

He is in total control of the dice. His roll is the model for the Golden Touch roll.

78 numbers

The Captain made a point here. I had three green chips and three white chips for the 78 numbers. The cocktail waitress came over and the Captain ordered an orange juice, no ice, and I ordered bottled water.

"When you come over with the drinks," I said to the waitress, "bring me his drink if he's still rolling, okay?" I put five dollars on her tray. "Okay," she said.

Kenneth Frasca reappeared. I squeezed over so he could get next to me. The table was now packed.

"How's he doing? How did he do last roll?" asked Frasca.

"It's the same roll. He's at 78 numbers," I said.

"Oh, man!" he whispered in my ear.

"I thought we were going to walk the Boardwalk?" asked Linda.

"Not now," said Kenneth who bought in. Linda did not seem pleased. But she wandered away.

As the Captain shot his Come-Out roll, new chips were brought in. We had seriously damaged the casino's chip area and new chips, big and little denominations both, were now being counted on the table.

The Captain ignored it. He rolled. He established a point.

79 numbers

Most of the other players were now betting green and black chips. Somewhere around roll 45, most of the players started to press their bets. Some had become almost insanely aggressive. The table was full of players now – 13 players altogether, seven on my side with Frasca squeezed in, and six on the Captain's side.

80 numbers (three green chips, one red)

81 numbers (three green chips, one red, one white)

When the great Golden Touch instructor Howard "Rock 'n Roller" shoots, you can barely see the Hardway area of the layout. That slows the game to a halt because Rock 'n Roller has the delightful ability to hit those Hardways in bunches and it takes a lot of time to pay off everyone's bets. This was not so today. There were only a few Hardway bets. It was almost as if no one wanted to slow down the game with bets that take too long to pay off. Most of the players were good bettors – a rarity at a craps table but one that was making this game progress at a nice pace.

The Captain was in his rolling zone for sure.

82 numbers

83 numbers

84 numbers

85 numbers (three greens, two reds)

The Captain is a rarity. I am not. As a writer, a teacher and a speaker, as a former actor, I crave the public performance. I want a readership, an audience. I like the spotlight on me.

86 numbers

The Captain doesn't care about those things. He was the leader of "the Crew" because they made him the leader, he didn't ask for it. His nature must make other men and women want to follow him.

87 numbers

He never asked to share in the glory or profits of the books or tapes I wrote. He never asked to be on television or radio. He never asked me to write about him. He did his thing and he let the world do its thing.

88 numbers

Best selling gaming author, Henry Tamburin asked me, "How come the Captain doesn't want to go out in public and be recognized?" I told Henry the Captain is the guy everyone wants us to be. "You see when we are criticized some of it is, 'Well, if they are so good why are they writing about it? Why aren't they just doing it?' Well, the Captain is the guy who did it and is still doing it. He doesn't crave the public attention like we do."

89 numbers

I had hit 89 numbers in December of 2004. I wasn't keeping track of them but Dominator and one of our Golden Touch students were. I had two students at the table that day.

90 numbers

So much for 89! The Captain was now getting close to the magic 100 rolls.

91 numbers

The Captain was happy that I became successful as an advantage player and as a writer. He was happy my books sold so well. But he is content to do what he does.

92 numbers

He has slowed down now. His investing in real estate is over. He lives off his past investments and his once-a-week play in Atlantic City.

93 numbers

The Captain used to play several times a week. I can recall him in those days. He was probably 63 when I first played craps with him at the tables. He was not much older then than I am now. I first played craps at the Claridge, which at that time was a great casino for players.

94 numbers

"Pay the line!" shouted the stickman.

It was now another Come-Out roll. I remember this clearly. I put several stacks of black chips on the table to color them up. I was completely out of room in the chip rack in front of me. The Captain now sat for all the Come-Out rolls. Kenneth Frasca kept whispering in my ear, "I can't believe I'm playing with the Captain."

"Believe it," I said.

95 numbers (no point established – he rolled an 11)

96 numbers (another 11)

I noticed that the Captain's bets were with purple and orange chips now.

97 numbers (point of 4 established)

We were getting close to 100 numbers. Would he make it?

98 numbers

99 numbers

I looked over at the Captain. He had no idea how many numbers he rolled but the time was now 2:45 in the afternoon. He had rolled for one and a half hours.

He set the dice carefully. He aimed. I noticed that there were now several suits behind the boxman. Big money was being wagered at this table and it was the job of the suits to make sure that no mistakes were made with such big money in play. I could see another cart loaded with chips being wheeled to the table. Some players think that the suits gather on a hot game to cool it off. That is not so. They gather to make sure the money is being handled properly. With $500 and $1000 chips in play, a small mistake can cost a lot of money – to the casino and to the players too.

"This is number 100?" asked Frasca.

"Yes," I whispered.

"Oh, man," he whispered.

The Captain arced the dice giving them a gentle backspin. They hit the table, moved slowly to the back wall, and died, flat, dead at the base of the pyramids, having barely glanced off the back wall.

"Five! Five!" shouted the stickman. "No field five!"

That was 100 rolls. That was one black chip. That was, my God! 100 numbers for the Captain.

No one other than Frasca and I knew what a monumental moment this was but they all knew they were on one hell of a roll.

101 numbers

102 numbers

103 numbers

The new chips were brought in. One of the suits laughingly said, "This is it guys, these are our last chips. Don't take them all from us."

104 numbers

105 numbers

106 numbers

Then a bloated man at the end of the table started an argument. "I had a five dollar yo bet! Where's my money?"

"That was the roll before this one, sir, not this one. It's a one-roll bet, sir," said the dealer.

"Call over the floorman," said the large one.

I took $80 in chips and threw them over to the man.

"Forget the floorman," I said.

"I, uh, I…" said the large one.

"Take the chips and let this man roll for God's sake!" I said. The dope took the chips.

"Move the dice," said the boxman. "We don't want this table to cool down."

The stickman pushed the dice over to the Captain. He had been seated while the large one had stupidly slowed down the game. The Captain now stood, set the dice, aimed and released.

107 numbers

That was nice of the boxman to say he wanted the hot roll to continue. He would not be able to share in the massive amount of tips the Captain, several players, and I were giving the dealers on each and every roll but he looked genuinely happy that he was watching such a great afternoon's session.

108 numbers

Several players and the Captain had now reached table maximum bets on some of the numbers.

109 numbers

110 numbers

111 numbers

Which got me to thinking: Stanley Fujitake! The *record*.

112 numbers

Fujitake held the dice for three hours and six minutes. He did this on May 18, 1989 at the California Club in downtown Las Vegas. That feat earned him the title of "The Golden Arm." A whole inventory of spectacular tales has grown up around the man who holds the record for the longest craps hand in history.

113 numbers

Sure, others have claimed anonymously that they have seen shooters surpass that record but only Stanley Fujitake's record is taken seriously by anyone the least interested in craps. He did his feat in front of scores of witnesses and the time was verified by them and by the casino.

114 numbers

Fujitake's is *the* record.

115 numbers

How incredible is *the* record? Take Joe DiMaggio's 56-game hitting streak; Wilt Chamberlain's 100 points in an NBA game; Muhammad Ali's upset of big George Foreman, Secretariat's winning of the Triple Crown in stunning blowouts, and wrap them all up in a knot – Fujitake's record is more spectacular.

116 numbers

Three hours and six minutes! That might have been 200 rolls of the dice.

117 numbers

Fujitake. *The record.*

118 numbers

I looked over at the Captain just as he looked at me. A smile played on his lips. "I feel good," he said to me.

119 numbers

Of course, Fujitake was a random roller and not a controlled shooter as is the Captain. His great feat is the great feat of luck; while the Captain's great feats, and he has had many great feats, are the results of skill. While the Captain was rolling I had no idea at this point that he had actually beat the number of rolls Fujitake had in 1989 – which was 118 rolls before he sevened out.

120 numbers

Each stickmen at this casino was courteous as they moved back as the Captain threw. That gave him a clear vision down the table. The player at the end of the table never put his Pass Line bet down where the Captain landed his dice. That was very smart of him. The table was behaving as you would want the table to behave to help create and perpetuate the monster roll.

121 numbers

There were maybe 30 people now standing around the outside of the table watching. Frasca kept whispering, "Holy shit," in my ear. That was his day's religious mantra. An aggressive-looking guy with slicked-back black hair was about to try to squeeze in next to the Captain as the Captain was lifting the dice. The guy next to the Captain pushed the aggressive one and said, "Don't even think about it." The guy next to the Captain sounded and looked like a wiseguy and the aggressive guy slunk away, his girlfriend hanging on his arm saying, "Why can't we get in and play? Why can't we get in and play?"

122 numbers

123 numbers

124 numbers

For almost 20 years the Captain and his Crew owned Atlantic City. High rollers, fun lovers, 22 of the most interesting men and women one could ever meet. Strangely only one of them ever really understood that the Captain was winning all those years. His name was Jimmy P. In the early 1990s, Jimmy P., the Captain, and the Arm hit Tropworld (now Tropicana) for millions in wins and comps.

125 numbers (one black chip and one green chip)

126 numbers

This roll was the longest roll I have ever seen. Even the Arm never had a roll that was this long. At 126 numbers, the Captain was approaching two hours of rolling. I remember one of the executives, who worked at the Claridge, saying in 1992, "The Captain is killing us." Even the former president of the Claridge wrote about the Captain and his Crew in a book. He talked about how the Captain hammered them.

Yet no one has revealed the Captain's name. Interesting.

127 numbers

The length of a hand kept in time is not as descriptive as the length of a hand kept in number of rolls.

128 numbers

129 numbers

This roll was in the mega numbers.

130 numbers (one black, one green, one red)

We were at the two-hour mark now. Two hours of rolling the dice. The Captain would roll, sit in the chair as the payouts were made, then stand when the stickman moved the dice to him. He constantly set the 3-V. He was a machine. No, in fact, more accurately: He was in a gambling ballet. His every move was smooth and beautiful.

131 numbers (one black, one green, one red, one white)

How much luck did the Captain need to create this monster-of-monsters hand? He had rolled some sevens on the Come-Out. The 3-V is not a set for rolling sevens and those sevens were therefore mistakes. That was good luck for him and for the rest of us at the table. He rolled at least four sevens that I remember on the Come-Out. Had any one of those sevens been during the "point-cycle" of the game, he would have sevened out.

132 numbers

133 numbers

Good luck? I have had great good luck in my life. I have wonderful parents, a wonderful wife, wonderful children, wonderful grandchilden, a wonderful writing career and I have a few good friends.

134 numbers

135 numbers

I also have some people who – for God knows what reason! – hate me and hate my writing. Walter Thomason, the gambling writer, used to tease me by sending me Internet web posts by people who were attacking me. One famous gambling authority once said he would kill himself if he woke up and found out he had turned into me. As Golden Touch has become internationally known, the attacks have become even fiercer.

136 numbers

137 numbers

138 numbers

The Captain and the Arm were the most devastating one-two punch in the history of modern casino craps – even better than the Lee Brothers whom I wrote about in *The Craps*

Underground. The two of them won eight figures together. Although Atlantic City is not allowed to bar players, the Tropworld casino (now Tropicana) refused to give them any comps after they won 1.5 million in a few months. They even sent a letter around telling the other casinos to be aware of these two. I was able to read this letter when the Captain showed it to me. He got it from one of his casino-executive friends.

139 numbers

The Captain was in a rhythm.

140 numbers

Bing!

141 numbers

Bing!

142 numbers

Bing!

143 numbers

Bing!

144 numbers

Bing!

We were at 144 numbers! *There is only the Captain.* The very Captain who was now banging away at two hours and 15 minutes in a roll that will become legendary.

145 numbers

Bing!

146 numbers

Bing!

I looked over at the Captain, who was as calm now as he was when he first got the dice. *There is only the Captain. There is only the Captain. There is only the Captain.* Could he go to 200 numbers? Could he go for over three hours and six minutes?

147 numbers

Bing!

The Captain is the greatest craps player who ever lived. He is more than a master, more than a mentor. *There is only the Captain.* He is at two hours and 18 minutes. He has hit 147 numbers.

Now we just linger. Time. There is only the Captain.

The dice were lofted into the air. One die lagged a little and when they came down that lagging die just stopped dead. The other die went to the back wall, hit, and gently rolled over.

There was a pause.

"Call it," said the boxman.

"Seven," said the stickman, "Seven out! Line away, pay the don'ts."

There were no don'ts. There was only silence.

Now we just linger.

Time.

There is only the Captain.

"That was a great roll," I said.

"Oh, God," said Frasca.

"Great roll, sir," said the boxman.

"Great roll, Captain," said the Pit Boss.

"Great roll, Captain," said one of the other suits.

And then the applause started. The players and the spectators started to clap. It became thunderous. Even the boxman clapped. The stickman, with the stick under his arm, clapped too. Then people cheered and some yelled, "Bravo! Bravo!"

That roll lasted two hours 18 minutes. It was 147 numbers, with the 148th number being the seven out.

The guy next to Frasca said to us, "They called him the Captain? Is that *the* Captain? *The* Captain?"

"Yes," said Frasca as if he knew the Captain a long, long time.

"You know him?" asked the man of us.

"Yes," I said. "We know him." I included Frasca in the "we." Frasca smiled.

"My god I can't believe it," said the man. "I saw the Captain himself. Oh, my God," he said as he put down his stacks of black, purple and orange chips. ·

"Yes, you did," I said. "That is the man himself."

"Amazing," said Frasca. "One hundred and forty seven numbers."

"One hundred forty seven numbers," said the man. "God."

No one can take this achievement away from the Captain – 147 numbers, two hours 18 minutes of rolling. The man who first realized that rhythmic rolling, a synonym for dice control, was the way to beat the house in 1978, the man who figured out how to win money playing craps, had just completed a Babe Ruthian roll. Ruth once hit a baseball 626 feet, the longest homerun in history. And this was the longest craps roll in history – 147 numbers.

There is only the Captain.

We colored up our mound of chips and security escorted us to the cage.

"We'll have a late lunch in the suite and then we'll head back home," said the Captain.

"You rolled one-hundred forty-seven numbers, Captain," I said.

"It was a great roll," he said.

Yes, it was.

There is only the Captain

The Captain Holds
the Real World Record

I have always thought that Stanley Fujitake's three-hour six-minute roll in May of 1989 in Las Vegas was not only the longest craps hand in terms of total time elapsed but also the longest hand in terms of total numbers thrown before the dreaded seven-out. I always estimated that Fujitake rolled about 200 numbers in his mammoth run.

I was wrong.

According to Boyd Gaming at whose property this roll took place, Fujitake's epic hand was 118 numbers long before he sevened out. [*Boyd Buzz* magazine, Summer 2004, page 3.] While Fujitake still holds the total time record, his great feat has been surpassed, in a spectacular way, by the greatest craps player of all time - The Captain, who rolled 147 numbers before he sevened out. The Captain's roll took place in 2005.

The Captain's roll lasted two hours and 18 minutes.

The disparity in time between the two rolls is easy to explain. Fujitake was rolling on a 14-foot table, packed with players, most of them making the Hardways bets and other Crazy Crapper bets that took a lot of time to pay off. That table had at least 14 players at it. With only 12 other players at the Captain's 12-foot table and with most of them eschewing the bad bets, the Captain was able to get in many more rolls in much less time.

The fact that the Captain achieved such a remarkable roll at the tender age of 83 merely vindicates what Golden Touch and I have been saying for years. The Captain is *the* man when it comes to craps play and history can now record him as having had the greatest single hand of all time.

Oh, yes, there is only the Captain.

- Part Five -
Adventures in the Weird World - '73 to '84

In 1973, I lived in Far Rockaway, New York. Far Rockaway, in the borough of Queens, is at the very tip of New York City, right at the border of Long Island, and right on the beautiful Atlantic Ocean. At one time Far Rockaway had been a well-to-do section of New York City, more suburban than city, but then came public housing – monstrous apartment buildings to house the welfare recipients and others classified as "low income" – and in streamed the low-lifes and criminals. This happened all over New York City, not just in Far Rockaway. Some of the nicest areas were destroyed because the City and State built their "low-income" housing on choice waterfront property.

When I lived there Far Rockaway had been transformed and was now a neighborhood under siege. The muggers and drug addicts ruled the streets. It was punk city.

I was married to my first wife then. I was 26-years old, teaching English at a Long Island high school, and I also wrote for a new magazine in which I had invested $50,000 of my life savings (I take that back, it *was* my entire life savings), but thankfully I was paying an amazingly small amount of money for a gorgeous top-floor apartment with a spectacular view. Of course, the neighborhood was not so nice and the tenants of the building had a tenant patrol every night to scare away the muggers and burglars and other assorted monsters who prowled Far Rockaway's streets. So two nights a week I sat in the lobby on tenant patrol with a neighbor.

It was worth it.

But the tenant patrol is not the focus of this part of the book. Instead this is about the weird, the strange, the wonderful; in short, some of the things I experienced during those years I spent in Far Rockaway just before my first son, Gregory, was born and before I become heavily involved in theatre. This was also long before I discovered the joys of advantage play against the casinos.

I just wish I knew why I had these experiences and what they all meant in the broader scheme of things.

1973
It Begins
Anita Harrison

One afternoon I was taking a nap. That night was parents-teachers night so I wanted to get a little rest before I met the parents. The district where I taught was one of the best on Long Island at that time – mostly composed of successful professionals and business people – and most of their kids were heading for college. These kids were generally well behaved, motivated, and some were even eager learners. A small percentage of the school were of a distinctly different class, mostly working class Italian, or poor black and Hispanic but the scheduling segregated the ruffians from the refined and the ruffians took what were called "school" classes, which were shortened to "S" classes; while the refined took "regents" classes. The regents classes all had to take challenging state-sponsored tests at the end of the year. The "S" classes – well, the students and the teachers just had to survive those and make it to summer vacation.

That's not to say that there weren't some wonderful kids in the school classes or that there weren't some real shitheads in the regents classes but economics tended to win out in those days and the school classes were filled with kids who would be going to Nassau County Community College if they were decent in their studies, or into jobs, or onto the streets, or into jails, while the regents class students had the Ivy League and other fine institutions in their sights.

During that pre-parents-night nap I suddenly woke up – except that my body was still asleep. That I knew instantly. I was wide-awake but my body just wasn't there. My mind was completely conscious, my heart seemed to be pounding, and I knew a terrifying fact – that I couldn't even force out a sound from my throat. Was I having a stroke or something? Suddenly I could feel a kind of electric tingle going through me, up and down, up and down, toe to head, head to toe – almost like an invisible magician waving his wind up and down my body. I tried to move but I couldn't. I was terrified that I would be paralyzed for my whole life, however long that would be after this stroke or whatever it was. Then I made a *supreme* effort, calling forth whatever store of will power I had, and was able to sit up – *blink* – just like that.

Except I didn't stop by sitting up – I kept going up.

Yes, I sat up fast and then I floated up slowly to the ceiling. I bounced on the ceiling as if I were a helium balloon. I looked down and there I saw someone in my bed with my wife – oh, my God, that someone was Frank Scoblete. I seemed to be sleeping soundly – although I looked kind of weird since I was always used to seeing myself in a mirrored image and not as I really was. And where exactly was I? Up here on the ceiling floating and bouncing gently and also in the bed. I could see my wife asleep in the bed next to me. She was sound asleep. Hell, I was sound asleep too.

But I was also completely awake up here bobbing gently against the ceiling.

I reached my hand up to stop from bouncing and my hand went right into the plaster of the ceiling. I could feel the layers of plaster and then the wood of the ceiling, then concrete. I pulled my hand back. *Was I dead? Was this death?* My only thought then was simple and intense, "I want to get down; I want to get down!" With that I floated down to the floor level and stood by the side of my bed. Actually I didn't so much float down to the floor level as I shot down to it.

Standing by the side of my bed, the side where I slept, the side that faces the hallway, I looked at myself sleeping soundly. I wasn't dead. I could see myself breathing in and out, and snoring. I looked as peaceful as a baby.

That's when a whole bunch of elderly people came down the hallway and started to enter my bedroom. Who the hell were these old people and what were they doing in my apartment? They all looked anxious – and many of them seemed totally confused. Why were all these people in my apartment? What the hell was happening? I knew I wasn't dreaming because I was totally awake – the way you are awake right now.

Before I could answer my own question, I launched into a speech about not worrying about dying and that they could all go on to heaven now and meet all their departed relatives. I have no idea where this speech came from or why I said it or why any of this was going on. But the speech, I must say, was powerful; my voice was strong – I even glanced over to see if I had awakened my wife - or me – but we were still sleeping soundly. I kept telling these old people that they were free to go now. *Go now, you can go now, a whole new world awaits you. Go now.*

One old woman came up to me and squeezed my arm. She smiled at me and I smiled at her. I could smell her perfume. Something passed between us – some understanding but I really don't quite remember what we understood. I squeezed her arm and smiled and said, "You can go now."

The others walked down the hall away from me. They all seemed so happy. This woman smiled at me again and I smiled at her. "Enjoy your new life," I said to her.

Then I was back in bed, for real, in my body and I woke up with a start – I mean I really woke up, both body and mind, my heart pounding. My wife was lying just as I saw her a second ago when I was – what shall I call it? – while I was *out of my body*. I looked around the room; no one was there. All those old people, that nice old lady, all gone – if they had ever been there to begin with.

But the memory of the event was fresh and it did not have the feel of a dream. I could still see the old woman who had squeezed my arm. I remembered her perfume. And that crazy speech about the after life – what the heck was that? I didn't even know if an afterlife existed, yet I was lecturing about it to a bunch of – a bunch of what? Dream figures? Ghosts? The recently departed dead? Ouch! That was insane. But I wasn't drunk; I wasn't drugged; but I might be insane.

But one thing I knew without question. I had been wide-awake while this thing happened. I was not dreaming. This was real.

The next night I sat in the lobby on tenant patrol with Sid Sussman. Sid was about 80 years old, owned one of those long, frankfurter dachshund dogs that always slept except when being walked. The dog looked to be about a thousand years old. Old Sid loved to talk – even though he would tell the same stories over and over. I remembered the stories; it was Sid who didn't remember that he had told them to me over and over. So he kept telling them over and over.

This night he had a bunch of old photos too.

"I have been living in this building since it went up in 1954. It wasn't as bad a neighborhood then, the scum hadn't been moved in then. I was going through my pictures," he said. "My wife used to keep albums but I never put anything in them. I found these in a box in the closet I was cleaning."

He handed me a pile of them. I politely went through them. Some of the tenants from those early days still lived in the building. This was 1973 so they were here for 19 years. I saw Sid and his deceased wife looking 19 years younger in a few of the earliest photos. I even saw the sleepy dog as a puppy. Then I saw *her*, the woman who was in my – whatever the hell it was yesterday afternoon. She was real.

"Who is this?" I asked, holding the picture up for him to see it clearly.

"Anita Harrison," he said. "She lived here with her husband Anthony – he died in, I don't know, about 1966."

"She moved?"

"No, she lived in your apartment. She was living there when she died."

"She *died* in my apartment?"

"Yeah, a couple of months before you moved in," said Sid. "She had a heart attack, very sudden. She didn't have much of a family – a bunch of us helped to clean out the apartment – sent most of the stuff to the thrift shops in Cedarhurst. I took this picture a couple of weeks before she passed on. She looks very peaceful doesn't she?"

I looked at the picture of Anita, standing face front to the camera with a big smile on her face. She actually was pretty – for a really old lady. There was no doubt in my mind – this was the woman I saw in my bedroom. This was the woman who squeezed my arm. This was the woman whose arm I squeezed. This was the woman who smiled at me and I smiled at her. No question about it.

Oh, God. What happened to me yesterday was not just some kind of hallucination – as I had thought it might be. That woman, Anita, had been a real person because here she was and I know I had never seen her before in my life.

Was I communicating with the dead? That couldn't be, could it?

At 26 years old I was a confirmed atheist (the arrogance of youth!) and I didn't believe in an afterlife. Yet, there in my bedroom, totally awake, I had been floating out of my body, first bouncing up against the ceiling, and then meeting a dead woman who had passed away in my apartment – *and maybe all those other old people had also been dead* and – what the hell? – they were waiting for *my* permission to head on up to heaven?

My apartment was the dead person hangout? I was a dead person guru?

Insane! Truly insane and I found it hard to incorporate that into my belief system – which was a non-belief system actually.

Yet it had happened. Maybe not the giving them permission to go to heaven part – that may have just been me getting dramatic with them. Why would they need my permission to go to heaven after all – if there was a heaven, which I didn't even believe? But I had certainly given a stirring speech about not being afraid of death and I did tell them to move on, which they all did. That was some strong voice that came from me too – in that *Weird World* I was some gifted public speaker.

Strangely enough, that night and the next night I was not afraid to go to sleep. I actually wondered whether I would again go floating away to meet more ghosts or guests or people needing my permission to get to heaven. So I just fell asleep and nothing happened.

1973
Face Splotches
Madeline Lowell

Two nights later I felt that same electrical impulse going through my body just as I drifted off to sleep. My mind became instantly awake; my body again became paralyzed. I struggled to wake my body up. This time I could hear a whooshing sound too. I figured it was my blood whooshing wherever the heck blood whooshes to and from in the body. Or maybe the whooshing was the sound of the electricity or whatever the hell it was that was coursing through my paralyzed body. I made a supreme effort to sit up. Instead I again lifted myself out of bed and floated to the ceiling. But this time I went right through the ceiling! No bouncing around inside the room this time.

Instead of winding up on the roof as I expected, since I had the top floor apartment, I entered a great banquet hall. Now I knew this was all Weird World stuff because the people in this banquet hall had various colored markings on their faces (oranges, purples, blues, reds – more like splotches on their skin than markings) and they all seemed to be sleepy – as if they were sleep walking. While the banquet room looked, felt and smelled real, I knew I was not in any banquet room in the real world – at least any banquet room I knew of – and these people, quite frankly, really looked out of it. I knew my body was back in bed with my wife, and it was, for all intents and purposes, soundly asleep, probably snoring away – except "I" was in this Weird World banquet room with hundreds of splotchy-faced half-asleep partygoers.

Music played softly – the kind that plays at wedding receptions but not quite so loud as your usual wedding bands whose sole goal is to deafen everyone at the wedding. People danced – mostly waltzing. Other people strolled around. Some were talking. But still there was a noticeable sleepiness to the entire scene. I floated above everyone and no one seemed to notice me right above his or her head.

Then I was on the ground, standing next to someone, whose face I couldn't see. "They all look kind of asleep, don't they?" he said. I tried to turn my head to look at him because obviously he wasn't asleep but for some reason I just could not look in his direction. My head seemed to be blocked from turning.

But I could feel his presence.

I looked across the room at a very long, square bar in the center of the banquet hall. I saw someone I recognized – Madeline Lowell, the high school librarian. I didn't know her well at all – I would say hello to her in the hallway. That was the extent of our relationship – a nod and a hello. I guessed she was in her mid 50s at this time and looked somewhat the worse for wear.

But one thing I instantly saw, she had no colored splotches on her face. She was clear-skinned. She also didn't seem to be at all sleepy. She was wide-awake. I walked over to her. The guy next to me also walked with me but I still could not get a look at his face. I just knew he was right next to me on my right.

"Madeline?" I said when I reached her.

"Scobe?" (My nickname is Scobe and my students crowned me King Scobe in the early 1970s.)

"Yes, uh, hi, Madeline, do you see the people here?" I asked.

"They all have colors on their faces. Is this is costume party?"

"Madeline, we are in some kind of like a dream world here. They all seem to be asleep but you seem to be awake. You see all those colors on their faces? But you don't have any colors."

"You two don't have any colors either," she said.

"Say something she'll remember," whispered the guy next to me. *Who was this guy?*

"Madeline, I am going to come up to you in the library tomorrow and say something to you. When I do I want you to remember tonight, okay?"

She looked at me – not confused, not really aware, but not asleep or sleepy looking as the others at the "costume party" appeared to be. So I felt I had a good chance of getting her to remember this – if she were really here that is and it wasn't some crazy hallucination. Anita had been real, so I was guessing that Madeline was real too. *Would Madeline remember this?*

I grabbed her arms tightly. She winced. Then I said, "I am a whole soul. I want you to remember that! I am a whole soul. *I am a whole soul!* I say that tomorrow and you remember this party, okay? I am a whole soul."

I am a *whole soul* – what the hell was that? I had no idea what I was saying or why I was saying it but there I was Mr. Whole Soul himself. I had no idea what it meant or why I said it, but nevertheless it should be pretty easy to remember that. I let Madeline go and I drifted upwards and then I was instantly in my bed, wide-awake. Mr. Whole Soul couldn't fall asleep the rest of that night. *Would Madeline remember this?*

I got to school early that morning. I wanted to meet up with Cathy Poe, a good friend of mine (I dedicated my book *Best Blackjack* to her) so that I could use her as a witness.

Poe always arrived early and she was in the teachers' lounge sipping tea and reading the *New York Times.*

"Cathy I need a favor," I said.

"What is it?"

"I want to go to the library and say something to Madeline Lowell and I want you to watch her when I say it."

"Okay, but what is this about?" she asked.

"I don't want to tell you that. I don't want to influence you in any way. I just want you to hear what I say to her and watch her closely."

Ten minutes before classes started we walked downstairs to the library. Madeline was behind the reference desk. Cathy and I walked up to her.

"Good morning," she said.

"Good morning," said Cathy.

"Madeline, let's go into your office. I have a question I need to ask you but I don't want to do it here," I said.

So far it looked as if she had no memory of the events of last night. When she saw me there was no hint she had been in that Weird World banquet room with me. She walked ahead of us to her office in the back of the library. *She's not going to remember this.*

"What is this?" whispered Cathy.

"Just watch her closely," I said.

In her office, Madeline said, "So what can I do for you?"

I reached out, grabbed her arms as I had done in the Weird World and squeezed her and said, "I am a whole soul!" I squeezed her again, "I am a whole soul!"

I let her go.

"Are you nuts?" she asked. "What is wrong with you?"

"I am a whole soul! I am a whole soul!"

"Frank," said Cathy, "Are you okay?"

"I am a whole soul!" I said forcefully.

Madeline slowly backed away from me. She must have thought I was going to attack her. "I...oh my God, you, you..." Madeline looked confused. She stopped backing away. Cathy Poe was doing what I had asked her to do – intently watching Madeline's face. Madeline was reaching into her memory. "I remember you said that to me. Yes, I remember that now. 'I am a whole soul.' That was in a dream I had. That was a dream. A dream. We were at a wedding. I think it was a wedding, crazy kind of wedding. You said that to me and the people were like they had colors painted on their faces. I don't know if they were painted but they all had colors on their faces and you said that to me in my dream. I didn't remember it but now I do. You said for me to remember that. 'I am a whole soul.' But that was a dream. That wasn't real it was a dream."

"Do you remember anything else?" I asked.

"There was a black guy with you. He and you didn't have any colors on your faces," said Madeline.

That was all Madeline remembered. As Cathy and I walked out of the library, she said: "Okay, what the hell did I just witness?"

Then I told her the story of my floating out of my body and my meeting with Anita and now my entering Madeline's dream – if it actually was her dream. Maybe it was all the people at the party's dream. Maybe we all shared the same dream states? All those people might get up this morning and some of them might have a memory of being at a party or wedding. Who knows what it was?

"I don't know much about it," said Cathy, "but I know it's called astral projection or out of the body experiences. That's what it seems to be. You are traveling out of your body."

"So I am not just out of my mind."

"Well," she smiled, "you are out of your mind, but that doesn't have anything to do with astral projection."

The Astral World

It is possible that today there are great books on astral projection. I have no idea because I don't read much in those paranormal areas anymore. The last book on astral projection I read was in 1977 – four years after my Weird World travels started. Most of the books I read came from a religious perspective; none of them were very satisfying. Other than a book by Robert Monroe, a businessman, I don't even remember the titles I read. Monroe's book was interesting because he seemed as confused as I did. His second book was not so good because he started to speculate.

The books that purported to know everything about the astral world really seemed to know very little about it. If my experiences were any criteria, the astral world was not a part of any religious mumbo-jumbo understood only by Hindus or Buddhists or Catholic Mystics or Jewish Cabalists, but instead it was a real, distinct dimension that intersects this dimension, or overlaps this dimension, or is a part of this dimension that we don't experience consciously – at least not often. Our minds exist in both the Weird World and the real world – although most of us rarely remember our visits to the Weird World except sometimes as dreams. I am not even sure if all dreams are a part of the Weird World either. I know some are but I have no idea if they all are.

So I have no idea if what I am about to tell you is true of the astral world for everyone or just true for me. I had about ten years of regular travels into the Weird World and after a short while I had laid out a kind of territorial map. One thing to keep in mind – as weird as the Weird World is, I was totally awake when having these experiences. I know I said this before, but it bears repeating – these states of consciousness were waking states.

While the Weird World impinges on our physical reality – that's why sometimes you float around in your room or visit places in the world we are familiar with – most of the Weird World exists in a world of thought or, rather, a world where thought shows its profound impact on reality just like *that*! For example, in the Weird World if I wish it were raining out – it starts to rain. (Okay, you have to get used to having this kind of control, obviously.) This physical or *real world* (as I'll call it) and the Weird World interconnect – they overlap, they segment each other, they intersect – you can choose whatever word you like. They are pages in the same book. The Weird World might be the world where dreams take place, or an area where many minds dream together, and the law of this dimension, if I can call it a dimension, is more or less the law of your own mind and – this is just as important – our own desires. The Weird World is truly a world of thought – thought images, thought events, thought people perhaps. And desires – particularly of the carnal kind. And fear – of whatever it is you tend to fear. Fear is a major stumbling block in the Weird World.

You control everything that happens to you in the Weird World – or at least, most of it. If it is the world of dreams, most people seem to be in a kind of "sleepy" state as they take part in the Weird World. But not all. Like me, there are many people who seem fully awake and may be astral traveling. In fact, I have seen many people in lotus postures or other relaxed positions floating here and there throughout the Weird World. When you meditate you might be entering the Weird World too.

The idea behind astral traveling is quite simple really. You have a physical body and an astral body or, as some call it, a "soul body" ("I am a whole soul!") or "spirit body." The astral body can leave the physical body and travel in the Weird World. As I said it can also travel in the real world. And often both the Weird World and real world co-exist on a journey.

Now whether the astral body is actually a body or merely some element or power of your mind – or some sickness that manifests itself in this peculiar way – I have no idea. But when you travel you feel as if you are in a real body – even if that body can take on some very peculiar characteristics, including those of animals. Oh, yes, dog and cat lovers – and bird lovers, elephant lovers, and fans of *Animal Kingdom*, you meet your share of animals in the Weird World too. Stranger still, there are times when you get to be an animal. I'll discuss that in detail later.

So are ghosts astral bodies? Are demons? Angels? Gods and goddesses? And Leprechauns? Are these all astral bodies?

I don't know.

It is easy to speculate whatever scenario you wish but I have no proof of what the Weird World actually is – except that many of my events had other observers who confirmed what I experienced when I spoke to them back in the real world. So the Weird World exists and that's about all I can say about it.

In my travels I met up with many strange things – and some pretty strange people – and a few beings who were definitely not human, at least not as they presented themselves to me. Were all of them real beings as were Anita and Madeline and other people I was able to confirm my visits to? I have no idea. Are the people in your dreams, the ones you don't know from this life, actually real people who are dreaming their dream while you dream your dream?

It beats me.

But in my ten years of traveling I did map out what I could of the Weird World and every time I could get confirmation that I had actually visited someone real I would get that confirmation. Traveling around outside your body is strange indeed and I didn't want to think I was actually insane – so I always asked people who I had seen in their dreams if they had seen me and, more often than not, they remembered seeing me and remembered the dream we were in. I was always fully awake in the Weird World (I feel I must keep repeating this fact), but the people I visited in their dreams were dreaming – I was a part of their dream, even if only as an onlooker.

I went to the trouble to get confirmations merely to satisfy myself – I had no thought to publishing any of this material (until now) because I had no answers to any of my questions – the biggest of which was "What the hell is going on here?"

In truth, I still have no real answers. I have speculations only and these are all based strictly on my own experiences. I am not an expert in the astral world – if such expertise actually exists – and I prefer calling it the Weird World because it is a truly strange dimension. The astral mumbo-jumbo of the books I read back in the 1970s didn't help me one bit.

You might notice that I sometimes interchange the "dream world" and the Weird World because the one or the other could really be the same thing. As I said I often found myself in other people's dreams and even when these people remembered me and remembered the dream, I often remembered much more going on than they did. It was as if they had tunnel vision – they were seeing just their dream – while I could see many other things going on at the same time. Several times I was in two dreams at once – and both participants remembered me being there and remembered their part of the dream but were totally unaware of the other part of the dream going on with the other dreamer. The other dreamer was not in their dream, although I was in both dreams.

It was a Weird World for sure and for ten years it was as much a part of my life as the physical world I lived in.

1973 and Thereafter
Mapping the Weird World

The Weird World has a set scenario that you tend to go through time and again. This scenario does not happen every time but often enough that I wish to outline it first, then discuss it in more detail. Here are the steps:

1. You leave your body – maybe experiencing that vibration or electrical charge.

2. You float up to the ceiling or float a little above your body.

3. You hit an extreme state of fear and (probably) project your fear on the landscape in such a way that it scares the hell out of you. I call this area the *terror-tory*.

4. You learn how to fight the fear, get rid of the fear, laugh the fear away – if you can't get rid of the fear, you probably can't go any further than this state.

5. After the terror-tory, then another difficult area arises and that is the Sex Paradise – where carnality rules.

6. Once you learn how to handle the carnal appetites, you can now have Weird World experiences that include the following:

    a. Real world adventures

    b. Mixed Weird World and real world adventures

    c. Total Weird World adventures

    d. Entering other people's dream states

    e. Weird World experiences imposed on the real world while you are awake in the real world

    f. Prescient adventures later shown to be true

I think the first two states, the terror-tory and the sex paradise, are primal states and just as we must conquer these states in this life in order to function in a society, we have to conquer these states in the Weird World as well.

The Terror-tory

Here is what I found out about the Weird World in my 10 years of journeys.

I didn't have to go through the electricity part to leave my body. After a few trips out of my body in 1973, I would just wake up from a sleep (although my body was still paralyzed) and I would stretch my (astral) arms out toward the ceiling and *zoom* I was out. I felt no electrical current (or whatever it was) coursing through me. At first I tended to always do the "float to the ceiling" thing but after awhile I just decided I didn't have to do that anymore so – quick as thought – I didn't do that anymore, although sometimes I floated a little just as I was getting out.

Unfortunately, the Weird World was not all pleasant times and good companionship with gifted, intellectual and spiritual people. My first two trips were fine, as I related, but I shortly discovered that the first moments out of the body on many other trips could be terrifying.

The third trip occurred about a week after the Madeline incident. I felt the electrical tingle, woke up, was paralyzed, and yanked myself out of my body, started floating to the ceiling and then my ankle was grabbed by someone or, rather, some *thing*. I was brought down and swung around the room with terrific force.

The "creature" had me by my ankle and was whipping me around in circles – Zoom! Zoom! Zoom! I could hear what I thought was rumbling laughter – crazy in the extreme – and then I saw what was spinning me around. Okay, here is where I know I am going to sound nuts but…it was a big black smoky beast of some kind – it seemed to take up half the room. It had a human shape, but somewhat distorted. Whatever face it might have I did not see since it was whipping me around pretty quickly. And although part of me was in my bedroom, I was also spun outside the bedroom – right through the wall, and then I would spin back into the bedroom. I was intersecting in and out of the physical world and the Weird World.

And please keep this in mind. As nuts as all this sounds, I was wide-awake. It wasn't a dream where when you wake up you go, "That was some scary dream." You are already awake and you are asking yourself, "Am I crazy? What the hell is happening here?" while this bloated smoke beast twirled you in and out of the walls of your bedroom.

And I was scared. No, make that *terrified*. The more terrified I felt, the faster this thing whipped me around, laughing and rumbling. But at some point I thought, "What the hell can this thing really do to me? I am asleep in my bed. It can't kill me. This isn't even a real body I am in." And I started to laugh at how stupid this whole thing was. As I laughed the smoke beast slowly dissipated and I floated up to the ceiling, through the ceiling, and into the Weird World.

This world of terror seems to be the first plane of thought after you leave your body. You don't always enter it but you enter it more than you'd like to. This area of the Weird World holds all the monsters, demons, boogeymen and women – or anything else you might personally fear. Tax cheats are probably met by IRS agents here!

There is only one way to handle the absolute terror in this section of the Weird World – you've got to laugh your way through. Nothing can actually hurt you here – these beings, if they are even real, can only scare you. If you give in to the terror, you ultimately wind up back in your real body and terrified of ever astral traveling again. I guess some people could drive themselves insane with fear once they have experienced this Weird World *terror-tory*.

That didn't happen to me. Since I knew instinctively that I couldn't be killed – what had I to fear from these demented beings or my personal demon, the smoke beast? Nothing. However, just like any fear – any *unreasonable* fear – it is always in you just waiting to pounce on you. Since I knew I could make it through the world of terror by recognizing its harmlessness, that's what I did. That smoke beast always seemed to be lurking around in the *terror-tory* but I would just say, "Poof!" to it and time and again it did indeed go *poof*. There were times when I actually called it forth, pompously saying to it, "Present yourself!" Of course, it presented itself and I would look at it and say, "Poof!" Come to think of it, after awhile I became the tormentor of that particular tormentor.

1973 and Thereafter
Sexual Paradise

Once through the *terror-tory*, the most difficult part of the Weird World confronts you, which I call the sex-paradise. This second area creates an overwhelming desire for carnal pleasures. If you are not a masochist, you certainly will have no desire to hang around the *terror-tory* so your wish is to always get through that as fast as possible. Not so with the sex-paradise. Here your every sexual dream, desire, and fantasy comes true. Except that if you keep staying in the sex-paradise you never get anywhere else. The sex-paradise can be a real hang-up – it's a man's world (if you are a man, of course) bathed in a kind of Viagra and it can stop you from experiencing any of the other adventures the Weird World holds.

I hit the sex-paradise on my fourth trip outside my body, totally succumbed to its pleasures, and went nowhere else while outside my body. The sexual appetite stopped me from having any other kind of experience.

There were plenty of times when a Weird World woman was actually someone I knew – from school, from the neighborhood, from a local store – and sometimes I could see they were wide awake.

Okay was this portion of the Weird World real? I can't prove to myself it was – as I could prove to myself that I was visiting others in their dreams. You see I never asked the "real" women I knew in the real world if they had met me in the sexual paradise in the Weird World for fear of embarrassing them and, obviously, embarrassing myself.

It took me over ten trips to realize that the sex paradise, while overwhelmingly delightful in a purely (or *impurely*) selfish way, largely wasted Weird World time. No trip would last past the sex-paradise if you gave in to it – that was the fundamental problem. To get to have a real Weird World trip, you had to get past the sex-paradise.

Two very strong thwarts presented themselves to getting out of your body and into the Weird World in any meaningful way. You had to overcome incredible terror and then overcome even more incredible pleasure. The terror part I handled relatively easily but the pleasure one took real effort – and I didn't always succeed. The sex paradise was a Garden of Eden that I had to throw myself out of – or I'd never gain any knowledge at all.

1973 and Onward
The Real World
and the Weird World

Many of my Weird World experiences were journeys into my neighborhood or into other real world areas. I didn't always go into the dream world. In some adventures (yes, I guess I can call them adventures) certain aspects of the real landscape might change – much as they do in dreams – but the predominant sense was one of this reality first, the dream stuff second.

Of course, the real dream landscapes were all over the place – from somewhat familiar types (like living rooms, hotels, houses which I knew I had never been to before) to stuff that was truly wacky – profusely colored landscapes so startlingly bright and spectacular that they could take your breath away – if you actually had breath in the Weird World: underwater scenes, alien scenes and wild vistas. There was little end to the variety of the dream stuff as there is really little end to the variety of dreams that people have.

Some of the dream world stuff was so alien that even when I had finished an adventure my mind couldn't quite grasp what I had seen. Were those colors that I couldn't remember colors that really existed? Was I hearing sounds I had never heard before – is that why I can't quite remember what those sounds were? There was a percentage of dream material that just couldn't be incorporated into my memory banks – even though I was totally awake when I was having these experiences.

That was weird.

I guess the parallel to that is now watching my father-in-law (who is 85 at this writing) and my mother (who is 81 at this writing) having memory problems – my mother from several small strokes; my father-in-law from dementia caused by age. Both will be aware of what is happening but soon after the event they forget. When something happens and you question them right away – they remember. "What just happened?" "This just happened." One hour later, question them again – they have forgotten. "What happened about an hour ago?" "I don't remember."

The dream experiences were like that for me when it came to the unfathomable colors and the unknown types of sounds. When I experienced them, I was just fine and I knew what I saw and what I heard. It felt, for lack of a better word, natural. But as soon as I got back to my real body I forgot. Instantly forgot – not slowly forgot. If I gazed upon a landscape with unimaginable colors, I saw those colors, but once back in my body I remembered the landscape and only the colors that I can see in this reality were the colors I could remember. It might be that those "other" colors are types of radiation that are not really color in the true sense. Maybe I picked those up and translated them into colors in my mind.

I just don't know.

I had no real proof that the dream stuff was real either – except if I could find someone I knew who could verify that he or she remembered dreaming about it and saw me in that dream too, then that would be my evidence that I wasn't just crazy. A lot of times I saw someone I knew but they had that sleepy look – although I never did see those colored splotches on people's faces after that very first trip. Those "sleepy" people I would ask the next day but they didn't even remember dreaming, much less dreaming of me. Some people thought I was nuts when I asked them if they remembered a dream with me in it. To them, I just said, "Oh, well, I had a dream with you in it and I wanted to see if you had the same dream. Yeah, it is crazy, I know that."

But I had so many people remember that they saw me in their dreams that I didn't doubt the reality of my experiences. By extension then, I knew that even the weirdest kinds of the Weird World adventures probably had some reality in them but the weirder the adventure, the harder it was to fix just what that reality happened to be.

Many of the adventures seemed overwhelmed with meaning and importance – but I just couldn't figure out what the hell that meaning was. In retrospect, a retrospect I will share with you, some of the meanings were highlights of the future. Some were just coming from my own inner fears and desires. Some – who knows – were just things that happened.

So what you will read now will be a few of my Weird World experiences – those that I think are memorable or interesting or typical. Some are "real world" experiences where the landscape is much like the world we all share in physical reality – the reality where you are reading this book and saying, "I always knew that guy Scoblete was insane." Some of these experiences mix the astral world into the real world – the most frightening ones I ever actually experienced.

There are also "dream world" experiences and combination experiences of both.

Then I'll try to wrap it all up and figure out what actually went on – the meaning of it all – which, in truth, is this: I don't really know the meaning of it all. I am not even sure I know the meaning of small parts of it.

Journeys Into the Known

As I said before, I stopped having the electrical phenomena as soon as I decided I didn't want it anymore. Maybe my body still went through it but I have no memory of it after a few of the earliest trips. The normal thing was this – I fell asleep; awoke, often stretching my astral arms up towards the ceiling, and then I found myself out of bed or floating just over my completely asleep real body.

I did not have astral experiences every night. Some weeks went by without any; some weeks had one; some weeks had a few. I learned Transcendental Meditation in my early 20s and a few times I had such a deep meditative state that I just got up and left while my body was happily meditating in the chair. I was not one of the meditators who crossed his legs and did the lotus position. I just sat in a chair.

1974
My Guide and the Floaters

I rose out of my body, halted the upward drift and then stood on the floor next to the bed. I could feel a little tension in me and I knew that if I let that get me I'd be in the *terror-tory* and probably fighting that smoke beast. So I relaxed myself, pushed the suddenly onrushing carnality away and made it through the two primal states.

This time I was not at a party like my second trip but on a deserted city street – I guessed Manhattan but it was not the real Manhattan because some of the buildings looked more like the type you'd see in an Arab country – spires, minarets, even one temple. Yet, I felt I was in Manhattan so I thought of it as Manhattan.

I walked slowly down the street. No one else was there. I could even hear my faint footsteps. I looked at my arms, my chest – I was dressed in sweats. *So even though I am in the Weird World I am picturing myself dressed*, I thought. As I now know, the Weird World operates on the mind's view – when people don't picture themselves dressed then they are naked. But most of us usually picture ourselves dressed and most of us are usually dressed even in our dreams. Except for sexual experiences or when an animal, I was always dressed in the Weird World.

As I walked down the street I suddenly became aware of someone behind me. So I turned around. About a block away was this black guy – maybe in his forties, walking rapidly towards me. I waited for him to catch up to me.

Somehow I knew: "You're my guide?" I asked

He smiled and said, "Madeline told you she saw me?"

"Can you read my mind?" I asked.

"All of this is mind," he smiled, indicating all of this with a sweep of his hand. He had a faint accent – Jamaican maybe, but very faint.

"Yeah, well," I said.

"I can read some things, can't read other things. Does that help?" he asked.

"Can I read your mind?" I asked.

"Yes, you just did," he said.

"But you talked to me," I said.

"That's what it appears to be," he said.

"Is this a dream? What is this?" I waved to the deserted city.

"Partly a dream, partly real or, maybe, all real and all a dream at the same time."

"Are you with me every time I – do this? Are you here all the time?"

"Most of the time," he said.

"Are you real - in the real world I mean, the world I take to be the real world?"

"Yes, I am as real as you are," he said.

"I don't want you giving me answers that can be taken two ways. If I am not real then you are as real as I am and if I am real then you are as real as I am – none of that makes sense, okay – but I want a flat out answer, you understand. I need to get this straight in my mind," I said. "No ambiguity."

"I exist in the real world, just the way you do. I have a wife, a family, and two daughters in fact, very pretty; I have a job. I am not some ghost or disincarnate spirit…"

"Good vocabulary," I said.

"So I am as real as you are and that is not being tricky."

"Are you here to help me?" I asked.

"Show you around."

"Can I meet you in real life. Call you on the phone?" I asked.

"I have no memory of these trips. I would just think you were crazy. Many people are doing what we do but a large percentage has no memory of it. They would think they are crazy if they did."

"Great," I said, "My guide thinks I am crazy."

"It could be worse, you could really be crazy."

"Thank heaven for small favors," I said. "So you have no memories of this. You don't find that weird?"

"Yes," he said, "but in the real world I am a very down-to-earth person and I think this would scare me and make me think I was losing my mind, so I don't let myself remember any of this. Survival instinct I guess you could call it."

Just then a giant airplane went overhead. It looked like it was heading down about to crash. Before you jump to the conclusion that this was a premonition of 9/11 (the terrorist attack in 2001 on the World Trade Center in New York City) I have to disabuse you of that notion. In my early 20s and into my late 30s I was afraid of flying because of two very bad experiences I had on airplanes.

Both bad experiences occurred when I was 19 years old and visiting a friend in Puerto Rico, David Brownstone, during the Christmas holidays. David's mother could fly a plane and she owned a Piper Cub. We had gone to Ponce to visit David's grandparents and his mother was going to fly us back to San Juan late that afternoon.

I was seated kind of on a dashboard in the back. As we were approaching the airport, Mrs. Brownstone cut the engine and started to glide in. David must have seen a quizzical look on my face when the noise from the engine seemed to stop and so he decided to get funny. "Oh, my God! The engine went dead! We're gonna die!"

I almost died right there.

"No, no, I'm kidding," he said quickly. "You're white as a ghost."

"You fuck!" I said.

I had diarrhea all that night. I really thought I was going to die. I vowed I would never go up in a Piper Cub again.

The next day we went surfing and I almost drowned. I had to swim about a mile back to shore after losing my surfboard and hitting my head on some coral. I was in a panic swimming back to shore because some moron started yelling that he could see a shark in the water. I swam like a maniac because I really thought that today a shark would kill me.

I fell asleep on the beach for several hours from sheer exhaustion while my friends frolicked in the ocean. I got such a sunburn that I blistered. That had been my first and last experience with surfing. I vowed I would never go surfing again.

The very same night some stoned, slobbering, screaming, saliva-dripping madman chased us around a park in San Juan with a machete. We had been sitting listening to some really great guitar music, under a beautiful tree, and this maniac rushed towards us swinging that machete. I was up on my feet and running as fast as I could. Luckily in those days I was a fast runner – and all the guys and girls with me were also in excellent shape – so the mad machete-man didn't come very close to hurting or killing any one of us. But it was still scary as hell.

I vowed I would never sit in a park in Puerto Rico listening to guitar music again.

A plane crash (avoided), a drowning and a shark attack (avoided), a skewering by a machete wielding wacko (avoided).

Time to go home and boy I could use the sleep on the plane. Which then became the last straw.

I flew back to New York on New Years Eve into a blinding snowstorm during which the oxygen masks fell out of the overhead compartments and we were told to put them on. I thought I was going to die right there as well. The plane was humping and bumping and luggage was falling out of the overhead bins where people hadn't secured them properly during the flight when they took stuff out to use and the food cart was clanging and the plane rocked from side to side and up and down and you could see all the snow zooming past the window and I knew I was a goner – and atheist that I was – I prayed to God to let me live.

God came through, we landed safely as the last plane allowed into Kennedy Airport until the storm subsided, and I went back to being an atheist. I hope God has no ill feelings towards me – although today, some 35 years later, I am no longer an atheist.

I vowed then I would never fly in a plane again.

I kept all the other vows – but this last one I ultimately had to give up.

Until I went on my first trip to Vegas in 1989, I did not get back on a plane. It took me several years to get relaxed while flying – and I even used a drug prescribed by my doctor to help me relax and sleep on those long flights from New York to Vegas. Now I fly monthly, sometimes more.

So from 19 to approximately 42 years old, I was self-grounded. However, every once in awhile I would have airplane dreams – always of the plane crashing in Manhattan; except I was never on the crashing plane. I was always looking up at the sky and I could see the plane coming down and I knew it was going to crash. It was not a foreshadowing of 9/11 (which wouldn't occur for three decades), just my own fears up on the giant screen of the sky.

"It's not crashing," said my guide. "Look over there."

I saw a completely different scene, but still in Manhattan, a group of flying yogis – eyes closed, floating amongst the abandoned buildings, in lotus positions, all meditating. They were all Indians – from India.

The day broke during my viewing of these yogis floating through the air, and then people arrived, regular men in suits and ties, women in dresses – the real work force. The minarets disappeared, as did the temple. This now looked like the financial district – it didn't have any dreamlike quality to it anymore. As the people rushed past me heading for work, zip…

...I was back in bed. My wife was shaking me awake.

"I'm awake," I said. "I'm awake."

1974
The Girl in the Schoolyard

I left my body and the smoke beast hovered right there. I knew it intended not to give me time to get settled into the Weird World. He figured he could nail me and terrorize me if he caught me as soon as I left my body. What a stupid smoke beast because I always expected him and I said "Poof!" and he went *poof!*

"No women," I said. "Don't waste my time." The sex urge subsided. Then I was in the suburbs, somewhere on Long Island I assumed, and in the distance a schoolyard with about ten kids – probably about 16 years old or thereabouts – with every one of them smoking cigarettes and acting "cool." It isn't until you get older that you realize "cool" doesn't exist. Standing in a schoolyard trying to look "cool" really made you look like an idiot. But teenagers have no idea that they often appear to adults as idiots because they usually only watch other teenagers. If wearing baggy pants (today's style) and looking like an idiot clown from the 1920s is considered cool, well then cool it is.

Sad, isn't it? Teenagers want to be teenagers and not adults.

I walked toward the schoolyard. One dark-haired girl, in the middle of several, laughed, and chatted amicably with her friends. Something about this girl made it hard not to look at her. She was not beautiful in any classic sense, attractive, yes, but – but there was *something* about her, *something* compelling. I wondered if I had ever seen her somewhere else before.

I watched her take out a cigarette, Marlboro, and light up. Smoking didn't seem to go with her, even though she obviously smoked.

Then a big fat guy walked into the picture. He just stood there looking at the group. Then he turned to me and smiled. "Hi," he said.

"Hi," I said.

"You out of your body?" he asked.

"Yes, I am," I said. "How did you know?"

"I look for people who are super awake and not going through the dream motions."

Before I could ask him what he meant by "dream motions" he vanished. That is something you have to get used to in the Weird World. People just wink in and out of the landscape. You could be talking to someone, as I was with this fat guy, and then *wink* he disappeared.

"I am almost failing every class," said the dark-haired girl in the middle of the group. "I am on the borderline in all of them."

"I hate school," said one of the boys. "What the fuck is the point? I am never going to use anything that I have learned. I forget just about all of it." He took a deep drag of his cigarette. "I'm failing everything."

If he was "failing everything" how could he forget what he had learned since he hadn't learned very much.

"What's the point of math," said another girl. "Like I really am gonna use trigonometry. Like what the fuck?"

I turned and walked away from the schoolyard. I wanted to tell these kids that school was weight lifting for the mind but I had learned talking to kids about school equaled a large waste of time. They were parrots at this stage in their lives, just parroting each other to fit in. If one of them were a teenage Albert Einstein he'd also be dragging a smoke from a cigarette and saying how school sucks. Then he'd go home and discover relativity – but he wouldn't tell the other kids because he wouldn't want to be thought of as too smart. Smart was often thought of as stupid in high school.

I started to walk down a street. That's when I saw the schoolyard girl ahead of me. I turned around and she was still in the schoolyard as well. That is Weird World all the way – a person being in two places at once. I walked toward her on the road.

"Hi," she said.

"Hi," I said.

"That's the younger me in the schoolyard," she said. "It's not now. That's the past. I'm dreaming this scene about me being in the schoolyard. It actually didn't happen that way."

"So this whole thing," I waved my hand to encompass everything, "is just your dream?"

"Yes," she smiled. She had a beautiful smile.

"How old are you now?" I asked.

"I'm 19," she said.

"I'm 28," I said. "Uh, do I know you? You look familiar."

"Well, I don't know you yet," she smiled, then yawned, "I'm waking up. I'll see you in sometime," she smiled that beautiful smile and vanished just like that.

I doubted I would ever see her again since I had no control over whose dreams I entered.

When she *winked* away, everything changed. The schoolyard vanished, and I walked along a small town's main street. A man and a woman walked together towards me.

"We're dead," she said to me.

"Oh," I said.

"Yeah, we died a few days ago in an accident and we are just hanging around," said the man.

"Car accident," she added.

"Are you dead?" asked the man.

"No, I am not dead," I said.

"But you can see us. How's that if you're not dead? The people around here do not see us. We talk to them and they show no sign that we even exist."

"I am not sure," I said. "I think where we are is kind of like a dream state and some of us are alive in here and some of us are dreaming in here and some of us, I mean you, are dead in here."

"I don't get it," said the man.

"Have you seen other dead people?" I asked.

"Not really," said the woman. "We kind of just walk up and down this street here."

"Is this a real town or in your mind?" I asked.

"No this is real. It's Valley Stream in New York," said the man.

"We didn't live in this town but we always liked to come here to the movies," said the woman. She pointed at the movie theatre, which kind of wasn't there until she pointed to it and then it was there.

"Funny," said the man, "but we aren't exactly sure of what we are supposed to do here or where we are going."

Then for some reason I said, "Well, you two are not dead. You are both in comas in the hospital over there." I pointed. A hospital appeared where I pointed but it seemed to be somewhat far away – a real long walk.

"You are both going to be alright. You are not dead. It was close but you are not dead and you are not going to die," I said with certitude.

Where was I getting all this from? How did I know whether these two people were dead or whether they were in comas or whether they existed at all? I was speaking so authoritatively about something I knew nothing about.

"Thank you," said the woman. "Then we will wake up soon?"

"Yes, very soon. Just walk to the hospital over there and once you enter it, you will wake up in your beds – you'll both wake up within minutes of each other. Now go walk towards that hospital. And good luck with your lives."

They both started to walk towards the hospital. The hospital seemed real enough. There were some people walking out of the front doors. Some cars went by on the street in front of it. The air smelled fresh – an early morning smell, just before dawn. This "Valley Stream" seemed like the real Valley Stream, a town not far from where I lived. I could hear birds beginning to chirp and I guessed the time at about 5 AM.

Then I "woke up" back in my bed. It was still dark out. I could hear the birds chirping. Were those the birds I heard chirping when I was in "Valley Stream"? Were those two people really in comas? Should I call that hospital, what was the hospital's name? Should I try to find out if they had two people in comas or who had just come out of comas?

Franklin General, I just remembered, was the name of the hospital – I looked up the number when I got to school.

Screw it; I had nothing to lose. I called.

"Franklin General," said the woman.

"I want to learn if you have two patients, a male and a female, who were in a car accident and in comas or just came out of comas," I said.

"I'll transfer you to the nurses' station, thank you," said the woman officiously.

The phone rang and rang and no one answered. I hung up. I tried again. I got a different woman on the phone this time.

"I am sorry, sir," said the woman, "but we don't give out information about our patients over the phone."

This hospital was about 10 miles from where I lived. Should I go over there and see if these two people I had met were there?

I let it drop. What did it matter? I knew I was visiting people in the Weird World – and sometimes people remembered seeing me in their dreams – good enough for me. Also, if these two coma patients were real and I went to their room, I might kill them by telling them we had met in the Weird World where they thought they were dead – or maybe the security guards would usher me out rather quickly, or arrest me.

"Wait! Wait!" I would scream, "You don't understand. I fly out of my body and visit people in their dreams and in the Weird World!"

"Come along, sir, just put these handcuffs on and we have a nice place for you to go to, sir, with a lot of people who think they fly out of their bodies too, sir. Some of them think they are Jesus Christ as well."

1975
The Indian Camp

This time the smoke beast came at me with a vengeance but I flung my hand in his face and told him to "depart!" I have no idea why I said the word "depart!" as opposed to "go away." In the Weird World I sometimes spoke more poetically – insane but true.

Then I was in the desert (*whisk!* just like that!) – surrounded by mountains – and it was dusk. There was a campfire with some Indians around it – American Indians. They were dressed in somewhat traditional fashion except they all wore jeans. Then I saw my friend Cathy Poe at the campfire and I waved to her. But she didn't see me. She was busy talking to one of the chiefs – I guessed he was a chief because he was older and looked, well, chiefish. Actually I think I thought he was the chief because he looked the way the chiefs looked in the movies of the 1950s and 1960s – he looked Italian.

I was about 75 feet away from this campfire and I noticed that the Indians were settling down and sitting cross-legged. I watched intently and then they started to sing and hum and then they began a chant. Cathy chanted too. Then they did some kind of ceremony but I was becoming distracted. Before I lost focus on this event I tried to remember who was at the campfire – so I could tell Cathy when I saw her the next day at school. Since she hadn't seen me I thought if I could give her the details she would at least remember that she had a dream about a campfire and Indians who looked Italian.

Then I was running on all fours – I was a leopard. I wasn't in America anymore, I knew that instantly, but somewhere (I guessed) in Africa and next to me, running right alongside me, a black panther – who I instantly knew was my guide. Nice. I was a leopard; he was a black panther – how fitting. Did these animals hunt together? I doubted it.

But the tricky part about being an animal was that your mind was in back of the animal's mind – in the front of the animal's mind was the animal's mind. You were kind of taking a ride. That animal mind was filled with scents and an endless urge to eat, sleep and reproduce.

This was not my first trip as an animal – but it was my first time being a leopard, which I would be many more times in the future. I've been a wolf, a small cat, a hawk, an owl, and a horse as well. You are as awake as you are now but, as I said, your mind is in the background – completely in the background – and the animal controls or, rather, the animal's appetites control everything. The fact that my guide was running alongside me I knew to be a false moment. I could tell from my leopard's mind that he was not even aware of the Black Panther running right next to him – so I guessed that the panther was not really there as such but my guide was with me in some way.

Now I saw it in the distance – a wounded doe. If the doe scented me, or saw me, she just wasn't quick enough to move. I was on the doe's ass dragging it straight down. I ripped my way up her back and grabbed her throat in my mouth, shaking my head to make the cuts bigger and deeper. It was a mighty feeling – for the animal part of me, that is – and somewhat unnerving for the human part of me. Killing the doe exhilarated me. As a leopard I felt the power in my claws, my mouth, my front shoulders and the powerful thrust of my rump as I pushed the doe down, tearing at its throat. Everything in me felt strong. I ripped away at that doe until it died and then I ate it. The blood was warm and savory, the flesh delicious. My leopard in all my transformations never bothered carrying any food into the trees the way you see in animal documentaries. As a leopard I ate my kill where I killed it. I ate until I almost exploded and then I would leave the rest and go somewhere to sleep. A lot of times jackals or hyenas scrounged near me as I ate. I guess the scent of blood attracted them. Occasionally they would try to grab some flesh, but I'd lunge to bite them. When I finished they could have the remainders but I wouldn't share with them what I had killed.

My animal bodies all wanted to run (or fly), eat (what to us would be in excess) and then sleep. These seemed to be the three most important things – other than reproduction. I have always been a male animal in the Weird World – as far as I could tell – because my nose could sniff out the female scent – which was overpowering when the females were in heat and all I wanted to do to them was copulate. I would smell that female scent and it would drive me crazy. I was lucky that my leopard must have been made of prime mate material because I don't ever remember a female turning me down. Love making among the leopards is not a pretty sight – you just take the female, do it quickly, and desert her. Then you go to sleep. Typical male I guess.

I have no recollection of what I felt like as a hawk or owl – I might have been female in those bodies but I was not in them very long before I returned to bed. The flying felt natural as could be – because, I guess, it was natural. In the air, I never said to myself, "Oh, my God, I might fall." I just soared. As both of these birds were predators, I flew to hunt. When I saw what I wanted, a mouse, a rabbit, I would fall through the air, then scoop up what I wanted and before I would touch the ground I was in flight again with a wagging animal in my beak.

When my leopard left his pray, he went to sleep somewhere away from the kill.

And I woke up in bed.

The next morning at school I met Cathy in the teacher's lounge. She was eating a bagel and having a cup of tea.

"Did you dream about me last night?" I asked.

"No, I don't remember any dreams," she said.

I told her the whole incident about the Indians who looked Italian and the campfire. I described the Indians I got a good view of.

She shook her head, "No, I have no memory of any of that, sorry. Maybe you were just dreaming?"

"Well not every trip do I have proof for," I said. "But it wasn't dreaming. I was as awake as I am right now."

By accident I hit my hand against the coffee pot, almost knocking the whole thing over. "You don't seem too awake," laughed Cathy.

And so that particular Indian event stood until two years later, on the first day back from summer vacation, when Cathy came rushing into the teacher's lounge. "Where's Scobe? Did he get in yet?"

"I'm here," I called to her. All the teachers were saying their hellos after a summer off. I was in the back of the room relaxing before we had to go to a boring meeting to meet the new principal.

"Let's talk," she said. So we went for a walk outside. "Do you remember that astral travel where you asked me about the Indian camp and the fire and the Indians who all looked Italian?"

"Yeah."

"Well, I didn't dream it," she said.

"I know, you already told me that."

"No, no, what I mean is, I experienced it this summer – exactly as you described it. We went to Navajo country and I met with a whole bunch of Navajos and one night we did the campfire thing. The chief did look like those Italians who play the Indians in the movies in the 50s and two of the guys were spitting images of what you described. I'm telling you, this was where you traveled – into the future. You caught a glimpse of a future event. I was even chanting just as you remembered it."

1976
This World and That World
Simon Michael

I knew Simon Michael for three years. He was a student at the high school where I taught. He came from Jamaica (yes, as did my guide), a lovely young man – a good student, respectful, hard working and super intelligent and a founding member of the school's Science Fiction Club – a club that at its peak once had 400 members. I was advisor of the club.

His story has nothing to do with any astral traveling on my part but I believe that Simon had extremely intense astral experiences of his own – all geared to a single future event. Here is a typical conversation we would have – because we would have it several times a month over the three years he was a student at the high school:

"Scobe, I had that experience last night," said Simon.

"The same events?"

"Exactly the same. I get out of my body and I am very scared and I find myself on the train. I am going between cars and that's when they attack me. I feel a warm feeling in my back and when I turn around I catch this guy's face – with a big ugly grin. And then I feel a pain in my stomach and many knives are stabbing me now one after another and all at once. My face is cut, my throat, I feel the warmth running down my chest. The stabbers are laughing and calling me names. I think there are three of them, maybe four. I am very bleary now and can't see too well. I am choking too. They stab me with long knives and then I am losing consciousness and I feel them pick me up and they throw me off the train. I feel air. Then nothing. Then I wake up."

"You saw their faces?" I asked.

"I saw their faces in a blur."

"Is this always the same? Is there ever a change in how this dream happens?"

"Nothing is different from one time I have this to another time I have this. It is always the same, always the same. What scares me is that it does not seem like a dream. I do not seem to be sleeping. I am awake when this is happening. I even think to myself that I am awake and that this is really happening. But when I am thrown from the train I feel the air and then I am back in bed, sweating, shivering, and I feel as if this really happened to me and it wasn't a dream, but I am back in my bed now, I am alive, so it couldn't have happened in the past. But I am afraid that it is going to happen in the future. I feel this is a future event that I am to be murdered. It is not a dream."

"I don't think you are going to be murdered because you are having this dream," I said. I never told him or any students at that time about my Weird World experiences. And I always referred to Simon's astral experience as a dream.

"It does not feel like a dream, it is real," he said.

"I really don't think you have a greater chance of being murdered than anyone else," I said. "I think this is a fear thing with you. I don't think it is real. I don't think it is a prediction of the future."

"It is the same all the time, Scobe."

"That's why I just feel you are experiencing a fear situation. If this were real I think you would notice different things," I said.

I went to the school psychologist – Dr. Harthman – a woman who was stranger than the strangest kids who went to see her. I figured she might be able to help Simon – or at least ease his fears somewhat. I really did not think that his astral experiences were predictions of the future. I actually thought this whole train thing was his version of the smoke beast. My guess was that we all had certain fears that manifested themselves in the Weird World – mine was a smoke beast, his was being murdered on a train, who knows what yours would be should you someday join the Weird Worlders.

I asked Dr. Harthman's secretary if she had anyone in with her. The secretary gave me a quizzical look; "She almost never has anyone with her." So I knocked on Dr. Harthman's door. A few seconds later Dr. Harthman opened the door.

She was smoking a pipe.

In those days, this was the 1975-76 school year; there were no smoking bans in public buildings. So teachers and administrators could smoke in their offices and in the faculty rooms to their hearts and lungs' content. Inside Harthman's office looked like a foggy day. You could barely see to the end of the room.

"Yes, yes?" she said.

"I am Scobe, an English teacher, and I have a student who is having nightmares," I said.

"They all have nightmares," she said. "What has that to do with me?"

I would guess that Dr. Harthman was about 60 years old, but she looked much older. She had leathery skin, blood-shot eyes with bags under them and black rings in those bags. Frankly, she looked awful – almost insane looking had this been a movie about a female serial killer working in a high school.

But she was the school psychologist and her job was to help students with their mental health.

She puffed on her pipe, "So why do you think he needs me? I am very busy you know."

"He has a recurring dream that he is murdered. It is the exact same dream every time, I think, exactly the same details," I said.

"That's what a recurring dream is," she said snootily. "It's the same every time."

"I thought maybe you could ease his fears," I said.

"Oh, all right, you send him to me," she said. "I'll talk to him. Now I have work to do." She took another puff on her pipe.

I sought out Simon a few hours later during my lunch period and told him I thought he should see Dr. Harthman.

"From what I heard she's insane," said Simon. "I don't mean any disrespect."

"No, I know, but maybe another person, someone who deals with these things, psychological things, can give you a perspective that I can't give you," I said.

"Okay, I'll go," he said.

A couple of days later I was on my hall duty. One period a day teachers had to sit at select areas in the halls to make sure the kids did what they were supposed to do – have passes if classes were going on; quiet the kids who were loud; break up any fights. Simon Michael came up to me.

"I saw Dr. Harthman," he said.

"And?"

"If I am not murdered on a train I could die of smoke poisoning," he said. "She not only smoked that pipe she also smoked cigarettes."

"Did she help at all?" I asked.

"We didn't talk about me much," he said.

"What did you talk about?"

"Her Christmas plans; where she was going on the Christmas break. She doesn't have much family, a cousin in Syracuse, and she isn't married. She has no children. She once had a boyfriend but he left her I guess."

"She told you all that?" I asked.

"She is thinking of retiring too," said Simon.

"Did she say *anything* about you," I asked.

"Yeah," said Simon. "She said I was stupid to worry about dreams."

In the yearbook for that year of the Science Fiction club there is a great picture of the young men who started the club, a sharp, clear picture of these really terrific kids. I hated to see them graduate – they were such a great group.

Simon Michael graduated in 1976 too.

He was accepted into an Ivy League school.

Eight months later, his body was found in a ditch alongside a railroad track. He was commuting back to his school it seems. His body had multiple stab wounds from several different knives – some of the knives went right through him, they were that long. Simon Michael was evidently thrown from the train, as there were broken bones but the police think he was dead before he hit the ground.

Simon Michael had been murdered as he had foreseen. As far as I know the police never caught the thugs who murdered him.

Several years after his murder, I told someone about this awful event, about the idiot psychologist, and Simon's insistence that what he experienced seemed real and was not a dream, and I decided to get the yearbook and show the person

Simon's Science Fiction Club picture. I opened to the Science Fiction Club and there was the picture of all these great students – still a sharp picture – except that Simon Michael's image had faded in the picture – had faded quite a bit in fact. Every other kid's image was still sharp but he had faded. Recall the scene in *Back to the Future* with the photograph that kept changing, well Simon Michael had faded in the picture sometime after his murder.

His astral experiences had indeed been a sharp glimpse into his future and what I had left in memory of him was a faded image in what is now an old, old yearbook.

1976
Through the Plate Glass Window Darkly

I was out of my body and this little fat deli clerk from the super-market around the corner stood right there in my room. From her perspective though it was not my room but a hotel room of some kind – very swanky too, nice smelling. So to start this journey into the Weird World I saw two rooms imposed on one another. I stood by my bed, where my wife and I slept soundly, and I could see my own room clearly. But I could also see the hotel room superimposed over my room.

Then my room faded and there was only the hotel room.

I knew I was in the deli-clerk's dream but I also knew this would be a dead end experience, so I dismissed this experience and I willed myself out of the hotel room and onto a street in Queens somewhere, not far from a highway. There were many stores on this street – although it was late at night, maybe 11 o'clock or so, but there was still traffic on the streets. The stores were all closed.

Then I was inside a store looking out of the plate glass window. I don't even remember the store because I had my back to the merchandise. Then I saw this kid, whom I recognized from my school, skate boarding, coming right towards the window, and I thought, *What the hell is he doing out this late in Queens?*

There was another kid behind him, also riding a skate board, and laughing loudly and hooting, and this other kid pushed the student just as the student was about to turn away so he wouldn't crash into the store's window. With that push the student went smack into the store's window and the glass came crashing down. I saw some blood on the student's face and the other kid stopped laughing and just had that "dopey" kid expression on his face.

Teachers, and parents, know what the "dopey" kid expression is – it is the equivalent of "Gee, I didn't know that was gonna happen." The kid jumps off a roof and slams to the ground, breaking his leg, "Gee, I didn't know that was gonna happen." The kid lights a fire cracker in his hand and throws it out the car window at another car, except the window is closed, and instead the fire cracker explodes in his lap, "Gee, I didn't know that was gonna happen." The kid lays down in the middle of a road, imitating some stupid movie, and gets run over and paralyzed, "Gee, I didn't know that was gonna happen." The kid rides atop one of his friend's moving auto, which is called car surfing, and falls off breaking his neck, "Gee, I didn't know that was gonna happen."

I moved towards the student to help him but then I shot back to the schoolyard I had been in before. There was no one in that schoolyard now.

My guide was next to me.

"I left an accident," I said.

"I know," he said. "I was there. You didn't see me though."

"Were you a Black Panther?" I said.

"No, I was just not in your vision," he laughed.

"So what am I doing here?"

"Hi," said a female voice.

I turned and it was that girl I had seen the last time I was in this schoolyard. *God, I knew this girl, but how did I know her?*

"Is this your dream again?" I asked.

"I am twenty-two now," she said.

"I'm thirty," I said. "We're looking for a house on Long Island."

"This is Long Island," she smiled. She had a beautiful smile. *Who the heck was she that all I wanted to do was talk to her?*

"I'm a father," I said. "I have an infant son, Gregory John Scoblete, he was born a year ago. I love him more than anything in the world. We are moving to Long Island because my wife just missed being mugged. The mugger ran to the elevator but the doors closed and my wife and son went up. The mugger got on the next elevator and mugged some old lady. There are a lot of old people in my building. They are sitting ducks for the muggers. My wife missed getting mugged by a second or two because the elevator doors closed and my infant son was with her. Far Rockaway is too dangerous for a family. I am moving. We're going to look for a place."

Why was I telling this girl all this? But I kept talking.

"My magazine folded a couple of years ago – in 1974 – it was called *Island Magazine*. I might write a book about that experience. We published for three years. The title of the book will be *Clawing My Way to the Bottom*. It's a good title I think. And true. I couldn't get many advertisers and the ones I had didn't pay me – half of them went out of business. Even Jupiter's, the nightclub in Franklin Square, really famous nightclub, where we held singles dances on Monday nights didn't make me enough money to survive. They went out of business too. We booked big names for those singles dances there too. Ray Charles was the last act we booked. He was great. But we just couldn't make any real money with the magazine, even with those dances and other events I planned. But I paid back everyone I owed money to – I didn't declare bankruptcy. I felt I owed money to people who believed in me and I made sure I worked extra jobs in teaching and I made sure that I paid everyone back. Some of my articles brought some good attention to me but the magazine just didn't take off. I am writing a book review column now for a weekly and they pay me twenty-five dollars for a thousand words. But writing is writing."

"I am going now," she said.

"You know, I really feel as if I know you," I said. "Have we met before, in the real world, not in your dreams?"

"I haven't met you yet," she smiled.

"Will I see you again?" I asked.

She was gone.

"Will I see her again?" I asked my guide.

"I don't know," he said.

"What do you know?"

"I know how much fun it is to be a Black Panther," he smiled.

A few days later in school the student I had seen in the skate-boarding experience was walking towards me. He had some bandages on his forehead and on his hand.

"Excuse me," I said. I didn't actually know this kid; I had only seen him around. "What happened to you?"

"I was skate boarding with my friend and the idiot pushed me into a plate glass window," he said.

1977
Buying A New Home

If the Weird World and the real world are side-by-side, or overlapping dimensions, then at times both might intersect while you are awake in the real world. Going into the Weird World you absolutely know the intersection of the two worlds and you see this overlapping all the time; but rarely do you experience that overlapping while in the real world. At least that was my experience.

This adventure, if I can even call this an "adventure," took place in the real world – at least most of it did. I think this might be the scariest thing that ever happened to me in my life. It's left a lasting impression.

It was the end of 1977 – November – and my wife and I were looking for a home on Long Island, shortly after her experience of almost being mugged. We could afford about thirty-five thousand as our maximum – a moderately priced house in those days on Long Island.

My father and mother, truly generous people, gave us fifteen thousand dollars as the down payment – not as a loan but as a gift. My father and mother were always so generous with me and generous to everyone they knew.

At first we looked for houses near the high school where I taught but they were much too expensive – over one hundred thousand dollars. We kept going farther and farther out on Long Island to find homes in our price range.

Each weekend, we'd get a babysitter in on Saturday morning and head out by 10 o'clock to look for our "dream" house. We did this for many weeks. Finally, early November 1977, we were out in Massapequa and we stopped in at a real estate office. There was only one salesman in the office at the time, a young man; I'd guess about 24 or 25 years old.

We introduced ourselves. Then we filled out some paper work too.

"I am looking for a house at no more than thirty-five thousand," I said.

"Let me look and see what we have," he said. "You can also look on the wall over there while I look through the circular file here."

My wife and I got up and went over to the wall of pictures – hundreds of pictures, some in color and some in black and white, of houses – every size, shape and price range in that community.

"Look at this," said my wife. "This can't be thirty-five."

The picture looked like what today we would call a "McMansion," a relatively large house with maybe an acre or slightly more land. That, by the way, on Long Island is considered a *lot* of land. It was unheard of that such a piece of property as this would be just thirty-five thousand.

I took the picture down from the wall and brought it over to the young agent.

"Is this really only thirty-five thousand?" I asked.

He looked at the picture and said, "Let me go ask the broker in back. This is a very big house with a lot of land. I think this might be a mistake. It's probably one hundred and thirty-five thousand."

My wife and I sat down at his desk. When he came back in the room, he placed the photo in front of us. "This house is only thirty-five," he said. "The owner just lost his wife and decided on the spur of the moment to move to Florida. The man is in his late sixties." Many of you reading this should realize that Florida is to New York City/Long Island what the elephant burial ground is to elephants. You retire from work and then you retire to Florida and then...well, you retire forever.

I looked at the photo, a truly beautiful house.

"I'd like to see it," I said. "It's hard to believe this is only thirty-five."

The real estate agent drove us to the house. It was well north of Sunrise Highway – a rather busy road on the South Shore of Long Island. We pulled up to the front. This area did not have sidewalks – it was extremely suburban – with houses set well apart.

"Let's take a look. Let's go up the path and see the front first, then we'll go in," said the real estate agent.

The house looked as if it were plunked in the center of a park, with pathways and bushes and plenty of trees.

"This is lovely," said my wife.

"It really is," said the agent.

The beautiful weather contributed to the loveliness of the surroundings, a clear blue sky, the sun shinning almost directly overhead, with the temperature a nice 55 degrees, a perfect fall day.

Then the agent opened the front door and we stepped inside.

And it seemed as if the weather now changed – instantly – because I could feel with my skin that it was a deeply cloudy dark day with rain. But I looked out the window as we entered the foyer – no, it was still a beautiful sunny day. So why did I feel as if it were raining? Why did it feel as if it were dark outside?

At the time I didn't bother to ask my wife or the agent if they were experiencing this as well. After all it was pretty weird (yes, yes, I know – this whole section of the book is weird). I actually didn't talk much with my wife about my astral traveling. She knew about some of it, although not most of it.

"Why don't we go bottom to top – let's check out the basement first, then we'll go around the first floor and then we'll hit the second floor," I said.

"You're the boss," said the real estate agent.

Down in the basement it again felt more like a sunny day – not quite as sunny as my eyes were seeing through the basement windows; however my skin did not feel that rainy feeling. So I wasted time. I actually didn't really want to go back up to the main floor – it was much nicer in the basement.

The basement was completely finished, except for a small patch at the very extreme end – with a saw, some paneling, and a workbench. I speculated that the owner of the house was someone who liked to do his own handiwork – very unlike me.

I took several tours of the basement – as did my wife and the real estate agent. I didn't connect the idea in my head that maybe they too wanted to linger down here instead of going upstairs again.

But all good things must come to an end and we finally headed back up the stairs to the main floor. The house was decorated in a way that I knew my wife hated – and in a way I also didn't particularly like – a lot of blacks, and some other deep colors, a little too much stuff all around – not quite Victorian clutter but close to it. You could call it littered. The main floor had a large dining room, a living room with a magnificent fireplace, several smaller rooms, one with a television and a lounge chair, a kitchen – quite large that looked out at the back of the house to a tremendous back yard which, like the front of the property, was heavily packed with bushes and trees, and pathways with some benches here and there.

One larger downstairs room, an office/library had been decorated much differently from all the other rooms on the main floor with shelves of law books, many hardcover volumes – novels, non-fiction books, even some small books of modern poetry – a beautiful wooden desk; a stereo; several hundred record albums – and right in the middle of the room, several boxes, partially packed with some books and papers inside them and also books and papers beside them on the floor – but all of this packing now left unfinished as if the owner just got up and rushed out. He must have been in some hurry to get to Florida.

And going through each and every room, I still had the overwhelming feeling that it was a dark day outside with lots of rain. Also I felt slightly nauseous. But out of every window, and this house had many large windows, the day looked magnificent. My eyes saw one thing and my feelings experienced something totally different.

"I guess we should take a look upstairs," said the real estate agent. He seemed kind of glum.

We went to the stairs and started up. With each step, I felt an increasingly strong pain in my knees and an increase in my nausea. The real estate agent was leading us and when he got about three-fourths of the way up the staircase, he turned around, deathly pale and said, "I am not feeling too good. Check out the upstairs and I'll meet you outside." He then headed back down the stairs. My wife was behind me and I kept climbing the stairs. It was difficult to actually get to the top because my damn knees were killing me.

I didn't ask my wife if she were feeling the same thing and I also didn't connect the real estate agent's feelings with mine. In retrospect, obviously something was going on that we all felt but at the time I just didn't make any connections. I thought my knees hurt because I had been doing a lot of long distance running – some of it on pavement; my head disconnected itself from the reality I experienced during my time in that house.

The upstairs of the house had been converted into two huge, and I mean *huge*, bedrooms with a large bathroom between them. The stairs went up in such a way that you faced the "guest" bedroom (I guessed it was the guest bedroom) on the right; with the master bedroom on the left. I was really nauseous at the top of the stairs but I made my way to the door of the guest bedroom and opened it.

The room was clean and orderly, again with way too much stuff in it. I looked around as my wife entered. Then I went into the bathroom with my wife following. She had not seemed too interested in the guest bedroom. In retrospect, she looked somewhat dazed.

In the bathroom, this world and the Weird World merged – at least that is what I think happened. I could see with my eyes that the bathroom was spotlessly clean yet I could also see gouts of blood everywhere. The bathroom had a pine scent but atop it there was another odor – extremely unpleasant – filthy swamp water mixed with death. The two scents, clean and dirty, did not merge together – they were both completely distinct in my nostrils. Can nostrils actually smell two different scents simultaneously without one dominating and one receding?

I was dizzy. I was nauseous. I was also in pain because my legs hurt and felt numb. I looked around the bathroom and at the other end was the door to the master bedroom. I passed the toilet on my way to the other door and made the mistake of looking in it – spotlessly clean, yes, but also filled with blood and blood clots swimming in the water – *oh, God*, I thought, *the clots make the form of a face, a screaming, agonized face.* I averted my gaze and literally staggered to the master bedroom's door. My wife had just gone through it – she had sped her way through the bathroom and it was then I wondered if she had also seen what I had seen in the toilet.

I entered the master bedroom.

This room was empty of furniture except for a large four-poster bed with a covering on top. My wife was at the foot of the bed, her back to me and I thought, *I am going to kill her. I have to kill her; it's the only way.*

Behind that horrible thought came another thought - what the hell was I thinking? Even many years later, when we went through a very long, grueling six-year divorce, I never wanted to kill her. We just weren't suited for one another, I readily grant that, and our marriage ended in a bitter six-year divorce struggle, but at the worst, there was never one moment where the thought of murder ever entered in my mind.

Except now.

At this moment, standing in the doorway of the bathroom and looking at her back as she looked at the bed, I knew that I would kill her and how simple it would be. Just place a pillow over her face and press down hard – suffocate her. No one would know what I had done. She was a dead woman anyway; I was just speeding up the process.

I can tell you this, I hated that woman so immensely at that moment that I could have torn her heart from her chest with my bare hands and eaten it, licking the blood off my hands in joy – just as primitives ate the hearts and drank the blood of their enemies.

So I started towards her to kill her.

It was not as hard for me to walk in this room and I didn't feel the nausea either. Instead, I felt a savage rage. That was the only emotion I could feel; a rage against this filthy, stinking bitch who had pushed me around for almost 40 years – *40 years? 40 years? What the hell was I thinking? 40 years?* –and destroyed my life. She was a dead woman!

I saw her standing by the foot of the bed but I also saw her in the bed under the covers, skinny, eaten away by evil, but the "her" in the bed didn't really look much like my real wife at all. My real wife was a beautiful woman – spectacularly beautiful in fact – but now she looked like something else. I knew something was seriously wrong with me. I knew I was thinking two thoughts – thinking of my wife as she really was – a 30-year old beauty and the mother of my son – and I was also thinking of her as an old, shriveled, decayed bitch who needed killing right now, right now!

I had to kill her, right now, and that would be that.

My wife moved from the bed and headed towards the door of the bedroom, in slow-motion – time seemed to be expanded or our movements repressed – call it what you will, but I knew that if my wife made it out of this room, I would not be able to kill her. I had to get her before she left the master bedroom. But I still saw her in the bed. She was in two places.

I could have gone directly at her as she headed for the door but for some reason I went to the bed. She was in the bed and she was at the door. She was in the bed. She was at the door. She was in both places at once. I had to kill her.

I could see a large closet to the left of the bed, the door ajar and two prosthetic legs against the closet wall. That bitch would never use those legs again! *What the hell was happening to me?*

I froze at the bed and that allowed my wife to get safely out of the door and once out of the door, the wife on the bed went away too. I headed out the bedroom door. My wife went down the stairs. I was behind her.

And I was nauseous again. My knees were killing me again.

I went down the stairs. With each step the nausea decreased; the knees started to feel better. Downstairs I just felt a little sick, not the waves of nausea I had experienced upstairs, and my legs also felt fine.

I had no desire to kill my wife – not since she exited the bedroom – and now she exited the house with me close on her heels. It still felt as if it were raining outside when you were in the house but outside the house was a beautiful sunny November day.

I stepped outside the house. I closed the front door. All the other feelings vanished completely.

I walked down the path, maybe ten feet behind my wife and then she, then I, got into the back seat of the real estate agent's car. The real estate agent sat at the wheel. We were all silent for what seemed like minutes. Then the real estate agent turned to us and said, "There is something wrong in that house."

My wife and I then started to talk about what we experienced – the exact same things; hers from the wife's perspective (she feared I would kill her) and mine from the husband's (I wanted to kill her).

Then the real estate agent took us back to the office. We said our goodbyes. A couple of weeks later we saw a house in Valley Stream that we liked – at forty-five thousand dollars and bought that one.

We never discussed the incident again.

Twenty-five years later, my younger son, Michael, asked his mother, who was now living in Texas with her second husband, about this house because I had told him the story – and she told him what she had experienced. The only difference between her story and mine was that she thought the real estate agent had been waiting on the path for us. I thought he was already in the car.

The rest of the story was the same.

You can take your guess as to what all of it meant. The fact that three of us felt the same things and that two of us had the same experiences upstairs as well leads me to conclude what happened was real and also a part of the astral phenomena. The Weird World impinges on us, perhaps all the time, even though we often don't know it. We had experienced a strong impingement that day.

1978
Butter Nut and the Killers

I was out in the street of Far Rockaway – even though I was now living in Valley Stream, hopefully safe from any muggers – and I was watching a bus at a bus stop. A bunch of kids were getting on the bus. The time, I guessed, was about 10PM since I had gone to sleep about 9PM.

My guide was with me too.

"Do you ever wonder why we wind up where we wind up?" I asked him.

"Not any more," he said. "I think there is some force or mind or soul or something that is directing this for us individually, although I am not certain of that."

"I don't know if I have learned anything from all the trips I've taken," I said.

The bus started down the street and my guide and I just took flight after it. Yes, in the Weird World you can fly. Somewhere in the spinal area of your "astral" body exists this ability. You can actually feel the force down there when you are in the Weird World. When you want to fly this force just lifts you off the ground. The same force does not exist in the real world – unfortunately. Flying is fun and gives you an exuberant feeling. What's more, no one seems to notice that you are flying. You can be zooming above their heads and they don't seem to care. Either that or they just don't see you.

We flew alongside the bus, looking in.

The kids inside the bus were goofing off and causing trouble with several other passengers. Then I saw a student from my school, Tony Butter, known as Butter Nut to his friends. This was a kid I had a year ago when he was a senior. He was still a senior. He failed my course and every course except gym where he got an A. He was a dull-eyed, stupid kid and he was now standing saying something to the "leader" of the gang of youths who were on the bus with him. Butter Nut and the "leader" were mouthing off at each other. They were in each other's faces – maybe an inch apart.

"There's trouble there," said my guide.

"This doesn't seem like a dream," I said. "They all look awake."

Then a big fight started as Butter Nut threw a punch at the "leader." The other kids headed towards Butter Nut and…

…my guide and I whisked away to a lavender forest of immense trees.

"What the hell is this?" I asked. "What happened on the bus?"

"I don't know," said my guide.

"This is a lavender world," I said.

"Can lavender trees and plants do photosynthesis?" he asked.

"Isn't that green?" I said.

"Yeah, I guess so."

"The sky is pinkish too," I said.

We landed in a field; the tall grass a very light shade of lavender – beautiful but of course, completely bizarre. The whole world that I could see was shades of lavender and pink.

I saw my guide turn into a bird unlike any bird I ever saw in real life, more like an insect mixed with a bird, and I could feel that I too was now an insect-bird. Then we took off. We were like jets, soaring through the sky. These insect-birds were powerful. I was thinking of food because my mind was an insect-bird's mind now – although my human mind was in the background as it always is when I am some other type of creature. So what does an insect-bird eat in the lavender world?

I don't know because before I could eat I whisked into Africa (I am guessing Africa) where I was now a leopard again and I was running full steam after something that I could smell but couldn't see. My guide was gone. I was running like crazy, a powerful, hungry, determined animal looking to rip into his next meal – whatever I smelled that drove me to run like the wind.

Then I was back in Far Rockaway and I could see police cars and what seemed to be the same bus I had been witnessing before now stopped at the curb. My guide was standing next to me watching this scene too.

"Do you have any idea what this was all about with the bus and the lavender world?"

"No," he said, "I don't."

Then I was in bed, in Valley Stream, awake, staring at the ceiling.

The next day at school I debated whether to approach this Butter Nut kid. The kid was an idiot and I really didn't want to go up to him and say, "Did you have a dream about a bus last night and a bunch of morons causing trouble and a fist fight?"

I went into the teachers' lounge and got a cup of coffee. Do I search out Butter Nut or not? I decided to hell with it. I had proven to myself that these experiences were real over and over again – so what was the point in scouring the school for that idiot? – I was either at that bus stop and he was on the bus – and he would either remember it or not and if not – well, really, by this point, who cared?

The next day, Friday, I came into school early after a really long run and there was a sign posted on the sign-in desk: "Anthony Butter passed away two nights ago. Funeral arrangements will be announced when they are completed."

I asked the secretary what had happened. She said, "It was on a bus Wednesday evening and he was in a fight and some kid stabbed him right in the chest. He died yesterday in the hospital."

Now here is a question I ask myself: What did the lavender world, being an insect-bird in that world, then a leopard back in this world, have to do with Butter Nut's killing? If some super mind was guiding these adventures what had been the point of it all?

I still haven't figured any of that out to this day.

1978
The Death Speaker Once Again
For Jews and Christians

This trip was a strange one because it centered on philosophy with me playing the role of a philosopher surrounded by his students – some young, some old, some dressed as if they were from past centuries – in short, strictly Weird World stuff from start to finish – with me speaking in a very commanding voice, much deeper than my normal voice I should add. I thought of myself as exhibiting a "voice from on high" while this adventure happened, which struck me as strange then and strikes me just as strange now. Weird World events such as this happen but you always have this split consciousness – you know when you are the "you" of the real world and you know when you are being someone or something else.

Speaking in that authoritative voice made me someone else.

I was in an amphitheatre, much like the ones you see in ancient Rome or Greece with people seated all around me. I stood there, commandingly, smiling knowledgeably (about what I had no idea), and asking if anyone had any questions.

"Speak to us," shouted a young man in 1950s clothing. He had that slicked-back Elvis hairstyle too.

"Let me answer all the questions that I can while I have time," I said. "I see many of you from many times and I know many of you are confused and some of you might even be upset. The entire worlds of your lives have themes. If you are a Catholic, you know perfection when you receive Holy Communion. But that is a moment where you and Christ come together and you sense the magnificence of him but that fades fast. Then you live in a world where you find no perfection, especially in yourselves, and you know that perfection exists but you can't seem to get to it and keep it inside you.

"Jews have a different problem. Wherever they are most of them are successful but the world persecutes them. Some think it is just Christian anti-Semitism fueled by the New Testament – and some of it is – but the hate goes back much further. It goes to ancient Rome and before that ancient Greece. As a Jew we question, why does God make us have this burden? But our very name means we struggle with God and struggling with God means that we struggle with all things from God – our families, our professions, jobs, politics, in fact the entire world around us."

Okay, the real me thought, *what the heck was I saying?* Even as I was saying this I kept thinking where was I getting this speech? What was the purpose of this talk? I wish it were a dream but I was wide-awake, as always in the Weird World. And why was I referring to myself as a Jew? I'm not Jewish. I was brought up Catholic. Now during all these Weird World experiences I maintained my atheism. I was a card-carrying (so to speak) anti-religious atheist until I hit about 44 years old.

But I kept pontificating.

"So the Catholic looks to perfection and fails to find it or live it or enjoy it. The Jew looks to the world and fails to find contentment. This doesn't just have to do with religion. You don't have to be religious to experience what I am saying. These are the themes of your lives. And if you look closely enough you discover meaning in these themes."

I saw heads nodding in the amphitheatre. I'm glad they understood what I was saying because I thought what I said really made little sense. Why would a Catholic have a sense of perfection that clouds his life? Does Holy Communion – which is the eating of the bread – really bring the real Christ into your body and soul? Do Catholics really feel spiritual perfection for an instant during this time?

And are Jews, as individuals, struggling any more than anyone else? Okay, maybe. After all, over the centuries they have been persecuted and it did go back well before the advent of Christianity. But each individual Jew suffers more than each individual Catholic or anyone else? What I was saying was nonsense, I thought, but that didn't stop me because I just kept going. My audience was rapt.

"We all want to know the meaning of life or if there is a meaning to our lives. But there is a meaning, oh yes, there is. Every human being knows instinctively that there is a meaning to life in general and his life in particular. Even the lowest intellect thinks he is here for some reason or senses some reason for what is going on. All people and groups of people of the same religion or nationality have themes running through their lives – and each and every one senses deep meaning in it all. There is meaning to life and there was meaning to all of your lives. Your lives were not meaningless at all."

Evidently I was giving a "death speech" as I now referred to them. A small percentage of my journeys saw me giving death speeches to people – maybe they were really dead people and if they were then maybe there is some existence after we die. And maybe there isn't. I could not find proof of any of these people's existences, those in front of me now and those whom I had lectured in the past – except for that first woman Anita Harrison. I never got the names of any of the other people I lectured.

Was what I said true? Did everyone think there was some meaning to his or her life? Does the stupidest person you know really think he has some meaning to his life – some grand scheme? I don't know if he does. I think we tend to assume the idiots of the world have some sense of grand meaning to their lives but I have no idea if what we sense about them has any validity. Yes, as I made this speech, my voice knew that what I said was right but my inner consciousness kept thinking, "This is nuts."

But the audience liked it. I could see them nodding and some of them smiled. Some looked as if they were getting a great revelation from me. And I continued talking about meanings, and life. I guessed it was a damn good speech. As I said, the audience liked it and by this time I was just starting my acting career so an audience eating me up "on stage" (so to speak) thrilled me.

Then I was back in my bed, looking up at the ceiling and thinking, "So what is the grand meaning of all these trips? What is the point of all this? Will I ever know the point if there is a point?"

1979
Could I Kill Someone?

Until this book, I have kept from talking or writing about two subjects – my teaching career and my Weird World astral experiences. While my Weird World experiences happened from 1973 until 1984, I only talked to several people about them. Although I did ask maybe a hundred people if they had dreamed about me, I never told them that I flew out of my body and entered their dreams because, let's face it, that's nuts. Of the slightly more than one hundred dream-visits, maybe 40 percent of the dreamers had strong memories of what happened – just as Madeline Lowell did.

Once I made the mistake of telling someone, whom I shouldn't have told, about my Weird World experiences. In 1979 I had already formed my theatre company with a partner and we were casting one of our first shows. Lewis earned himself a co-starring role in the play.

One night after a particularly strenuous rehearsal, I went home and fell asleep in two seconds. Maybe five minutes later, based on looking at the clock in my room, I floated out of my body and entered the Weird World of Lewis's dream.

Lewis was strangling someone. I knew this had nothing to do with reality so I didn't do anything – in fact, had it been reality I couldn't have done anything anyway because in reality I was – I guess you could say this – nothing.

Lewis looked up at me. He was wide-awake.

"What do you want?" he asked me.

"I'm just visiting," I said.

"What does that mean, Horace?"

"It's Frank, not Horace," I said.

"The elephant graveyard is filled," he said.

This dream stuff will not conform to our normal logical ideas of conversation or flow of events. Lewis must be thinking of elephants and someone named Horace. When I first encountered dreams I always wanted them to be logical and understandable. Now, I knew that many of them would be illogical and totally un-understandable.

"I'm sure there's room for more elephants," I said.

"Frank, are you friends with Horace?" he asked.

"I don't know Horace," I said.

The man on the ground under Lewis said, "I am Horace."

"You are dead," screamed Lewis and started strangling Horace again.

At that point neither Lewis nor the gurgling Horace bothered with me. I watched for a while and then Lewis flew off into the sky hooting like an owl and Horace stood up.

"He can't kill me," said Horace, looking right at me.

"No?"

"I'm already dead," said Horace. "He kills me all the time."

Lewis came flying down but Horace popped away. Lewis didn't notice me this time as he was taken up with his flying and hooting. Then everything became really jumbled and elephants and zebras strolled around the park – now I saw we were in a large park – and African beaters hit the ground with large branches. Several Swiss guards for the Pope strolled amidst the animals.

And I was back in my room wide-awake. I went through everything I saw and then fell back to sleep.

The next day at rehearsal I took Lewis aside and asked him if he had dreamed about me the night before.

"Yeah," he said, "I did."

"What was the dream about?"

"I was killing my father – I have a lot of dreams of killing him – and then I saw you standing there and we talked about something. Then it all got crazy and I was flying."

"That was some dream," I said.

"Why did you ask me?"

"Oh, I had a dream about you that's all. I always want to see if the people I dream about dream about me," I said.

"And what was your dream about?"

"Uh, I, really…it…" I stammered. I hadn't expected him to ask me what my dream had been.

"You didn't have a dream, did you?" he asked.

"Yes, yes, of course…"

"No, there's something else going on," he said. "Come on, you didn't have a dream about me but you knew I had a dream about you. Right?"

Then I told him the truth.

"I've read about this," he said. "I think I did it once, when I was a teenager, but I've read of people who do this. So you actually visit people's dreams, huh, that's wild."

"That and other things," I said. Then I explained about how the Weird World and the real world intersected, I explained some of the other adventures I experienced, and I figured that would be that.

"Can you kill someone?" he asked.

"You mean can I kill someone in their dreams?"

"Yes," he said. "Give them a heart attack or scare them to death or something like that?"

"Never thought about that," I said.

"You got any enemies you could just kill them," he said. "That's power."

"What if you had stepped in when I was killing…" he paused. "Okay, what was his name?"

"Horace," I said.

"Oh, man, yep, yep, that's his name," he said. "Wow!"

"Why do you kill him?" I asked.

"He's my father; he *was* my father. He's actually dead now," said Lewis. "But he was a mean bastard and I guess I have a lot of stored up hate against him."

"Makes sense, you get that hate out in dreams," I said.

"You know, you could kill someone and no one would ever know," he said. "You could kill anyone and no one would know."

"I'm not sure that could happen," I said. "It might be one of the restraints on the Weird World stuff. I mean people could try to kill the president or other famous people."

"Maybe they have safeguards against this," he speculated. "You know, like astral protectors? People who do what you do but more powerful and they protect the famous."

"I have no idea about that, my experiences have nothing to do with that," I said. "What you're saying would make a good science fiction movie but it has nothing to do with my experiences.

"So let's try it," he said. "Kill someone for me."

"Very funny."

"No, really, I got this guy who has been a real thorn in my side, my former agent, a real prick if you want to know. I'd love him dead. His name is Gerard Hollingsworth. [Editor's note: This is not the man's real name.] Let's kill him."

"Lewis, Lewis, I don't want to kill anyone," I said.

"Kill this guy, come on," he said. "You wouldn't be caught for murder and a real bastard would be dead. Think of your enemies too, wouldn't you like them to die of a heart attack or something? Or maybe you could tell a diabetic to eat sugar and cause some kind of insulin shock by suggesting this to his mind when he is dreaming, or tell someone who has anorexia that they are looking fat and get them to subconsciously not eat anything and kill themselves? Man, you would be like a superman, Frank, a fucking superman."

"Lewis, you have a lot of hate in you," I said. "I'm not going to attempt to kill someone, even if I could do it, which I probably can't."

"You know when I go to sleep at night, I am going to send you thoughts about Hollingsworth, his face, where he lives and works, and I am going to try to get you to see him and see what a bastard he is and then maybe you will kill him for me and everyone else he has screwed. You would be doing the world a service, Frank."

Then the break was over and we went back to rehearsing.

That night when I went to sleep I wondered if I would visit Hollingsworth. Thankfully, I didn't that night or any other night, but Lewis was persistent. Just about every night of the rehearsals and of our four-month run of the show, he'd try to get me to kill Hollingsworth and others. This man had death, or rather murder, on his mind.

I, however, wasn't filled with hate and had no intention of finding out if I had the power to kill someone.

1980
My First Trip
to Las Vegas

Gambling did not appeal to me in 1980. Other than some poker games in my early 20s, I never placed a bet on anything. So this trip seemed quite strange because I left my body and walked the Strip of Las Vegas – although my mind told me I was in Las Vegas, it didn't look like Las Vegas. Even in 1980, people had knowledge of what the Strip in Las Vegas looked like and this did not look much like the Strip. It kind of looked like a miniature New York City with casinos and many skyscrapers too.

Yet, my mind said, "Scobe, you are in Las Vegas." Everything glitzed and glittered. I passed people on the sidewalk but no one seemed to see me. These people all seemed awake, fully awake, and enjoying their walks in Sin City. This did not seem like anyone's dream.

I'd never been in a casino before so I flew into one. I didn't have to stay on the ground with the pedestrians because I could loft myself up and over them, which I did.

In the casino, before I could reconnoiter, I saw the girl from the schoolyard – except she had become a woman, maybe 25 years old, standing by a long bar, waving to me to come over.

"Hi," I said.

"Hi," she said.

"We meet again," I said.

"Yes," she smiled. "We are destined to meet it seems doesn't it?"

"Do you think this is destiny, our meetings? Or is it just one of your dreams that I am visiting again? This is supposed to be Vegas but it doesn't really look like Vegas," I said.

"You think it's a dream?" she said.

"Well, I've gone into your dreams before," I said. "When you woke up did you remember meeting me?"

"No," she said. "I have no memory of you from my dreams. We haven't met yet."

"You don't consider this a meeting?"

"Yes, but not in the real world. I don't know what this is," she said.

"Las Vegas," I joked. "Las Vegas, although it doesn't look like Vegas from the pictures I've seen."

"I'm leaving," she said. "I'm waking up."

"Will we ever meet in the real world?" I asked her.

"If it is our destiny," she said.

"Do you believe it's our destiny?"

She smiled and vanished.

I heard someone scream at a slot machine and then I was back in bed. Destiny? Is there such a thing as destiny?

1984
The Point of It All

It ended in 1984. Through the early 1980s, my Weird World experiences slowly became fewer and fewer and they finally stopped.

My Weird World adventures lasted about ten years – until I was about 36 years old and well into another exciting career, this time producing, directing, writing and acting in plays. What did I learn from my Weird World adventures?

Plenty.

And nothing.

I have no doubt that they were real – after all I received so many confirmations that I had seen individuals' dreams that I couldn't discount all that as hallucination. Some of these adventures did seem prescient as well.

Some seemed to be actual real world events that I witnessed. The fat guy I met in my travels to the schoolyard appeared several other times in my adventures. He was always friendly but a little "off" as well. I always had the feeling that I would meet up with him in the future in the real world. So far I haven't – at least I don't think I have.

I never found out who my guide was. He didn't seem much more knowledgeable than I once I got started on these adventures. I did meet that beautiful girl/woman from the schoolyard again too – in the Weird World and in the real world. I'll have more to say about her shortly.

Was the Weird World really "soul travel?" Was I a "whole soul" as I had said to Madeline on my second trip? Did the soul really exist and were these adventures taking place in my soul?

I didn't think that was the case, at least not in the traditional sense of the soul. There was nothing heavenly about these experiences. My journeys, even into alien landscapes, seemed real and not the least spiritual – at least as I imagined spirituality to be.

I could actually go through walls and other things that we think of as solid. When the smoke beast would throw me around the room, I went in and out of the walls, the ceiling, and furniture. On several Weird World trips, I did experiments to see if I could actually control going through "solid" objects. I could if I thought about it with some force. However, when I was in somebody's dream – meaning the other person was controlling the scenery and environment – if he thought a wall was real, I tended to think it was real too.

I could fly, as I've said, both as myself and as a bird. But when I was in the Weird World I never thought to fly straight up and go into outer space. In retrospect that would have been a very interesting experiment.

Was it possible that the Weird World was a cosmic consciousness where all our individual minds joined as one? Could be, but I have no idea if that's the case. I can speculate as well as anyone else but speculation is not fact. My travels in the Weird World do not prove the existence of the soul, or of a cosmic consciousness, or of God, or of anything, really – except that they happened; that another world of some type co-exists with this one. I experienced that world for slightly more than a decade before the experiences slowly stopped.

I should tell you one last thing – to confuse you, as it has confused me. In 2003 I had to go for an MRI and the doctors found that sometime in the past – at a time that the doctors couldn't determine – I had several mini-strokes. At least the images on the scan indicated that. I also had a very old brain injury revealed by a CAT scan – probably caused by my boxing career.

Were my Weird World travels stroke induced, as I feared on one of my first trips? That is as possible as any other explanation. Were these events caused by the same boxing injury that caused my seizure in 2007? I don't know. Still I saw what I saw, experienced what I experienced, including enough evidence from other people, that stroke-induced or injury-induced or seizure-induced or not, the Weird World is as real as you are.

Happily enough, I finally met the girl from the schoolyard in real life. It was 1985, and she came in to apply for a job with my theatre company, yes, the beautiful A.P. She has no idea that I saw her long before I ever met her in real life (she will discover that when she reads this book) – and falling in love with her at first sight was simply seeing her in the flesh of real life.

It did take us years to finally become one but it happened and we married in 1993 and being with her now is even more fun than my travels into the Weird World

With the Weird World, with life in general, with my own individual existence – I wish I could explain it all.

Unfortunately, I can't.

- Part Six -
Adventures in Fighting - '63 and Today

When I was a high school kid at St. John's Prep in Brooklyn, there was another kid named Sullivan who tormented me day after day. Sullivan was an ugly kid, his ugliness highlighted by an even uglier disposition, and he was big – almost six feet. He lifted weights, too, and looked like the Incredible Hulk – a comic book character that didn't exist at that time, although maybe Sullivan was the inspiration for that creature. For some reason, or due to some chemical reaction, he hated me from the first day he laid eyes on me in 9th grade.

I was not a nerd or a bookworm, although I was a decent student in high school. I was also a good athlete, on a four-year scholarship to this great Catholic high school. I had no other enemies. In me there were none of the obvious reasons for a bully to do his bullying. I was not a member of an outcast group, and although I only had a few close friends, I was certainly no loner. It was not racism (we were the same race); it was not my religion (we both went to Catholic school); it was not that I wore glasses (at the time I didn't); it was not that I was a wise ass and insulted him in any way (I actually hadn't noticed him until he noticed me). I have no idea what the "root cause" of Sullivan's animus was – it just was.

He'd say things to me under his breath: "Fuck you, Scobe, and your mother." I'd ignore his taunts. Once I asked him why he always got on me and he replied: "Cause you suck."

I turned the other cheek so many times that I had a neck ache. The more I turned my cheek, the more Sullivan must have felt empowered because he kept up the steady stream of harassment.

On the basketball court Sullivan would try to physically hurt me. Thankfully I was much faster than he and a much better player – I had a scholarship for basketball and baseball to an outstanding sports school and this lummox couldn't keep up with me on the court, thank God. His inability to play at my level frustrated him no end too. Although he did occasionally slam me hard, he never could get in the licks he wanted.

As my 9th grade year wore on, and our basketball team made it to the New York City finals, Sullivan's verbal assaults increased in ferocity and decibel level. It wasn't just a whispered "fuck you and your mother!" – it was now loudly shouted put downs in the presence of others with bumps on the lunch line, and the occasional rock thrown when we were on the field and the priests' attention diverted. I often tried to avoid him, but he always seemed to find me; he always seemed to be there. He could sniff me out.

Big, ugly, powerful Sullivan was getting more and more daring, more and more assaultive. "If I ever get you alone, Scoblete, I'm gonna eat you." [This was long before Mike Tyson ever threatened to eat the children of one of his opponents.] Finally, one day he "accidentally" knocked over my lunch tray, spilling my lunch all over me. Although I did nothing at that moment, that moment I knew I had to do something drastic or Sullivan would finally get me alone and, indeed, as he was a tough and incredibly strong monster, he probably would "eat me." I didn't kid myself into actually thinking I could beat Sullivan in a fair fight – he was one bully who loved a fight and he had beaten up plenty of his classmates over that 9th grade year. He just hadn't beaten me up – yet.

I actually planned my strategy, how I would employ it and who I wanted to see it. We were in the schoolyard playing a pick-up game of basketball. There were a lot of kids in the schoolyard. Sullivan came along with two of his surly friends and called "winners." That meant whichever three-man team won, Sullivan's team would take them on. My team won. Sullivan and his bunch took the court. I was warmed up and ready. Sullivan was cold, having just come from wherever he had been smoking cigarettes – you could smell the smoke all over him – with his low-life friends.

"I got Scobe," Sullivan called loudly so the world could hear him trumpeting his challenge. That meant he guarded me. My teammate took the ball out of bounds under the basket and threw it to me past the foul line. The game was on. I didn't wait either – no sense letting Sullivan warm up. I started backing into Sullivan. He started bumping me. I faked a jumper. Sullivan went for the fake and jumped up to block my shot. As he was almost at the height of his jump, I took my jump shot all right – right into his ugly face with every ounce of strength I had. His nose exploded (he had a big red freckled nose) and blood gushed and spouted everywhere. Sullivan went down on his back on the blacktop, the wind knocked out of him (I could hear him lose his breath), his head hitting the ground hard as well. He was completely dazed. And I came down right on his chest. I didn't care if he was conscious, semiconscious, unconscious or dead, I wailed away at him. In the space of a few seconds, I paid him back for all his torture. My friends and his friends dragged me off him.

I had blood all over my hands and my clothing and, as I recall, I snarled like some rabid dog – that was for effect more than an unconscious response. At first it looked as if his friends were going to jump in, but my growling probably stopped them. They lifted Sullivan to a sitting position but he was in no position to stand. I took one last kick at his face, just grazed it, and walked slowly out of the schoolyard.

Probably 40 kids saw the end of that fight; 40 witnesses to the utter destruction of big, ugly Sullivan.

Unlike today, in those days if a kid got into a fight, the parents didn't sue. Sullivan returned to school several days later, his nose bandaged, and his eyes blackened, with black and blue lumps on his ugly face. He never tormented me again. In fact, he ignored me and I ignored him. There is no doubt in my adult mind that had I not finally launched my attack on Sullivan when I did, he would have eventually gotten me alone (probably with a bunch of his moronic friends) and beaten me to a pulp. Sullivan only understood one thing – power – he was more powerful than you, or you were more powerful than he. Period. There were no other ingredients in his zeitgeist.

The pacifist ethic, taught by Jesus Christ, Gandhi and Martin Luther King Jr., does not work with the Sullivans of the world. Adolph Hitler, Joseph Stalin, Mao Zedong, and Osama bin Laden were monstrous versions of Sullivan. They could not be assuaged ("Gee, Sullivan, why do you hate me so?" "Cause you suck!"); they cannot be avoided; they are either more powerful than you or you are more powerful than they. Period.

Had Mahatma Gandhi been Jewish, with the fate of *all* Jews in the world hinging on his decisions during the Hitler years, and had he tried to use his pacifistic philosophy on the Nazis, there would be no Jews in the world today. Had Martin Luther King Jr. used "peaceful resistance" in a society with no sense of human values – again we can reference Nazi Germany, Stalin's Soviet Union, Mao Zedong's China – America would not have instituted the Civil Rights Act.

For pacifism to work the society has to have some inner core of shared values with the pacifists, otherwise the pacifists are looked upon as dross to be swept away. Obviously, America has had its share of pacifists. The Quakers come to mind. They refuse to fight in any war. In truth, the Quakers survive because others have kept them safe – others died violently so they could live peacefully. Just picture an entire nation of Quakers facing the threat of an advancing Adolph Hitler. It's a bloody picture, indeed.

The great playwright, George Bernard Shaw, a pacifist, when asked what he would do if he were Prime Minister and the Nazis entered England, said: "Welcome them as tourists." Witty, funny, and dead wrong. Those "tourists" would have ravaged the country, perhaps even killing old George Bernard himself.

Today, we see another anti-war movement in America, especially among naive college students and their cynical professors. It has been reported that students at some universities are singing the old "all we are saying is give peace a chance" chant. In an ambiguous war such as Vietnam where national interests had to be defined in broad political brush strokes, a "peace movement" could be defended. After all, no one attacked us directly. But an anti-war movement against the war on terror (or whatever you want to call this war), which has been etched in the brush strokes of innocent blood, cannot be defended. The ones who attacked us are not tourists, they're terrorists; their goal is world domination for their religion – a religion that hates the values of the very people who are "giving peace a chance."

As Hitler revealed his true plans in Mein Kampf, so the Islamic terrorists have told us in their many unambiguous, public statements their plan as well – they wish to wipe our way of life from the planet. They wish to make the world Muslim. They believe America is, at heart, a land of cowards. Terrorists cite our withdrawal from Somalia, after losing "just 18 men," as proof that America is weak. The anti-war folks, the college socialists and politicians hungering for votes merely fuel the delusion of American weakness and embolden the terrorists to continue attacking. The true irony of the "peace-movement" is that the "peaceniks" will be the first people put to death if the terrorists win. I'm guessing even something as idiotic as coed dorms will be enough motivation for beheading or stoning the co-eds.

I do not deny that some pacifists are brave men and women. Pacifism is not necessarily a synonym for cowardice, despite the fact that the bin Ladens, Hitlers, Stalins and Zedongs (and the Sullivans) of the world think it is. Many pacifists are willing to die for their beliefs. But in the face of those with no equivalent moral compass, the deaths of brave pacifists are utterly without meaning. Such men and women are not dying so that their children might live. They are dying so that their children might die too. Clearly, pacifism, while laudatory in some respects, is ludicrous in others. Does anyone really think it is praiseworthy to sacrifice one's life in order to facilitate the sacrifice of other lives as well?

Truly, even Christ's statement, "There is no greater love than this, that a man sacrifice his life for a friend," was never intended to have as a corollary, "so that his friend might die as well." The intent was plain – so that "his friend might live." Pacifism in the face of monstrous, conscienceless evil is an evil in itself, as it allows evil to win.

When dealing with terrorists we must hit them in the face with the basketball if we hope to survive their evil onslaughts.

- Part Seven -
The Virgin Kiss: An Adventure in Love

Our Lady of Angels elementary school in Bay Ridge, Brooklyn; those were the days! I played on an undefeated basketball team, winning a championship, and I fell in love – starting in second grade – with Mary Sissallo.

Of course, in second grade I had no idea of what love was – the reality of which actually eluded me until I hit college – but every time I looked at Mary my chest felt tight and I felt weak in the knees. I thought she was the most beautiful girl on the planet.

From second through fifth grades I watched Mary from afar, since I sat in the back of the class with the dumb kids and she sat in the front of the class with the smart kids. That gave me time to gaze at her all day long. Mary was the smartest girl in the class as a matter of fact, sitting right next to Hugo Twaddle, who was the smartest boy (that was his *real* name). The Sisters of Charity, the nuns who manned Our Lady of Angels, did not know about modern educational concepts like all kids are equal (even when they aren't), and these nuns sat us based on how well or how poorly we performed in their classes. The dopes were in the back; the smart kids in the front – the natural order of things now and, if the dopes continued their ways, in the future as well.

I performed poorly. I was stuck in the back of the room, with Stephen Gatowski, Valentine Zammit, Quincy Padookie, and Farashaula Pedanda, the coterie of dopes of our Lady of Angels elementary school. I don't know if these guys stayed dopes for the rest of their lives as the nuns predicted they (we!) would – I hope they didn't.

It wasn't until I was much older that I realized as smart as Mary was in elementary school, she was still innocent in terms of the real world, that is to say the non-Catholic world.

It wasn't until eighth grade, when I was playing on our great basketball team, that I finally got up the gumption to ask Mary Sissallo out. The boys and girls at our Lady of Angels had been separated in sixth grade, the girls going to one building with the nuns, the boys going to another building with the Franciscan brothers. That kept all of us from distraction as puberty set in. Needless to say this change of climate caused my grades to soar since by beautiful distraction was no longer within eyesight. I went from being a "your son is about to be thrown out" student, to a 95 student. Love certainly had taken a toll on my early elementary school career.

Still I did get to see a lot of Mary since we had dances in the gym where we could meet and we had those basketball games which were attended by most of the boys and girls of the school. Indeed, after most games there were dances.

I was starting to get some courage since I had earned some notoriety by being one of the two big stars of the team – the other being the devastating six-foot-eight Patrick Heelan.

At one dance in February I asked Mary to go on a date with me after I had asked her to dance. In fact, I had some help. Billy Bell, another great ballplayer on the basketball team, had egged me on. "You like her, so ask her to dance. Man, man, everyone knows who you are. She'll be happy to dance with you."

"You think?" I asked.

"The worst that can happen is she'll laugh in your face and tell you to go to hell," he said.

"Mary would never use the word 'hell'," I said.

"So then you got nothing to lose," said Billy.

I asked her to dance. She said yes. I asked her to dance again. She said yes. Then a lady's choice dance was announced and Mary asked me to dance.

What did I have to lose?

"So you want to go, you know, uh, ah, on a, uh, ah, uh, date?" I stammered.

"Sure," said Mary.

And that was that...well, not really.

I told my mother about the fact that I was going to take Mary out to see *West Side Story* that weekend and my mother gave me her typical lecture. "You must always respect girls. You must not act like King Kong. You must never take advantage of a girl, even if she wants you to. Do you understand?"

"Yes," I said, having no idea of what "taking advantage of a girl" actually meant. So I translated that as best I could to "don't kiss until you are married." I thought of my mother as very old fashioned because of this attitude because I knew from my religious training that you could kiss a girl without sinning if you didn't have evil thoughts when doing it and you didn't do it for too long. The brothers told us that in class and I assumed the brothers were right; they were God's emissaries on earth. After all I thought, what else was there other than kissing? I had no idea. Kissing Mary loomed as the biggest thing in my life.

Unlike today where Mary and I would probably be discussing birth control methods, those days were totally different. Even in eighth grade I only had a hazy, fuzzy, foggy extremely dim notion of what went on between a man and a woman, which meant, translated into today's language – I knew nothing.

I had a simple plan for my first date – *West Side Story*, which was playing at the Dyker Theater on 86th street, and then a big hot fudge sundae at Grossman's Soda Fountain. Then I would walk her home and give her a kiss.

It couldn't get simpler than that...well, not really.

I had been practicing my kissing method for about six months, always with the hope that it would be Mary Sissallo to whom I would give my first kiss. In fact I was determined it would be her. I knew from basketball that no matter how talented you are, the thing that separates the winners from the losers is practice. Obviously I had no one to practice kissing with but I had figured out a way any way. I would tuck my folded thumb under my pointer to simulate a mouth and then I would kiss it. I always used my left hand for this so that my head would go right when I bent it a little and planted my kiss.

I wanted to get down what I called "the cling." I had overheard some women talking about "the cling" on a bus, debating who had a better "cling" style, Paul Newman or Clark Gable. The idea was that you kissed in a way that made your lips cling to the other person's lips so that as you parted your lips and her lips they gently separated in stages since they were "clinging" together. This cling was not easy to do because if you had too much spit in your mouth you would slide off too fast but if your lips were too dry they couldn't stick to hers enough to make the "cling."

I gave myself 15 minutes of practice a night and I was getting darn good at this cling business – about 90 percent of the time I had that cling perfectly. The other 10 percent of the time I tended to slide too much because I was drooling, having wet my lips too much before the kiss. But the sequence when done perfectly went like this: plant the kiss softly, then press a little more, then lighten up while slowly parting your lips with the cling. Mary would love it if I could do it properly – and I was determined to do it properly.

Of course, I assumed Mary would want to kiss me, a big assumption I realized. I knew Mary was a "good girl" and "good girls" might not want to kiss boys, certainly not on the first date. I would have to play that aspect of my first kiss by ear. I knew I would be walking on eggs or eggshells, whatever the saying was, but I so wanted to kiss Mary that I existed in a Mary-mania of wishing and hoping and desiring.

The night of our first date arrived. I dressed casually, which meant I wore the best clothes I had. I picked Mary up at her house on 74th Street between 4th and 5th Avenues. While I lived in an apartment above a store, Mary actually lived in her own house with her sour mother, a widow.

We walked to the Dyker Theater on 86th Street. It was a great movie theater in the good old days but today it has been converted into an "Everything is 99 Cents" store. Since *West Side Story* was all the rage with the girls in my neighborhood, Mary talked excitedly about the movie as we walked from 74th to 86th Street.

"I'm so happy you decided to see this movie," said Mary. "Patty saw it and said it was A-one."

"I'm glad," I said.

"It's supposed to be really sad. Tony dies."

"Who?" I asked.

"Tony, the star of the movie. Dies. After he kills Maria's brother," said Mary.

"Too bad."

"A big knife fight at the end," said Mary.

"Gee," I said. I actually wished Mary wouldn't tell me the whole movie beforehand because if I knew the whole story, why go see it?

"You know this movie was rated 'objectionable in part' by the Legion of Decency," said Mary. "We had to swear in church that we would be very careful if we went to see it."

"Really? It must be good," I joked.

"Didn't you have to swear in church too?"

"Uh, I don't remember," I said. I didn't tell her that I rarely paid attention when I went to church every Sunday.

"My mother said she didn't want me to see it. It's about Puerto Ricans."

"Aren't there any white people in it?" I asked.

"Oh, yes. It's about this white gang called the Jets and this Puerto Rican gang called the Sharks...and a police officer named Officer Cupcake," said Mary.

"Does he get iced?" I laughed.

"What?"

"Does he get iced? It's a joke. Cupcake. Iced," I said.

"A joke?

"Not too good I guess," I said red faced. Well, I bombed on that one.

After we took our seats in the movie theater, I got buttered popcorn and some candy for us.

"Mmmmm, this butter is delicious," said Mary. "You think they use real butter? My mother says they don't use real butter in buttered popcorn."

"Of course it's real," I said with authority. "They wouldn't say buttered popcorn if it wasn't butter. That would be lying."

"My mother says there isn't a real Betty Crocker either. My mother eats all those Betty Crocker cakes which have made her so fat but she says that Betty Crocker really doesn't exist."

"That's like they say there isn't one Lassie because they use a lot of dogs on the show," I said. "Now how could they get so many dogs to be so smart? People say stupid things like that."

"I know," said Mary in agreement. I hoped that my Lassie analysis made up for the bad joke I had told about Officer Cupcake. I felt pretty good at that moment.

"Oh, great; the movie is starting," said Mary as the curtains opened. In those days the movie theaters looked like playhouses and the curtain would open when the movie started. That added dramatic tension.

In the darkness I wanted to put my arm across Mary's shoulders but I just couldn't move. I was frozen to my seat. Also, I didn't want to offend or upset Mary by being too forward. My mother's words rang in my ears, "Never take advantage of a girl." Was putting my arm across Mary's shoulders taking advantage? On the first date, it might be. Caution was called for. Also, I was, I'll admit, terrified and I had a bead of sweat falling down my forehead which I wiped off before she could see it.

So we watched the movie. Mary ate popcorn and I ate popcorn. Mary ate candy and I ate candy. Mary drank soda and I drank soda. My frazzled nerves were acutely aware that Mary was sitting next to me and I could smell her perfume. I half watched the movie but I fully basked in the presence of the girl I had loved since second grade. Sitting next to Mary was as close to heaven as I had ever been up to that point in my life.

When the movie ended and the lights came on in the theater, I knew I had scored big time. "Oh that was great!" said Mary. "I never ate so much in all my life."

"His name was officer Krum-key, not Cupcake," I said.

We headed for the exit.

"Wasn't Maria beautiful? She had such a lovely voice. No wonder they picked her for the role," said Mary. Neither of us knew that Nathalie Wood's voice had been dubbed in by singer Marnie Nixon.

"Krum-key like in crumb cake I guess," I laughed. Mary didn't get that joke either. Maybe I wasn't so funny. Nerves can do that to you.

"I never realized that Puerto Ricans could be almost white," said Mary.

"Got room for a hot fudge sundae?" I asked.

"Always! Mmmmm, I just love hot fudge!"

At Grossman's Soda Fountain on 73rd Street we talked about the movie some more and Mary had two hot fudge sundaes with a ton of fudge. "I love a lot of fudge and also nuts," she told Mr. Grossman who delighted in feeding this young girl, although he skimped on my sundae. Back to the movie, Mary said she also liked Maria's brother, George Chiclet, who was the actor. She liked his straight black hair. Nuts! I had curly blonde hair. I hoped that didn't put me at a disadvantage.

We spent two hours at Grossman's and then I walked Mary home. I made no move to kiss her. I didn't want anything to interfere with my love for this girl and you never knew if she would get angry if I tried it. I could wait. In addition, I was sweating under my arms and I had no idea if I smelled bad. Best to stay at arms distance.

When I got home I realized that I had made a big mistake that evening. I had given her a great night – a great movie, great popcorn, great candy, great soda, two great hot fudge sundaes loaded with fudge and nuts – but I hadn't followed up by asking her out on another date. I knew she had a great time because she told me so. "Frankie," she said, "I had a great time." Mary was not a liar and therefore, I surmised, she had a great time. But I had been dumb. I was so taken up by being with her that I hadn't made the move to be with her again.

So I called her house right away to speak to her. Mrs. Sissallo answered.

"Hello," said Mrs. Sissallo.

"Hello, Mrs. Sissallo, this is Frankie, uh, ah, is Mary there?"

"She's in the bathroom throwing up," said a stern-voiced Mrs. Sissallo. "How much did you give her to eat. She's green."

"I, uh, ah, uh, um, ah," I said.

"Wait," said Mrs. Sissallo, "she's coming to the phone."

"Frankie?" asked Mary.

"How are you feeling?" I asked.

"I threw up a lot of chocolate," she said.

"We ate a lot of chocolate," I agreed.

"With nuts," she added.

I needed to change the topic even though I was quite surprised that Mary was capable of throwing up – she was an angel; did angels throw up? That threw me somewhat.

"I enjoyed the date," I said.

"I did, aaarrrrgggghhhh!"

I heard Mary's mother's voice in the background, "You couldn't run into the bathroom? You had to throw up all over the phone and rug?"

"Mary would you like to go out next weekend too?" I asked.

"Yes, aaaarrrrgggghhhhh!"

"Jesus Christ," said Mary's mother closer to the phone this time.

"Great!" I said.

"Aaaaarrrrgggghhhhh!" said Mary.

"Holy mother of God!" said Mary's mother. "What did you eat?"

"See you next Saturday at seven o'clock," I said.

"Aaaaaarrrrgggggghhhh!"

"God!" screamed Mary's mother.

"Bye!" I said and hung up.

I went on 38 dates with Mary over the course of the next year. By now I was a freshman at St. John's Prep in Brooklyn. I still hadn't kissed her. As time passed I became more and more worried that if I made a move on her she would repulse me and never see me again. My mother was constantly cautioning me to "never take advantage of a girl" and I froze every time Mary and I stood on her porch before she went in after our dates.

I became an expert too in *West Side Story* which we saw 23 times during the course of our dating. I figured that if *West Side Story* worked once it would work always. We followed this movie from the Dyker, a first-run house, to the Harbor Theater (which is now a gym), to the Fortway – which was the last step a movie took before it went into oblivion. As we followed the movie, the prints became grainier and the sound became scratchy. The buttered popcorn wasn't as good and several times we found worms in our candy.

The only thing that really scared me about these dates with Mary was that she seemed to be constantly throwing up when she got home. She just ate too much I guess. Also, Mary's mother didn't seem to like me – at all. When I would call, Mary's mother would say, "Guess what? It's *him* again."

But I knew this kiss couldn't wait any longer. I had kissed my left hand so much I thought I might have to give it an engagement ring.

I made up my mind that on the 39th date I would make my move – come hell or high water. I figured I would take her to the Harbor Theater to see *West Side Story* and then we would walk down to Shore Road where they were building the Verrazano Bridge across the Narrows River to Staten Island. I figured we'd pass up those two hot-fudge sundaes at Grossman's – to make sure Mary didn't throw up on me when I kissed her. We'd look at the lights along the shore and the sparkling water that always had these strange white balloons floating in it, all very romantic I figured, and then as I walked her home, I would hold her hand (sad to say, I hadn't yet held her hand either) as a prelude to the kiss. My "cling" was now at 98 percent according to my well-kept records.

On that final trip to *West Side Story* I learned two things. The name of the police officer in movie was Krupke and Mary let me hold her hand. Not being a fool I never let go of her hand once I had it locked in my grip during the movie, which made eating the popcorn and candy difficult, and I didn't let go of her hand as we walked along Shore Road looking at the sights.

Then we were at Mary's porch and I knew this had to be the night. But I was again frozen by fear.

"Whew! That was some walk," said Mary. "I think my hand has fallen asleep. Wow! I think you've cut off all the circulation, it's almost blue. We should have switched hands."

"I, ah, thought you might not want to," I said lamely.

"No, it was fun holding hands. Look, your hand is blue too."

"Yeah," I said. "It's all pins and needles."

We disengaged hands. The blood rushed into my hand and it felt really swollen.

"I'm glad I slept in the movie," said Mary. "Or I wouldn't have been able to make that walk."

I was going to do it. I was going to kiss this angel who stood before me. My God, I had played with and against the best ballplayers in New York City – how could I be afraid of a little kiss?

"Mary, I…uh, ah, uh, uh, ah."

"What?" asked Mary.

"I, uh…" I was totally losing my courage so I changed the subject to recoup. "Do you know how many grains of sand there are in the Sahara Desert?"

"Should I?" asked Mary.

"Not as many grains of sand as there are stars in the heavens."

"Really?"

"In fact, a camel trying to count the grains of sand would finish faster than a scientist trying to count the stars," I said definitively.

"Why?"

"Why what?"

"Why would a camel want to count the grains of sand in the desert?" asked Mary. "It would get pretty boring, even if a camel could count, which he can't."

"I don't know. I read that in a book I got out of the library," I said.

"Oh."

"And did you know that five thousand years ago the Sahara Desert was only one mile square?" I said. I was dying inside.

"A perfect square?" asked Mary, really interested now.

"I don't know."

"What did the book say?"

"It just said one-mile square or one square mile," I said.

"Then it must be a perfect square if the book said so. Don't you find that strange?" asked Mary.

"What?"

"That there'd be a perfect square in the desert?" she said.

"I guess." We were getting further and further away from the kiss.

Mary was now enthused and she had a revelation. "I'll bet God planned it that way to show He really existed. To show the evil Egyptians that he was God."

Okay, okay, I thought, I got her happy now. I would follow through. "And the universe is some trillion trillion square miles," I said triumphantly.

"You see!" Mary was really into this now.

"See what?"

"God made the universe square!" shouted Mary.

"Uh..."

"Then how can people say He doesn't exist?" she asked thoughtfully.

"I never heard anyone say that," I said.

"Oh, they do, the atheists do. The sisters at my high school told us that all the atheists say that God doesn't exist."

"Do you know atheists?" I asked

"No! My mother wouldn't let me even if I did."

"I don't think there are any atheists in Bay Ridge. I never met any."

"Sister Jerome Drake says that atheists are everywhere – they could be your best friend and you wouldn't even know it," said Mary. "Sister says they infiltrate everywhere, even the White House."

"Really, no kidding?"

"All of Russia is atheist…"

"Did you know in South America," I started.

"And all of China…

"There are still cannibals," I threw in.

"And Cuba now…

"They're these little pygmies," I said

"She says the Jews are atheists too, only they don't know it…"

"They file down their teeth into sharp points," I added.

"Who? The Jews do that? File their teeth?" asked Mary shocked.

"Really? I never knew they did that!" I said stunned.

"Mmmm, yes, that would explain everything," she mused thoughtfully.

"Come to think of it, Kaplan, the butcher down the block, boy are his teeth sharp," I said. "He's a friend of my father but he has this crazy tattoo on his arm. It's like numbers."

"You really think they eat people?" asked Mary, putting it all together.

"The pygmies do, sure," I said.

"And the Jews?" she asked

"I don't know."

"Oh, Frankie, they eat something called Cocksure or Corning-ware or something – maybe that's a Jewish word for people!" said a wide-eyed Mary.

"So you think when Christ said, 'Eat my body, drink my blood,' he really meant it?" I asked.

"No."

"Then why did he say it?"

"You're forgetting one thing," said Mary.

"What?"

"Christ wasn't Jewish. He was Catholic," she said.

"I thought he was born Jewish."

"How could that be? Christ was God and the Jews are atheists, they don't believe in God. How could Christ not believe in himself? That would be pretty silly," said Mary, having now reasoned it all out. "Aren't we lucky to be Catholic?"

"Yeah," I said.

"All the other people in the world are going to hell but us."

"I don't really think that's true," I said.

"Sister Jerome Drake says."

"I really feel sorry for the other people if that's true," I said.

"Not the atheists?"

"No, no, not them," I corrected. "But the other people. I mean they all believe in their religions and they're all wrong. They spend their whole lives following their religions and when they die they go to heaven only to be told they have to go to hell."

"Sister Jerome Drake says that Catholics have a mission to be pure in mind and body. So we can be an example to the world," said Mary, her face red with realization.

This whole conversation was going in the wrong direction. I didn't care about religion right now, or that crazy Sister Jerome Drake, the ugliest woman I had ever seen in my life, or whether Jews ate people or not. I knew they didn't eat people or my father wouldn't be friends with Kaplan the butcher. I had to get this going in another direction.

"Yeah, ah," I said. "Did you know that Christopher Columbus brought syphilis back from the new world?"

"What's that?"

"I think it's a disease. I read it in a book," I said.

"What kind of disease?"

"I don't know, the book didn't say. I think you get it when you are on the ocean a long time without oranges."

"What does it do? Sis-a-lisp?" asked Mary.

"Maybe it makes you talk funny," I said.

"Isn't it wonderful that God designed the world so that everything bad you do you get punished?"

"But what bad could you do being alone at sea?" I asked.

"Maybe they had impure thoughts. I never have impure thoughts."

"Never?"

"Nope," said Mary. "Do you?

"No! Never!" I lied.

"Sister Jerome Drake says that impure thoughts are the fathers of impure deeds."

"She really knows a lot doesn't she?" I asked desultorily.

"She's a nun. I want to be just like her when I grow up."

"You want to be a nun?" This whole night was going into the dump. Mary wanted to be a nun!

"No. I want to get married and have four children, two boys and two girls. And I want to practice virtue. Sister Jerome Drake says that the practice of virtue is a woman's highest calling."

"Oh," I said somewhat relieved. At least Mary was normal.

"My mother agrees. She practices virtue." That figured.

"Did your father?"

"I don't know. He died when I was four."

"I don't think fathers do."

"Father McKeveny does," said Mary knowledgeably.

"I don't mean that kind of father," I said.

"I always go to Father McKeveny for confession."

"You do? Even though you don't have to? He's really hard."

"My mother says he is a real priest. I never get more than two Hail Marys for my sins," she said.

"Wow!" I exclaimed. That *was* something. That priest loved to yell and scream at you for your sins and he was always giving big penance for little things, too. None of the guys went to him.

"How many prayers do you get?"

"Not many," I lied.

"But how many?"

"I don't go to McKeveny. I go to Father Egghart," I explained.

"But he doesn't speak English too good."

"I know."

"My mother says that only bad kids go to Father Egghart because he doesn't understand their sins because he can't speak English. He gives easy penance."

"Well, not me," I said, putting my foot firmly into my mouth.

"He gives you *hard* penance? What did you do?"

"Oh, no...not that...I go...because..."

"Why?" asked Mary.

"Speaking of sin..." I was trying to get out of this bind and get back to the main thrust of the evening, my first kiss.

"Sister Jerome Drake says that every time you sin, you drive a nail through Christ's heart," said Mary.

"I thought they drove a spear?"

"I think a nail hurts more because it has a thick head."

"Yeah, maybe...you know this book I read..."

"She says we always have to be on guard against sin."

"Mary, ah, what do you think the worst sin is?"

"I don't know." She thought a moment. "Probably murder...and prolonged kissing."

"How long do you think? Ten minutes?"

"No, with a gun, instantly."

"No, kissing," I said. "How long before you commit a sin?

"I don't know."

Okay, Frankie, I thought to myself, *it is now or never! Get to the kiss!*

"Ah, Mary…"

"Yes, Frankie."

"We've been going on dates a lot."

"I've memorized the movie," she said.

"And I was thinking that…"

"What?"

My mother's words popped into my head ("never take advantage of a girl") and I said, "I don't want to offend you."

"No, you always smell good with your after shave."

"Thanks, that's not what I meant."

"Then what?" she asked with a slight smile on her beautiful lips.

Now! Now! Do it now, Frankie! "I want to…kiss you. Not a prolonged one. I mean I don't want you to think I think of you in that way…"

"Of course, silly," said Mary quietly.

"Because I don't…"

"Of course…" said Mary

"I mean I really like you and respect you…"

"Fine…"

"A lot," I said. "A real lot."

"Okay," she smiled.

"And if you wouldn't mind…"

"Okay."

"I wouldn't tell anyone. I wouldn't even confess it," I said.

"Do it."

"And I'll even think good thoughts while I'm doing it."

"Okay."

"You mean it's okay?"

"Yes," said Mary.

"You're sure?"

"Yes."

"I mean you don't have to do this if you don't want to." What the hell was I saying? I was going to talk her out of it! I was an idiot!

"I want you to kiss me, Frankie."

"Okay…ah…so how are we going to do this? Ah, maybe you should close your eyes."

"Okay." Mary closed her eyes. Then she made the sign of the cross. So what? I was "this" close to kissing the girl of my dreams, so what if she was religious. Then I realized as I moved closer to her that I hadn't practiced. I wasn't warmed up. I wanted to make sure my lips were perfect. I quickly lifted my left hand, made the faux mouth with thumb and pointer, and frantically planted several kisses on it until I had the cling just right.

"What are you doing?" asked Mary with her eyes still closed.

"Practicing...I mean, uh, I'm trying to get the right angle." I almost blew that one.

"Well, hurry, my mother will be out soon to tell me to get in," said Mary.

"All right, here goes," I said and I cupped her checks in my hands, very gently, and I planted the perfect kiss on her wonderful mouth. As we parted several seconds later our lips clung to perfection. All my practice the past year had paid off. She opened her eyes and stared at me. I stared at her. She smiled. I smiled. I was so overcome with joy that I made the biggest mistake of my life to that point. I burst into song!

I sung "Officer Krupke" from *West Side Story*! As bad as that was, I did something even worse. I forgot all about Mary standing on the porch. I leaped off it and clicked my heels, singing like a maniac; so happy, so relieved; so overwhelmed with a joy I had never felt before. Winning a City championship in basketball hadn't been as wonderful as this.

I headed down the street at a rapid pace, singing, ecstatic. I then heard from far away: "Frankie, don't you want to see me to the door?" But I was in a fog.

I slept like a baby that night but the next day it dawned on me how stupid I had been. I had experienced the most beautiful kiss in the whole wide world and I ran away from the very girl I had shared that kiss with.

So I called Mary that night.

"Oh, it's *you*," said Mary's mother. "She isn't home. She's helping with religious training at the church. Don't bother her. Good night." She hung up.

I called thirteen nights in a row. Mary was either out or taking a shower or indisposed, whatever that meant. Obviously she didn't want to see me ever again.

It was over. The most beautiful kiss, indeed my *virgin kiss*, had ended in disaster.

For a whole year I nursed my disappointment in losing Mary Sissallo and then one of my friends at St. John's Prep suggested I get back into the action by going after a slut.

"You know," he said, "the type of girl who'll let you hold her hand; kiss her, stick your tongue in her mouth on the very first date. That type. Stop worrying about what happened with Mary and go after a slut. That will make you feel good about yourself."

"Where do you find sluts?" I asked.

"Oh, man, they are everywhere," said this guy.

Then I thought of a girl that was probably a slut. I had seen her on the Staten Island ferry when I went to the pool in the St. George section of Staten Island. She was always in black and white; a short black dress and a white blouse that you could see her bra through. It was hard not to look at her on the ferry going across the Narrows heading back to Brooklyn. That bra was like light to a moth.

She had only two things wrong with her; she smoked like a fiend and she had silver braces on her teeth – she looked like she had electrical wiring in her mouth. I mean when the sun hit her face you could be blinded by those braces.

Still, the way she sat, the way she walked, the way she looked around, if she wasn't a slut there was no such thing in the whole wide world.

But, of course, I had to meet her before I could hold her hand and kiss her, maybe even putting my tongue into her throat. So one sunny day in July as I was coming back from the pool, I made my move. She was sitting on one of the benches, with her back to the skyline of Manhattan.

"Excuse me," I said suavely. "Is this seat taken?" I pointed to the spot next to her.

"What?" she said somewhat distracted.

"Can I sit here?" I asked again.

"It's a free country."

"Not until eighteen sixty-five, until after the Civil War," I said trying to show her how intelligent I was. I figured girls would like an intelligent guy.

"What? What are you talking about?" She looked at me suspiciously.

"America wasn't really free until after the Civil War."

"What's that?" she asked.

"The war between the states," I said, somewhat flustered. Didn't everybody know about the Civil War?

"Oh, you mean the Nazis."

"No. The Civil War was in the eighteen hundreds."

"Do you read books?" she asked. "Cause I hate guys that read books. They think they're so smart."

"No…books? I hate books."

"Then where'd you get this stuff about free Nazis and the states?"

"I think I heard it on Cousin Brucie," I said trying to cover my tracks. Cousin Brucie was a very popular radio show in New York City at that time.

"He's a creep. He calls everyone his cousin. I'm not his cousin, are you?"

"No," I said. She had me really off balance now.

"He thinks he's hot stuff 'cause he's on the radio. I hate guys that think they're hot stuff."

"Me too," I said strongly.

"Hey are you some kind of fag?" she asked.

"What?"

"You like to kiss boys?" she asked.

"What? Are you kidding?"

"Oh, well, you like girls then, right?"

"Yeah, I like girls," I said. I had to get this conversation onto another topic. "Would you like some Almond Joy?" I showed her an unopened Almond Joy bar, my favorite candy at the time.

"No. The chocolate sticks to my teeth," she said challengingly. "If you haven't noticed, I wear braces."

"Oh, no…really?"

"Everybody notices them."

"They're very, ah, shiny," I said.

"I hate them. But my skinny pimply stepmother makes me wear them because she says I look like Bucky Beaver."

"I'll give you one of my almonds then," I said trying to comfort her. She seemed wound up.

"I told you they stick."

"The almonds too?"

"What of it?"

"Nothing."

"Everything sticks," she said.

"How do you get nourishment?"

"I drink Coke."

I had to change the topic, get away from the stuff that upset her.

"Oh," I said. "I love looking at the water."

"That water's dirty. Some guy caught a rat on the 69th Street pier when he was fishing. Caught it right on his hook." She took out a pack of Marlboros from her purse. "You smoke?"

"What?"

"I love guys that smoke. They look so manly."

"Yeah, yeah, of course I smoke. I've been smoking for years." I had never even tasted a cigarette.

"I've been smoking for six years, ever since I was ten."

"You're sixteen?"

"I'm fifteen and a half. I can't wait until I'm sixteen. I'm gonna drop out of school."

"You're going to drop out of school?"

"Who needs school?" she said. "What do they teach you anyway? What has that got to do with me?" She took a deep drag from her cigarette and blew out the smoke. "How old are you?"

"Thir...four..fifteen...years and thirty-four days," I stammered.

"Want a cigarette?"

"Uh...sure, sure." I took the cigarette.

"Everybody says that smoking causes your teeth to turn yellow."

"You don't have to worry about that."

"What'd'ya mean?" She eyed me.

"Won't the braces protect you?"

"My drunk smelly father says I'll have two-toned teeth, yellow and white, after they take off the braces. I say who cares? My future husband will have to love me no matter what, right?" she asked.

"Right."

"How come you're not smoking?"

"Oh, here," I said and put the cigarette in my mouth. "Could you light it for me?"

"If you smoke, how come you don't have matches?" she asked.

"They got wet at the pool and I had to throw them out."

"That's stupid, swimming with matches."

"I forgot they were in my bathing suit," I said. God this conversation was nuts. I was doing all this for a kiss?

She lit my cigarette.

"My father is a zero. That's why he married my stepmother. They're both zeroes. My stepmother is a beautician. She has a big nose that always has snot in it. How come you don't inhale? Men should inhale."

"Uh, ah, I like to warm up my mouth first."

"That's pretty stupid," she said.

"It's a habit I got as a kid."

"How old did you say you was?"

"Thirty-four," I said. "Uh, no, no, I mean thirteen years and thirty four days."

"You said you were fifteen," she said eyeing me.

"I mean that's what I mean, fifteen. I just forgot."

"You gonna drop out of school too, huh? I mean you're not too good with math. Inhale."

"Oh," I said and took a puff, trying to imitate the men I saw in the movies. I had to look like a big shot or I would never get to first base, although I wasn't really sure I wanted to get to first base any more.

"Like I told my friend Anne…"

The smoke hurt my lungs like crazy and I said in a falsetto, "Anne?"

"My girlfriend, stupid. Like I says to her. I don't care if she's this great beautician, all that snot up there…"

I leaned over the railing and puked.

"Hey, hey, what are you doing?" she asked.

"Aaaarrrggghhhhh!"

"You sure you smoke?" She looked over the railing. "Hey, great! You got vomit all down the side of the boat. I think you hit a couple of cars. Yeah one of the drivers is looking up. Yeah, what are you looking at buddy? Can't you get enough at home?"

"I was a little sea sick," I said.

"Here, have another cigarette, it'll calm your nerves." She handed me another cigarette.

"Thanks."

" I'll light you up."

"I'll save it for later, when I get home."

"Where do ya live?" she asked.

"Bay Ridge."

"I figured that. Everybody does. Where?"

"On Third Avenue. I live over my uncle's store," I said. "My uncle repairs TV's."

"Sounds boring," she said. "You got a big one?"

"A big what?"

"T.V., stupid?

"No...I mean, yes. A big one, huge."

"My ex-boyfriend had a big one. The biggest one made. But he thought everything he had was the biggest. What a jerk!" She then laughed at some joke. I had no idea what she found funny.

"We're pulling into the dock," I said.

"Don't you love it when it bangs into the dock? I love that! Well, I better be going. Nice talkin' to ya."

"Wait a minute!" I had put up with the craziest conversation with this slut and I wasn't going to waste that by seeing her just go away. "I was just thinking...Saturday night...there's this dance at Our Lady of Angels...and I was wondering if you...weren't doing anything."

"You wanna take me to a dance – at the church?" she asked skeptically.

"You're not Catholic?"

"Of course, but I hate dances at that church."

"You've been there?" I asked.

"Once," she said. "And those stupid nuns always come around with a ruler to make sure you was dancin' six inches apart. I like to dance close, you know?"

"Yeah, me too," I said. Now I was getting somewhere!

"But my ex-boyfriend said that he didn't care. He said six inches wasn't enough to keep him away, ha! ha!"

"Ha! Ha! Uh, what did he mean by that?" I asked.

"Ha! Ha! Ha! You're pretty funny. I like guys who can make me laugh. Okay, Saturday night. What time?"

"Seven-thirty," I said. "Where do you live?"

"Oh, ninety-two twenty-seven Ridge Blvd, apartment 6D."

"Got it," I said.

"See ya," she started to walk away.

"Wait, what's your name?"

"Jane. Jane Minichelli. What's yours?"

"Frank," I said. "My friends call me Frankie."

"Okay *Frankie* I'll see you at seven-thirty Saturday."

I knew I had to carefully prepare for Saturday evening. This Jane seemed like such a hard nut, or maybe just a *nut* nut, that I knew I would have to get the conversation away from all the nutty stuff that upset her – which seemed just about everything. So I bought a joke book, *A Thousand and One Jokes for the Amateur Comedian!* (or something like that) with which I would keep her entertained.

I had it all figured out. I would get her laughing at the dance. Then as I walked her home, I would hold her hand. Then when we got to her building we'd go into the elevator and I would kiss her, *bang!*, just like that. If the kiss clung, it clung; if it didn't cling, it didn't cling. The idea was to just get the kiss and get rid of the image of Mary Sissallo forevermore.

I picked up Jane at her apartment. Her mother and father weren't home. "They are out drinking and getting loaded," she said.

We walked to the dance. Jane smoked four cigarettes in about a mile. She gave me some of her philosophy, too. "You have to know what you are doing around boys and you know why, right, because they only go for one thing. They are animals but what are you gonna do, they are the only game in the world and I like boys and what is so wrong with that? What do they want me to like – rats?"

When we got to the gym, "Smoke Gets in Your Eyes" was playing. That was appropriate because all of Jane's smoke seemed to seek me out and get into my eyes.

A lot of the guys enviously watched me with Jane. They all knew she was a slut and that I had her! She was dressed to kill with a short black dress and sheer white blouse with a noticeable black bra. We danced really close and several times one of the nuns came over to tell us to get "some inches between you." One nun even criticized Jane for how she dressed.

When that nun walked on, Jane said, "Fuck her. Look how she's dressed." I had never heard a girl say "Fuck" because my parents never cursed and none of the girls I knew in Our Lady of Angels cursed – at least I never heard them curse. Some of the guys I knew cursed though. I figured cursing was also a sign of a girl being a slut, so that "Fuck" was a good thing because I figured my plan was working to perfection.

So now I had to soften Jane up and I would do that with humor. I told her several jokes I had memorized but she didn't find any of them funny. She would just say, "What the fuck are you talking about?" She was using that word a lot now.

After awhile, Jane said, "Wanna go out for a cigarette?"

"But you've had ten already," I said.

"This dance is so boring. There's no action."

"What action? We're dancing."

"Fights, stupid," she said." I like dances where the guys fight."

"They don't have many fights here. We kinda all get along."

"Who's that stupid nun that keeps looking at me all night? What the fuck is her problem?"

"That's Sister Jerome Drake," I said. "She teaches in a high school near here."

"I'll bet she's a fucking dyke," said Jane.

"No, she's Irish."

"Ha! Ha! That's really funny! That's the first funny thing you've said all night."

"It is? What about the joke about the farmer?" I asked.

"That was stupid.

"But you laughed."

"I laughed because it was so stupid. Where'd you get such stupid jokes?"

"I read…my friend, Red, told me," I said trying to cover up that I had read something.

"He must be a pretty stupid kid," said Jane. "Let's get outta here."

"But the dance contest is coming up."

"Who wants to see that? A stupid dance contest."

"But I entered us," I said.

"Ha! Ha! That's funny. You make me laugh – let's go make out!"

"Make out what?"

"Ha! Ha! You kill me," she said.

We walked back to her house and I tried to tell her a few more jokes but she wanted to talk about her ex-boyfriend who had been jailed for breaking into a local bar and getting so drunk he fell asleep on the floor.

When we were outside her apartment building, she said, "If my parents aren't home, we can make out in my living room. If they are home, I'll tell them we're going to the movies and we can make out on the roof. I love making out, don't you?"

"Oh, yeah, all the time."

In the elevator I saw that there was this big red STOP button which could stop the elevator between floors. "Does the stop button make an alarm?" I asked her.

"Naw, it stops the elevator but there isn't no alarm anymore. The kids ripped out the sound to screw up the older people who sometimes hit the button and get stuck. Ha! Ha! That's really funny those old farts getting stuck. You can hear them screaming sometimes. I let 'em scream. It's fun. They don't even know if you hit the floor button the elevator works again. Stupid dopes."

So I knew my plan in that instant. I pressed six for her floor but when the elevator went three floors I pressed the STOP button and took her by her arms and moved her towards me.

"Aren't you the man," said Jane and then she leaped at me and planted a fierce, wet, hard kiss on my lips. Her mouth was open and then …

"Ahhhhh!" I screamed. "I'm sthuck! I'm sthuck!" I was stuck to her braces! I tried to pull myself off them but my lip hurt too much – and I was starting to bleed.

"Spresh the buthin!" screamed Jane but her voice was too muffled to understand.

"Whaaa?"

"Spresh te floo buthin!" she screamed.

"Ahhhh! Ahhhh!" I screamed. I could feel blood coming down my chin. Blood or spit.

I pressed the button for her floor and the elevator went up. That hurt too as it jarred my lip.

At her floor Jane said something, "Whee ath ma fo…"

"Whaaa?"

"Ma for! Ma for! Ow!"

With little, painful, stutter steps we exited the elevator – still attached to each other's lips. Apparently , it wasn't just food that stuck to her braces.

"Haap! Haap!" I screamed.

"Shtop it! Shtop sowting! Illya!"

"Ahhh!"

"Ge ta ma doo," said Jane.

"Whaa?"

"Ma doo! Ma doo!" Jane pointed to the door of her apartment. We shuffled down the hall to the door.

"Isthen," said Jane.

"Whaa?"

"Isthen fo ma arins!"

"Whaa?" I could feel wetness on my shirt.

"Ma arins! Ma arins! Ou iyot!"

"Yo arins? Ga ta," I said

We listened at the door to hear if her parents had come home. Jane had told me when they got home from their drinking they would be loud and probably having a blow-out fight. I could hear them. They were home. Her father's voice was getting closer. "O od! O od! Air eeving! Air eeving!" said Jane.

"Whaa?"

Jane started to nudge me down the hall again. I was in agony but I realized that her parents were coming for the door. We shuffled as fast as we could back into the elevator.

"Uthon! Uthon!"

I pressed the button for the first floor and as the doors to the elevator closed, the door to Jane's apartment opened. I heard her father, "You schtupid fuck..." but the elevator drowned out the rest as it headed down.

In the elevator Jane said, "Ull! Ull!"

"Whaa?"

"ULL!" she screamed. Oh, God, she wanted me to pull my lip off her braces. I was in agony and didn't even want to move, but I also knew I would have pull myself off or I would be stuck on Jane for the rest of my life.

"O! O! Ee urts!" I said.

"ULL! ULL! ULL! ULL!" Jane was screaming furiously.

And I pulled and my lip came away – I poured blood. "Aaaaaaahhhhhhhhh!!!!!!"

Jane was none too happy. "YOU CREEP!"

"I'm bleeding!" I said.

"You zero!" she screamed. It was echoing in the lobby. "You left skin on my braces!"

"I'm gonna need stitches," I said.

"Get this skin off me, you creep!"

I could see that the elevator was coming down. That would be Jane's drunken father and mother heading out for their second round on the town. So I ran out of the building but behind me I heard, "YOU CREEP! YOU STUPID, FUCKIN', ZERO CREEP! YOU LEFT SKIN ON MY BRACES!!!!!"

That was my second kiss. It had a cling I would never forget.

Afterward

Mary was my first love; my kiss with her was my virgin kiss; and I did take her to *West Side Story* over and over and over again. Yes, I did sing "Officer Krupke" and, yes, I never saw Mary after that idiotic display of excitement because of my first kiss. Her mother ran interference for her and I finally gave up.

Until....

In the year 2000, my wife, the beautiful AP, and I went back to Bay Ridge to go to my old church, Our Lady of Angels. We were meeting the Captain and his wife for dinner that night and we thought it would be fun to see my old neighborhood and attend Mass at my old church.

God works in mysterious ways, the saying goes. He sure does.

I was kneeling, having just come back from taking Communion, when I saw Mary – the *teenage* Mary, looking as she had so many decades ago – walking right towards me down the center aisle of the church. Obviously this couldn't be the Mary of my youth, the Mary of my dreams unless I was hallucinating. My eyes followed her to her pew and there she was – the *real* Mary, probably 52 years old now, with her four children (two girls and two boys!) and her husband. She looked well dressed and contented. She had handsome children and her daughter looked just as she used to look.

I nudged A.P. and said, "I can't believe it, there's Mary." A.P. turned around. "She's very pretty," said AP. "After Mass go over and talk to her."

I didn't do that. I couldn't do that. I don't know if it were cowardice or my desire to keep Mary where she belonged – in my memory.

- Part Eight -
Adventures in Teaching

Quick preface: I was a teacher for a considerable period of time. I taught about 6,000 kids in my career, most of them juniors and seniors in high school. I was a great teacher. Of course, all teachers think they are great – even the rotten ones, and a lot of rotten ones can be found in a profession with over eight (or is it nine?) million workers. I taught Advanced Placement English, Classics, Science Fiction and classes for non-academic students, called "S" classes (the "S" stood for the word "school"). The kids I taught ran the gamut from murderers (I once had a class with six major felons – two who had been convicted of murder), maniacs, nice dull kids, average kids, brilliant kids and geniuses. I had kids whom I respected and liked. I had kids I hated. It's an interesting profession since you have to deal (and control) people you wouldn't give the time of day to in real life.

Teaching in school is like driving on a highway. It's the great equalizer. Good, intelligent, law-abiding drivers such as you, driving alongside major morons and maniacs who have no idea of the dangerous things they are doing on the road.

My schedule usually had three advanced classes and two "S" classes. There were teachers in my school who couldn't handle the "tough" kids so they never had to teach the tough kids. There were other teachers who couldn't teach the "bright" kids because the bright kids made intellectual mincemeat out of them. I taught them all.

The powers that be offered me many awards locally and from the state for outstanding teaching – I turned them all down when I saw some of the idiots who had gotten the awards in previous years. I only accepted one award for teaching, The Teacher of the Year Award, given by the students of my school. An award from students is an award worth accepting.

How good was I really? I'll leave that to former students to say. But I can say the facts: In my years of teaching about 6,000 kids I never once had to throw a kid out of my class; I never once had to yell at a class or a kid; I never once had to write up a disciplinary referral for a kid who was a pain in the ass. My students did well on the standardized state tests they had to take – tests I didn't grade by the way.

Now I once thought I would write a book about teaching but to tell you the truth, I find the whole occupation a raging bore. I don't even know if I believe in public education anymore. While I knew many great teachers, I knew more bad teachers.

There are some students I do remember as well, not always fondly – the true nuts and the truly eccentric, for good or ill. Coming up are a few of the many who crossed my path and also some interesting events in my teaching career – which still goes on today with my Golden Touch Dice Control classes, Golden Touch Blackjack classes and my Casino Killer College classes in advantage-slot play, video poker, casino poker and Pai Gow poker.

I think of myself as a person who can *do* and one who can *teach* as well. I've never bought the old saw that "those who can do, and those who can't teach." After all, Jesus was a teacher, so was Aristotle, Socrates, Plato, Maimonides, Einstein, and my parents, and hundreds of thousands of others – they could do and they could teach. I might not be in their league but at least I am in their class.

1969
GERRY
The Rat Boy

This is the story of the craziest kid I ever taught who also taught me a valuable lesson; that lesson being that I wouldn't love every kid I ever taught – and some would be out of their damn minds. Getting your eyes opened in the very first year of your teaching career – starting on the very first day of your teaching career – was more of an education than I ever got taking the education courses that I needed to get certified in New York State.

Okay, let me set the mood. I came out of college with three majors (literature, history and philosophy) and decided that I didn't want to work the business world and so I went into education. I wanted to be the best teacher that ever existed and also become a world famous writer. That's a character trait of mine – I always want to be the best I can be at whatever I try – be it basketball, baseball, boxing, teaching, writing, and casino advantage play. I was filled with fire and with insane ideas I had learned in the education courses I took the summer before my first teaching assignment. I actually thought I could reach every kid I taught. It never dawned on me that there would be some kids I didn't want to reach or even touch for that matter, Gerry being one.

That first class was huge, thirty-seven 7th graders. Now some of you may have forgotten what 7th graders look like. They're a disconcerting amalgam of adult and infantile characteristics; mature bodies with elementary school heads sitting atop them; or little kid bodies with adult heads; or diminutive creatures with huge feet, or somewhat proportional bodies hosting teeth so monstrous that it's a wonder any mouth could accommodate them. If a normal 7th grader is a wonder to behold, imagine what a wacko one looks like.

And Gerry was wacko.

He sat in the second seat of the middle row. I didn't see him at first because he was so little even the little Korean kid (Peter Kim) who sat in front of Gerry actually obliterated Gerry from view. Gerry tended to hunch over and he looked like a bizarre crossbred rodent – part rat, part ferret, and part squirrel – with teeth that would do a chipmunk proud. To this day I fondly recall him as "Rat Boy" because when I first glimpsed him I thought, "Jesus, that kid looks like a rat."

I realized as I took attendance that first day that something was amiss. When I called out his name instead of the standard yo's and here's, I heard growling noises coming from his area. I looked over to see who it was and I saw Rat Boy growling into his notebook. Actually he was growling while eating the cover of his notebook.

"Excuse me," I said, "notebooks are for writing in, not eating."

"Ignore him," said Peter Kim. "He's crazy."

"You shouldn't say that," I said in my best adult tone. Keep in mind I was a just-turned 22 year old and my mind was filled with the unreal educational idiocy that a 12-year-old kid couldn't be Looney-Tunes. "We should respect each other," I concluded.

"I respect him," said Peter Kim. "He's just crazy."

I glanced at the rest of the class. No one seemed to care in the least that Peter called this poor, shriveled rat-kid crazy or that, in fact, the kid was crazy. Indeed, a few kids nodded in agreement.

I decided to move on.

"In any case, Gerry, I don't think it's a good idea to eat your notebook," I said lamely.

Gerry looked up and I saw his eyes for the first time – beady, bloodshot, rodent little eyes. He looked at me as if I were a piece of cheese. Then he put his head down and continued eating his notebook. I didn't really know what to do so I let it ride.

If Gerry had confined himself to only eating his notebooks and assorted other classroom products, this story would be about some other kid. As any veteran teacher knows, kids will eat assorted school supplies, sometimes in great quantities, including pen tops, pen tips, pencils of lead or graphite, paper, hard or soft book covers, book bindings of string or glue, and some kids will go as far as to nibble on film strips or the edges of their desks. In short, a kid's culinary palate can easily handle the mundane aspects of the normal classroom menu. If a kid isn't learning, he's eating.

But Gerry took his Epicurean treats into the realm of the unique. Several days later, as I was teaching a particularly boring lesson on subject-verb agreements, I heard a snap, snap, snapping coming from his area. I figured he was eating another pencil since he had eaten several #2 soft pencils in prior days. So I didn't pay it any mind. However, the snap, snap, snapping continued and occasionally I'd hear a little flutter, flutter, flutter – at least in the beginning of the snapping.

Finally I looked over Peter Kim's shoulder to see what was going on. Gerry was eating a little bird – it resembled a destroyed Tufted Titmouse. He had snapped, snapped, snapped the little thing to pieces on his desk and he was devouring little snippets of wing and leg. There wasn't much blood because he hadn't yet gotten round to the underbelly, but his razor-sharp incisors gnawed away like mad. By this time the bird was mercifully dead.

The other kids in the class ignored him; an unusual thing as you all know because kids, even big, high school ones, will use anything as an excuse to justify an assortment of groans, whelps, catcalls, farts, burps and other noises in order to annoy their teachers and diminish work time. But not when it came to Gerry. No sir, Gerry could have been eating an African lowland gorilla and the kids would have pretended nothing was out of the ordinary. You see, Gerry the Rat Boy was truly, magnificently crazy and the truly, magnificently crazy can silence any forced craziness even 7th graders adopt. No one wants to mess with the truly crazy – that's why we put many of them away in hospitals.

Of course, I didn't let him finish his meal; it would have ruined his lunch. I took the bird away and threw it out the window. Being a first-year teacher, I thought the principal would be helpful. He wasn't. He told me that all the students had "individual needs" and that I should try to meet those individual needs. I tried to explain to him that short of opening an ornithology workshop in the class, I didn't see how the feeding frenzy of a Rat Boy came under the province of subject-verb agreements. I ended the conference by sarcastically showing the movie *Rodan*, about giant birds that eat Japan, to the class.

This principal and I never got along after that. I alienated my first principal within a few days of starting my first teaching job, not a good thing to do.

In the following weeks Gerry ate an assortment of flora and fauna, furniture and fixtures that could have earned him a lasting spot in *The Guinness Book of World Records*. And all of us in the class ignored him.

Until he started eating himself.

That's where I drew the line in the sand.

I'm not kidding, one day Gerry started to nibble away at himself. It would have been an interesting, albeit bloody, experiment to see how far he could have gotten. He was pretty skinny so he probably could have finished himself in a week. But I didn't let it go that far. Even back then I had some standards.

He jabbed a Bic extra fine point pen into his hand and nibbled off the pieces of skin that separated. He slurped up the blood and ink as he did so. Now, him eating himself didn't bother me the most but the noise did. Do you have any idea of what it's like teaching "The Tell-Tale Heart" and in the background there's a constant gnashing and slurping? Not an easy feat, I'll tell you.

So I walked over to him and grabbed his hand – not the one he was eating since that was all bloody – but the one he was eating with – and said, "Now, Gerry, it's impolite to eat yourself in class."

And with a fierce growl, he bit my hand!

I tried to continue with my lesson – since I was one of those teachers who thought his lessons were important – but Gerry had a strong hold. I guess I should have seen it from his point of view, which is what you learn in education courses; repeat after me, *no one is responsible for his or her own behavior.* Hey, I had this big, meaty hand and Gerry had this skinny, almost bony hand – which would you rather eat? But at the time the pain was rather intense for me to see his side of it. All I wanted was to get the Rat Boy to let go of me.

So I yanked and yanked again and yanked yet again as strong as I could and he released my hand from his mouth. I was bleeding. Even though my hand was no longer in his mouth, his teeth were chopping away – like those monsters in the movies that are killed but their skulls keep snapping away trying to eat the hero and heroine.

I grabbed Gerry by the throat, gently of course as he was a student and I was a teacher, and said, "I think you should see the school nurse."

Before I could utter another syllable, Gerry jumped up and out of my grasp. "I'll die first!" he screamed and ran to the window and before anyone could stop him, he opened it and jumped out.

Unfortunately, my classroom was on the first floor. Gerry plummeted all of three feet. I could see the top of his little rat head at the windowsill. I reached out, grabbed him, and hauled him back into the classroom. I then carried him to the nurse's office, right across the hall from my classroom.

Now the nurse, Mrs. Delaney, was a kindly woman, always on a diet. She was eating her lunch at her desk, her daily custom, from an assorted array of Tupperware containers. I informed her that Gerry had been eating himself, then tried to commit suicide by jumping out the window. She looked kindly at Gerry, put her fork into her Tupperware container, and rang for the principal.

By this time, Gerry sat in a chair, growling softly, and eyeing the nurse's Tupperware container. *Could he still be hungry? What an appetite this kid must have,* I thought.

Seconds later the principal arrived. He asked me what was going on. I related the story. The principal looked at Gerry, no longer growling and looking innocent as a lamb (well, innocent as a lamb that looked like a rat) then back at me. "It seems you didn't heed my advice," he said. "You have to individualize instruction and meet the needs of the students."

"The kid was eating himself, Doctor Denton, *eating* himself! Should I have given him some salt? And then he bit me!" I held out my left hand to show him where Gerry had taken a small piece of my hand. (If you ever meet me, ask me to show you the scar.)

"You probably provoked him," said Doctor Denton knowingly.

"He'd eat you if given half a chance," I said.

"I am sure it is not half as bad as you make it sound," he said.

Gerry saw his half a chance. He grabbed the fork from the nurse's Tupperware container and in one, smooth, swift motion plunged it through Doctor Denton's gray, thin, pinstriped, polyester suit jacket and into his back, just next to the shoulder blade. The one thing you should know about polyester is that it doesn't absorb blood as well as good old-fashioned cotton or corduroy. A big, red blot appeared almost immediately on the principal's back, the fork still embedded there.

The principal picked Gerry up – and none too gently I might say – and carried him down the hall to his office. What a sight – the principal barreling down the hallway, Gerry hissing as he hung over Doctor Denton's shoulder, with the fork sticking out of the other side of Doctor Denton's back.

Then the bell rang and hundreds of junior high kids streamed into the hallway with Doctor Denton making his way through them – and none too gently either – as he finally staggered into his office.

I wish I could tell you that the story ended here. It didn't. Of course, Gerry did not come back to class that week, or the next, or the next. The following week, Doctor Denton told me to meet him in his office after school. We had some clashes in the three previous weeks, even without the presence of the Rat Boy, and I thought he would read me the riot act as he had every week since I started teaching there – or fire me (which he ultimately did during my second year at that school). So I went to his office after school.

"Mr. Scobe," he said (everyone called me Scobe or Mr. Scobe and when I taught in high school two years later I was called King Scobe – a title I feel I deserve). "I think I've been wrong about you – well, somewhat wrong, not totally wrong. But in some things I might have been wrong. Well, in one thing I might have been wrong."

"And that one thing is?" I asked.

"I thought you weren't able to reach each and every student – for example that Gerry child. But evidently you do."

"Thank you," I said. *What the hell was he getting at?*

"Yes, I was just on the phone with Gerry's mother. She says Gerry has really taken a liking to you."

"God, really?"

"Yes," he replied. "A real liking. That's why we want you to home tutor him."

"Excuse me?"

"Gerry's mother says that he can relate to you."

"We're both mammals (*a rat, a human*)," I said, then added, "Well, I guess that's nice but..."

"Oh, no buts about it. We've had our problems, you and me, but for me to ask you back for next year, I have to see some evidence..."

"That I'm crazy enough to go to that maniac's house?"

"I would not put it that way," said Doctor Denton.

"What way would you put it?"

"To be an educator requires a true commitment to the students."

" I *should* be committed if I went to his house," I said. I think one of the reason's Dr. Denton didn't like me is that I said what I said without too many "educationese" filters blocking out what I really felt. Also I had a fistfight with him – but that came in the second year, a day before he fired me. But I don't want to get ahead of myself.

"Okay, I will ask you one more time, will you home tutor Gerry?"

We eyed each other over his desk. I didn't want to get fired and Doctor Denton could fire me just like that since I had no tenure. After all, my wife didn't work – in fact, she only worked for a couple of months in all our 18 years of marriage because she didn't like to work. I knew she was home, reading a murder mystery where some husband who lost his job was probably brutally slaughtered, and I knew that there was only one answer to Doctor Denton's question.

"Hell, no," I said.

"Then I am going to terminate your employment here," he said.

"Just kidding," I said. "I'd be delighted to do it seeing as you'll let me finish out this first year and start a second year, yes?

"Of course," he said. "We always want to see fine, young teachers get a chance to establish themselves. And you will also get fifteen dollars per hour to tutor him too."

I nodded yes and shook the principal's hand, thus sealing my fate. I would actually enter the lair of the craziest kid I would ever teach.

When I returned home that evening, I informed my wife that I was going to the house of Gerry the Rat Boy to home tutor him the next day. After checking to see that our insurance was paid up, my wife said, "Sure, fine, go. We could use an extra fifteen dollars a week."

I didn't sleep well that night. I realized that I might have made a very big, perhaps fatal, mistake. This kid had shown himself capable of eating anything – including himself. What would his parents be like? A rodent doesn't crawl too far from the family tree, does it? Maybe this family did this every year. Maybe they were cannibals and once a year ordered out for a teacher to dine on. Maybe they wanted me as a snack? *Yes, please send over Mr. Scobe as we would like to dine on him tonight.*

I woke up in the middle of the night in a profound sweat. The next few hours might very well be my last on earth.

I then woke my wife up. "Honey," I said. "I might be facing death tomorrow." She mumbled something. "What was that? What was that you said?" I asked.

"Increase your life insurance," she mumbled and then fell back into a deep sleep.

That day I taught my classes but my mind was elsewhere. It didn't really matter because my students' minds were elsewhere too – as they almost always were every day anyway. I kept thinking I had never had a book published – or even an article – and now I would die never having completed my destiny to be a great writer. Damn! The hour was approaching when I would go to Gerry's house.

And the fatal last bell of the day rang.

After the students exited the building, I went to my car. Doctor Denton stood proudly in the parking lot waving goodbye to the buses, then he saw me, and shouted, "Good luck today Mr. Scobe!" His smile looked as if he were hoping I would be killed *and eaten*!

I turned the key in the ignition and then prayed. At that time I was an atheist but that didn't matter. I prayed to every god whose name I had ever heard of because maybe one of them was up there listening and would see me through this ordeal.

Now Gerry lived in a relatively rural area of Long Island with no sidewalks, no street lights, houses tucked into the woods so you couldn't see your neighbors and they couldn't hear you if you screamed as a knife was being plunged into your heart because you were stupid enough to show up to tutor the Rat Boy who was now ripping away at your body, tearing large chunks of your stomach out and eating them raw and *Oh, my God!* I thought to myself, as these visions passed through my mind. Then I said in a whisper, "Scobe get a hold of yourself."

I found his house. It looked almost normal if you ignored the little gravestones on the front lawn; yes, little grave markers covered parts of the front lawn of the property. Each one had a little something written on it in Gerry's weasely scrawl. I read one. "Here lies Ralphie, a good puppy." I read more. "Here lies Dino, a good lizard." "Here lies Bubba, the good blue bird." "Here lies Alphonse, a good friend." I hoped Alphonse hadn't been a human. A thought flashed – would a grave marker say next week: "Here lies Mr. Scobe, a good English teacher"?

Put this out of your mind, I said to myself. I took a deep breath and went to the front door. I lifted my hand to ring the bell and saw that my hand shook like mad. *What am I doing here?*

Then I heard a man singing, beautiful singing too, "I Get a Kick Out of You." Beautiful singing; great voice.

I rang the bell. Several heartbeats later, the singing stopped, and several heartbeats after that the door opened. I don't know what I really expected to see – probably some demented looking adult with wild, unkempt hair and pointy teeth wiping his face with claws – so it surprised me to see a normal looking man of about 40, maybe five-foot six inches tall, dressed immaculately in a tuxedo jacket, frilly tuxedo shirt, and black bow tie. Probably this must have been the man whom I heard singing. I later found out that this man was a professional nightclub singer of some renown which was unfortunate because he was shot dead in a mob hit while he sang "My Way." Indeed, before me stood Gerry's father.

He smiled, "Mr. Scobe?"

I had almost relaxed as I smiled back (*Whew! He's normal!*) and almost uttered hello when I realized something was wrong, seriously wrong. Oh, yeah, this nightclub singer, immaculately dressed from the waist up – but if you looked lower, from the waist down he was naked – *he's stark naked!* – with his, with his…microphone hanging there for all to see and that "all" was actually only me.

Now I don't know about you but when someone is exposed in front of me I want to look. Well, I don't mean I *want* to look, I mean I have an irresistible *urge* to look. It can be a man, a woman, a wildebeest – if their naked self stands before me my eyes keep going to you know where. I fought it this time. But my damn eyes wanted to look down. So instead I put my head up and kept looking at the sky.

"You Mr. Scobe?" he said once again.

"Uh, yes," I said, looking at the sky.

"Come on in," he said, swinging the door wide open. "Gerry's waiting for you."

I started to walk in but bumped into the side of the house because I was still looking at the sky. It's hard to see where you are going with your head pointed heavenward. So I angled my head down a little, just a fraction, so I could get through the doorway.

"You got a stiff neck?" Gerry's father asked.

"A stiff what!?" I reacted terrified.

"I asked if you had a stiff neck," he said calmly.

"Neck, God, great," I said.

"What?" he asked.

"No, no, my neck is fine…I have…a…a nosebleed," I lied. "I get them all the time. It'll go away."

"You know what's good for a nosebleed?" he asked.

"No, what?"

"Singing," he said.

With his microphone hanging there like that I wasn't about to sing a duet with the man, so I said, "No, no thanks, I'm in a bit of a rush…ah…I have to pick up my wife at work."

"My wife is in the kitchen. She wants to meet you before you go upstairs to Gerry's room."

"Okay," I said, "which way?"

"To your right and down the hall," he said and I could see out of the corner of my upturned eye that he was indicating the direction with his hand.

"Thanks," I said, then turned right and walked into the wall.

"No wonder you get nosebleeds," he said, "you're always bumping into things."

"Yeah," I forced a laugh, and thought, *And as long as you don't bump into me, I'll be all right.*

Get a hold of yourself, one part of me thought, *the man is normal, almost. He has a wife, a kid, he's normal.*

Oh, yeah, right, he's normal, the other part of me thought, *sure he's normal. You idiot! His son is Gerry the Rat Boy. The man probably doinked a giant rat to produce him!*

Shut up, my first part said to my other part, *Get this over with by just walking down the hall into the kitchen and meet his wife.*

Oh, Lord, and what a wife she was! She could have been four wives. She was a tall woman because even though she was kneeling on the kitchen floor praying she seemed almost as tall as me. She had to weigh 500 pounds if she were an ounce. Five hundred pounds in all directions too – a Mount Kilimanjaro but with this molehill of a head (there's that rat theme again), a teeny-tiny head sitting atop a flesh mountain. She chanted incantations about Satan and his demons swarming around her. "Get away! Get away! The Lord Jesus Christ of the Last Supper and the Cross and the Resurrection says to get away from me Satan!"

I coughed.

Her mole-head turned to look at me. At first it was as if I weren't there. Maybe she thought I was one of Satan's demons, but then she smiled and struggled to lift her mountainous bulk. She sweated profusely, with some little flecks of foam in the corners of her lips. Gerry had eaten pens, pencils, furniture – his mother had eaten a house!

"Mr. Scobe?" she panted.

Please don't eat me! I screamed inside my head. *Please don't eat me! God, don't let her eat me! I'll believe in you if you get me through this!*

She trundled towards me. "Are you okay?" she asked. Her voice coming from that monstrous body was soft and feminine. I came out of my trance.

"Yeah, yes, I'm okay, yeah, fine, okay," I said.

"Have Satan's hordes and legions gotten to you?" she asked sweetly.

"No, no, I think I have indigestion," I said.

"I have that sometimes," she cooed and then she angled her mole-head heavenwards, "but the good Lord cleanses me as does a physic I take each night."

"I'm in a bit of a hurry. I have another kid to tutor after Gerry," I lied and for effect looked at my wrist. I wasn't wearing a watch but I looked at my wrist as if I were. Actually I didn't know what I was doing, but as I looked at my wrist I thought: *My time is running out.*

Then I heard loud singing coming down the hall, which meant Gerry's father was heading this way.

"Can't I go tutor Gerry?" I pleaded.

"I must first rid you of all the demons that surround you. You have many demons in you young man," she chanted.

"I really don't have time for that," I said looking at my wrist again.

"Everyone has time for the Lord," she answered sweetly.

Just then Gerry's father entered the room. My eyes shot to the ceiling.

"Still have that nosebleed?" he asked.

"No," said Gerry's mother, "he is looking to God to rid him of his demons."

"Oh, ho! ho! ho!" guffawed the father.

"James," said Gerry's mother, "how many times have I told you not to walk around the house like that?"

Oh, good, I thought, *she's going to make him put on the rest of his clothes.*

"Now take off your good clothes immediately," she said.

"Yes, dear," he said and left the room.

"My husband doesn't believe," she confided in me.

"Oh," I said. I wanted to say, *you mean he doesn't believe in wearing pants?*

"He doesn't believe in Satan and his onions," she whispered.

Onions? Satan and his onions? She meant *minions*, but I didn't bother to correct her. If a woman that big wanted Satan with onions who was I to argue?

"Gerry? I'm here to tutor Gerry," I said.

"First, we must pray," she said and before I could respond, she wrapped her giant tree limb of an arm around me, squeezed me tightly into her bloated body, and started screaming, chanting and praying as if the world were about to end. I can't remember what she said, what she shouted, what she chanted, but as she shouted and chanted her mouth became full of spit and she spat in my face a Baptismal fount of saliva.

When she finished, she released me and I staggered into the kitchen table. Just then Gerry's father re-entered the room.

"Boy, you really do bump into things," he said.

I closed my eyes. *Why had I come here?* Oh, yeah, to save my job.

"I'm here to tutor Gerry," I said. Actually I think I croaked it.

"He has to pick his wife up soon," said the father.

"I thought you had to tutor someone else?" asked the mother.

"Both," I said. "I pick up my wife and then I go and tutor someone else."

"Gerry's room is upstairs," she said.

"Okay," I said and started to walk. Where? I had no idea, since my eyes were closed, as Gerry's father was totally naked now. I slammed into the refrigerator.

"Maybe," said Gerry's father, "you bump into things because your eyes are shut."

"I'll lead you," said Gerry's mother grabbing my hand, "as the Lord leads me away from carnality and into the light!" Gerry's father rolled his eyes and itched his balls. Yes, I had looked!

At the bottom of the stairs she let go of my hand. I noticed that she had a chair seat on a metal railing that went up the side of the staircase. She sat in the chair. It creaked like crazy. She pressed a button and up she went. *God, don't let the whole staircase fall down!* I climbed the stairs behind her.

We walked down the hall to Gerry's room. The hall was dark and musty. *Things have died in this hallway,* I thought. We stopped at Gerry's door.

"I will knock three times," said Gerry's mother. "On the third knock he will open the door and you count to six and then go in."

"Count to six," I repeated.

"Six," she repeated.

Gerry's mother knocked once, paused, then knocked twice, paused, and then knocked the third time. She turned around and ambled down the hallway back to the stairs. She walked much faster going away from Gerry's room than she had walked going to Gerry's room.

Gerry's door swung open slowly. I was alone, alone and entering Gerry the Rat Boy's room. Maybe I should have let Doctor Denton fire me.

He had huge furniture in his small, cramped, foul-smelling room – a giant armoire with swinging doors, an oversized desk from the 1940s, a large, murky fish tank that hadn't been cleaned since Noah's flood, and on the walls hideous pictures from newspapers and magazines of traffic accidents and murders.

I was standing in the center of the room, but where was Gerry? "Gerry?" I asked hesitantly. No answer. "Gerry, are you here?" I heard a movement behind me and just as I turned, a body came hurtling from the top of the huge armoire.

Gerry landed half on my shoulder and half on my back; his mouth open and about to take a chunk out of my arm – the same arm whose hand he had previously bitten. I spun around fast and grabbed him by the throat – none too gently I must say – and then pulled him off me and held him at arm's distance. The kid couldn't have weighed more than seventy pounds. With my hands on his throat, with his feet dangling in the air, Gerry smiled. "Hi," he growled. "He ha, ho, ho, who." (*What the hell was that?*)

"I'm going to let you go," I said. "But if you attack me I am going to beat the shi…I am going to beat you to a pul…you get the idea?"

Gerry nodded as best he could and I released my grip on him as I put him down so his feet were on the floor. Gerry smiled (he looked even crazier when he smiled); this was the happiest I had ever seen him. Maybe he liked to be strangled?

His beady, blood shot, rat eyes looked at me strangely.

"Wanna see my skull collection?" he asked.

"Not now," I said.

"Wanna see my dead fish?" he asked. "They are all skeletons."

"Not now," I said.

"Wanna see my moth collection?" he asked.

"No, no," I said, "I am here to tutor you."

"You hungry?" he asked.

"No," I said. "Let's get this over with, okay?"

"You wanna play?" he asked.

"No," I said.

"I like you," he said. "You're the best teacher I ever had."

"Get your books and let's get started," I said.

"I don't have books," he said with a slight smile.

"The school was supposed to send you two copies of all the books on a list I gave them," I said.

"They did," smiled Gerry. God, his teeth were sharp. Did he go to the dentist and have them filed? Would a dentist do that – file some kid's teeth like that?

"So where are they?" I asked but I knew where they were. They were where other books, pens, birds, bugs, frogs and assorted pieces of furniture were – digested.

Gerry the Rat Boy now started growling in very low volume. His cheeks started to twitch and his eyes started to glaze over. "So what you wanna do," he asked in a whisper.

I wanna get outta here, I thought and then I said, "I want to get out of here!" And I literally leapt out of his room and ran down the hall to the stairs. I didn't turn around to see if Gerry was chasing me – I certainly could outrun a rat. I ran down the stairs. I could hear Gerry's mother praying in the kitchen – a mountain praying to Mohammed (okay, to Jesus). I could hear Gerry's naked father singing into his microphone in the living room.

I didn't say goodbye to anyone. I just catapulted out the front door, through the front graveyard, and jumped into my car. I drove off like a demon – or Satan and his onions.

Three months later, Doctor Denton called me into his office. "Good news, Mr. Scobe. Gerry's coming back to school."

"Shit," I said.

"Don't worry," said Doctor Denton, "he'll be drugged."

"Strong drugs I hope," I said.

1970
The Principal
And the Principle

My second and last *almost*-year of teaching in junior high was no more pleasant than my first. Oh, I got along well with my students but I had a really strained relationship with the principal and some of my colleagues, one of whom thought I was an "arrogant, athletic scumbag." In fact that quote comes from my former English department chairman, Mr. Jonathan Moody – who was just like his name, moody.

I never said anything to him that would lead him to believe I thought I was great. He was kind of like Sullivan – he took an instant dislike to me. After school we used to play basketball and he was not very good at that. Somehow [I'm guessing at this] he must have felt that as my chairman he should be a better athlete than I. He wasn't.

But he also thought he should be a better teacher than I as well. I have no idea if he was a good teacher or one of the legion of bad teachers, but I do know he sent a lot of disciplinary referrals which tells me many of his students were tough for him to control.

The fact that I never had to send in a referral drove him nuts.

"You think you are a better teacher than I am?" he said to me one day at the copy machine.

"What?" I said.

"You heard me. As your chairman I want to know why you don't send in any disciplinary referrals. Why don't you?"

"I don't because I haven't had to," I said.

"You really expect me to believe that?"

"You've been in my class a dozen times, you walk by my class, I mean, you see what I'm doing. It's not like the kids are being bad or anything."

"Something is wrong here," he said. "I teach the same type of kids you do and all the English teachers do and you are the only one who has never sent in a referral in two years."

"There was Gerry," I said. "I had to drag him to the nurse."

"He was a psychopath, he doesn't count," said Mr. Moody.

"What's the point of this conversation?" I asked. "Shouldn't you be happy that I can control my students?"

"I know you think you are a better teacher than I am," he repeated. "But you are not. Just because you majored in three subjects just remember that teaching is not college, smart boy."

"Listen, I hate to tell you this Mr. Moody, but I don't think about you and I know teaching is not college," I said. Now, I know I said this with my voice dripping with sarcasm because I tended to get sarcastic with authority figures when I was young. I did think Moody was an idiot. As an adult, long gone from the teaching profession, I have to admit I have no idea if Moody really was the idiot I thought he was. But he certainly was uptight as I recollect his conversations quite well.

"The principal is fully aware of what a fuckhead you are," he concluded, walking away from the copy machine.

That afternoon, my team beat his team in basketball 62 to 24. These were pickup games in the gym and there was one other player, besides me, who could dominate the game – Howard Dodd, a big guy, maybe 6'3" strong and powerful. I happened to get him on my team that day and when the two of us were on the same team, well, we were unbeatable. Midway through that second year, the other teachers decided that Dodd and I could not be on the same team and we always had to face each other. He got the better of it, overall, as a good big man can beat a good little man. But the games were exciting nevertheless.

Except that Moody got really angry every time he lost. When Moody was on my team (Dodd and I were the "captains") he'd complain that I didn't pass him the ball much. He was right; I didn't, because he stunk.

The principal was also a pain in my ass. He didn't like the things I taught. I did a section of poetry and lead it off with some lyrics from the Beatles "Sergeant Peppers" album. The students and I discussed drugs and my message was very clear – don't do drugs. Please recall that 1970-71, the year I am writing about here, was the beginning of the big drug surge in America among junior high and high school students – following the college students' example.

In the middle of discussing one of the lyrics, Doctor Denton walked right into the room, shut off the record player, and told me to "get out into the hall so I can talk to you." My students were as stunned as I was, but that might have also contributed to them liking me – I was in more trouble with the principal than any of them.

"What do you think you are doing?" he asked.

"I'm doing the poetry unit," I said, faking innocence. I knew why he had dragged me out into the hall.

"You are doing stupid lyrics from the Beatles, who are communists," he said.

"I don't know if they're communists but what I want to do is get the kids to see that what they listen to every day is a type of poetry. Then I will do real poetry with them."

"I don't like this drug stuff," he said.

"Well, the lyrics I am doing are anti-drug stuff," I countered.

"We are not going to discuss drugs in the classrooms," he said. "It will only encourage them to take drugs."

"You know I think you are wrong here. You have to realize that today's kids are really getting exposed to drugs now. They need an anti-drug message."

"We are not discussing drugs in the classrooms of this school," he said.

"Look, you're the principal…"

"I'm glad you realize that," he said.

"But you are wrong on this. You're going to catch kids sooner or later using drugs and you're going to wonder how it all happened. You know 'an ounce of prevention' and all that."

"No," he said. "Not in this school. No lyrics. Go straight to the poetry section. I don't want any of this modern education crap that you are doing."

Just then Moody wandered by. As department chairman he only had to teach two classes so he had plenty of time to do whatever the hell chairmen in that school did – which was get paid to do almost nothing.

"What's up?" he asked.

"I am explaining to Mr. Scoblete," said Doctor Denton, "that he is not to do Beatle lyrics about drugs or any lyrics for that matter as a part of his poetry lessons."

"You call that education? Lyrics? What were you thinking?" asked Moody.

I didn't answer. What was the use? Both of them stared at me.

"You're the bosses," I finally said, "but if I were a betting man I would wager that sometime this year or next year you are going to wake up and find you have some kids right in this school who are using drugs. I'd put a bet on it."

"Not this school," said Doctor Denton.

"You think you know everything?" asked Mr. Moody. "You have to realize that out here in the suburbs we don't have that problem. We're seventy miles from New York City. These kids are not like the kids you know in the slums of Brooklyn where you grew up, they are innocent. We don't want you polluting their minds."

You idiot, I thought, *I didn't grow up in the slums.*

In April of 1971, the principal caught nine kids in the bathroom drinking booze and smoking marijuana. A couple of kids had some pills too – I never found out what those were. Doctor Denton took firm action. He suspended the kids for a couple of weeks. Then he got on the loudspeaker.

"This is Doctor Denton, your principal. As some of you know, we caught nine students using drugs in the bathroom today and they have all been suspended."

I watched the faces of my students. Most of them looked truly shocked. There had been some truth to the assertions by Denton and Moody that these kids were largely innocent.

"Because drugs are dangerous to all of us, I am now telling each and every student in this school that there is to be no talking between classes or in the lunchroom during lunch. It must be total silence. You are all being punished. If any of you are thinking of using drugs in this school look around you and realize that what you do will affect everyone else. If you use drugs the whole school will suffer because of you! This punishment starts immediately. Anyone talking between classes or in the lunchroom will be paddled [yes, in those days in that school you could paddle students – and Mr. Moody was the school's official paddler, something he seemed to enjoy immensely] and if it occurs a second time you will be suspended. This punishment will last five days. I hope all of you learn your lessons from this."

I looked over the classroom. Darby Colton raised his hand. I nodded to him.

"Can we talk in class?" he asked.

"Yes," I said. "Yes, of course."

There was silence and then Chuck Smith raised his hand. I nodded to him.

"Mr. Scobe do you think this is fair? We're all being punished for what some other kids did. There are a thousand kids in this school [actually 900] being punished for what a few did. Do you think it's right to punish everyone?"

"Okay," I said. "Do I think it's fair? No I don't. Do I think it's right? No. I think it is stupid. But I also know in life a lot of people get caught up in situations where they are innocent of anything but take it – a punishment, a beating, whatever bad thing it is – because of what others have done. That's a lesson you are learning right his minute but do I think this is fair? No."

Being young, being idealistic, being perhaps stupid, I went on to teach a lesson about how innocent people get caught up in all sorts of horrible things – like the Holocaust, war in general, disease. I thought it was a pretty good lesson.

After class, as the students went silently into the hall – these kids were terrified of having Mr. Moody paddle them – I roared into the crowded teachers' lounge, jumped on the table (I was always dramatic) and launched into a speech attacking Doctor Denton's idiot punishment of all the students for what nine students had done. I compared him to Hitler and his running of the school to a gulag. Most of the teachers just looked at me silently. Maybe a small group agreed with me but they were all afraid of Doctor Denton, who did run this school with an iron fist. I told the teachers that even my students thought this was an unfair and stupid punishment and that I told my students I had agreed with them.

At this point, one teacher walked out of the teachers' lounge and went straight to Doctor Denton's office where he ratted on me. This teacher was taking courses so he could become an administrator and I guess he figured getting my scalp on his spear would help him achieve his goal.

After I finished my dramatic harangue in the lounge, to a crowd that looked at me as if I were a total idiot, I then went straight to Doctor Denton's office to give him a piece of my mind, not knowing that Doctor Denton was already well aware of my opinion. I passed the future-administrator in the hall as I headed for Denton's office.

"That was fast," said Doctor Denton's secretary.

"What?"

"Doctor Denton wants to see you," she said. She rang Denton, told him I was there, and then said to me, "You can go in."

I walked into his office.

"Sit down," Doctor Denton said pointing to the chair in front of his desk.

"Doctor Denton," I started but he cut me off.

"I don't want to hear anything from you. I know what you did in the teachers' lounge, trying to incite the teachers against me, and I know you did something that no teacher should ever do – you criticized me in front of your class. How dare you? Who do you think you are? I am now putting you on notice that if you do one more thing I don't like, I am firing you. Do you understand that?"

I couldn't deny I had disagreed with his policy in my class – how did he know that? How did he know what I had just said in the teachers' lounge? Was this guy psychic – or bugging the school?

"I understand what firing means," I said. "Do you understand what free speech is?"

"You can have all the free speech you want, Scoblete, but you don't have tenure and I can fire you and not have to give a reason. So free speech away all you like young man but one more thing and you and your free speech are gone."

That "one more thing" happened the very next day.

I had a lovely student named Jennifer Van Hatton, an honor student with a 98 average in my class. Today she might be about 50 years old but then she was an as cute as a button 7th grader just on the verge of growing into a beautiful young woman. She was everything a parent could want in a child – smart, athletic, well behaved, and well mannered.

Jennifer's locker was right across the hall from my classroom. At the end of the day, Jennifer realized that she had left her notebook in a friend's locker and she whispered to her friend, "I need my notebook."

Unfortunately Jennifer did not realize that Doctor Denton loomed right behind her.

"YOU TALKED!" he screamed so loud that every kid in the hall and all the teachers could hear him clearly.

Jennifer turned around, saw him, and froze like an ice sculpture. I was about five feet away from them, standing outside my classroom.

In one quick movement Doctor Denton grabbed Jennifer by the collars of her blouse and shook her. "YOU TALKED!" he screamed and then balled his hands into fists with her blouse inside them and lifted her right off the ground. Jennifer looked as if she were in a state of shock.

I wasn't really thinking clearly – or maybe my subconscious was thinking clearly – I really don't know. I just know in two big leaps I grabbed Jennifer away from Doctor Denton, ripping her blouse in the process, then turned and hit Denton a left hook on his jaw that sent him staggering. I followed that by stepping in with a straight right and then pushed Denton as hard as I could. He fell to the floor – knocking over a student who was standing close to him. I then yelled at him, "Don't you ever manhandle one of my students!"

I could see that Jennifer was crying now.

"You stupid fuck!" I yelled at him again.

Some other teachers came running and got between Denton and me. Denton was standing now, still a little groggy, and he allowed himself to be lead down the hallway to the nurse's office. I could see the kids eyeing me as they walked past me to go to the buses. One kid whispered to me, "He deserved it."

Jennifer was helped to the buses by one of the hall aides and that is the last I ever saw of her.

When I got home I didn't bother to tell my wife that I had just punched out the principal over this talking principle. She never liked my rebelliousness. I figured I would be fired – maybe even arrested for assault.

The next morning I never made it down the hall to my class.

"Oh *Mister* Scoblete," said Mr. Moody in a great mood this morning and drawing out the word mister as if I were anything but a mister. "Doctor Denton wants to see you in his office."

I walked down the hall to Doctor Denton's office.

"Mr. Scoblete is here," said his secretary into the phone. "Go ahead in," she said to me.

"Doctor Denton," I said as I entered. I had given this some thought and I wanted to apologize for hitting him when Mr. Moody walked into the office and brought a chair over to sit next to Doctor Denton. I could see Doctor Denton had a little bruise where my right had hit his cheekbone.

"Doctor Denton," I started again.

"Please be quiet, meeeessssteeerrr Scoblete" said Mr. Moody. "Haven't you done enough to disrupt this school?"

"Mr. Scoblete," said Doctor Denton taking out a large folder from his desk. "As of today you are no longer working here. You are terminated." Well there was no point in apologizing now. I was a goner. He pointed to the folder. "In this folder is a record of your behavior as a teacher in this school. Mr. Moody I would like you to read some of the highlights of Mr. Scoblete's performance while he has been a teacher here for the past year and three-quarters."

Mr. Moody happily took the folder, opened it, and began gleefully reading, oh happy days – for him. Page after page of all the things I said which went against school policy, all the things I taught which I shouldn't have taught, and page after page of statements written by Mr. Moody about my "lack of respect" for all the educational philosophies he and Doctor Denton believed in.

He delighted in reading the never-ending list of my educational character flaws but I had heard enough.

"Stop," I said. "I get the picture. I'm leaving. You want me to leave right now? At least can I say goodbye to my classes?"

"No," said Doctor Denton.

"You've had enough influence over them – too much," said Mr. Moody.

"You know not one of those nine kids caught taking drugs came from my classes," I said. Yes, that was a stupid thing to say because I was not responsible for the behavior of my students outside of my classroom, but I was looking for something to say to defend myself against this inexhaustible list of my not respecting this, that and the other thing. The same holds true today when I teach my advantage gambling classes. I am not responsible for what my students do once they head for the casinos. If they follow my and my teachers' advice on betting and behavior, in addition to developing their skill, they will make out just fine. If they play like idiots, which many unfortunately do, well, then *they* are playing like idiots.

"Take whatever materials are yours and leave," said Mr. Moody.

"Mr. Scoblete, one last thing," said Doctor Denton.

"Yes," I said.

"If you go for another teaching job, if it is in the right district, I will give you a truthful recommendation. I think you should teach high school. You see, you are a good teacher, maybe even a great teacher; you just don't fit in here. And I am not going to press charges because you hit me because I was a little out of line myself. So you see you can still have a career in teaching – if you pick the right district to go to."

"Thanks," I said. "Actually I appreciate that. And I am sorry that I hit you. I should never have done that."

Doctor Denton nodded.

"I think you should find some other occupation because you don't have the temperament of a teacher," said Mr. Moody contradicting the principal.

I got up and left without a glance at Moody.

I took home all my belongings. I didn't tell my wife about hitting the principal but I had to tell her that I had been fired. It was the end of April and I was out of a job. My wife didn't work.

"What are we going to do?" she said to me. "You'll never get another teaching job."

"I don't know," I said. "Maybe you'll have to work."

She eyed me.

As a postscript to the above: I did get another teaching job. I went to 10 interviews at various high schools across Long Island and all of them said that because of my behavior on my last job they just didn't want to take a chance hiring me – "and good luck." I gave myself one more interview and figured if I lost out on number 11 I would have to look for another career. The 11th job interview, which was at the school where I experienced the Weird World adventures, consisted of four parts – an interview with the department chairman, in this case Gregory Monahan, then an interview with the principal, in this case Edwin Krawitz, and if both of them liked what I had to say at the interviews then I would be asked back to teach a lesson in front of a class. Then the students and teachers who were watching me teach would have their say.

I made it through the interviews. I never lied. I told the truth about everything that happened at my last district – except I never said anything about punching out the principal. When they called Doctor Denton he affirmed everything I said and, thankfully, he also did not mention my landing two solid ones on his jaw. He also told them he thought I was a great teacher. In retrospect – I am looking a long ways back in the past now – I might have – in my youthful enthusiasm and stupidity – underrated Doctor Denton. He could have blackballed me from teaching after all and he didn't. Mr. Moody on the other hand, even in retrospect, was an idiot.

I taught the class. I am good with an audience in front of me and I was the favorite for the job after my lesson. The teachers who saw me liked me and the students – the most important group – liked me too. Gregory Monahan, a new department chairman, now had to make a tough decision – hire a young firebrand that could give him enormous headaches if I turned out to be a maniac. Gregory Monahan spoke to two of his colleagues and dear friends, two of the best teachers I ever met and ever saw in a classroom, Gabe Uhlar and Lenore Israel. They both told Monahan to go for it. Hire me. "He's the kind of teacher we want," they said.

As a new chairman, as someone who could be inviting disaster by hiring me, Gregory Monahan decided to go for it. Now, I can't say I was perfect for Mr. Monahan but any disputes we had I have to say – he was right. I went from being a kid to being an adult under the tutelage of Gregory Monahan, Gabe Uhlar and Lenore Israel.

I named my first child Gregory in honor of Gregory Monahan. I have no idea how my life would have turned out had he not taken a big chance with me. And for that I am forever grateful. I actually hope he reads this book and knows that I still have the utmost respect for him.

The Stinking Truth

Okay, back to some fun, if being nauseated and tormented can be considered fun.

The time has come to blow off the lid of a serious educational problem many teachers, myself included, faced on that most horrible of occasions – parents/teachers night; those dreaded nights when Mr. and Mrs. (or Miss, or Ms, or single Dad, or Timmy has two fathers, or two mothers, or several illegal aliens, or Olaf is being raised by a goat) America come to find out how Johnny and Jillie are doing on their climb up the educational hilly.

For some reason I found it much, much better facing a classroom than doing this one-to-one stuff with the parents. I think a lot of teachers are/were in the same boat as I.

Now where I taught long ago you had so many parents who thought their kids were geniuses that the first half of the meeting was telling them, "No Doctor James and Doctor Joan, your daughter is never going to be a doctor and she is going to have a hard time passing because she is slow, undisciplined and never hands in her homework. But her lipstick and manicure look good."

In truth, most of the parents that I saw on parents/teachers night had great kids and these parents needn't have shown up. The parents whose kids were headed towards prison were the ones you needed to see but, of course, these parents didn't give a damn and never showed up – since many of them *were* in prisons. To the parents of the good kids I really had little to say. So I would mumble something to the affect that Nancy's doing fine, Harold's a nice kid, Brian has a lot of talent, Tamara is going places, and have you ever noticed it gets dark early in winter? I used to fill up the five-minute meetings with inanities and I'm guessing that many parents went away now knowing what was wrong with American education – me!

However, not all my meetings ran so smoothly. Sometimes you got a parent whose kid really had a problem – not just with education, but also with important things that effect the world all around him. This is the story of one such encounter with the parents of one such kid.

Once I had a "stinker." A stinker is a kid who stinks. This particular kid's name was Melvin Charles Palomius, but he was known around the high school as Mel Odious.

Now Mel smelled as if many small, nasty creatures had met their Maker in, on, under and throughout his body. He did not have that normal, everyday odor of rancid chicken soup that several days of not bathing can produce in people. No, I'm talking serious dead-animal smell for Mel.

I first realized I had Mel in my class on the very first day of school when I walked into the classroom and was appalled by the fact that the custodians hadn't cleaned out my garbage can all summer – for what else could cause such a stench? Some of the custodians at my school had the reputation for cleaning up on the job but not cleaning up anything else, if you get my meaning. But when I looked in the garbage can, expecting to see the rotted remains of the last lunch I had eaten just before summer vacation, I found to my surprise that it was relatively clean. If it weren't for the wads of fossilized gum, the bottom of the can could have passed for almost new.

So what was causing that horrible odor?

I looked up from the garbage can and there was Mel. I knew immediately that the scent from hell came from him. It was elementary my dear reader. The rest of the kids stood in the back of the classroom, pushing themselves against the open windows, all wondering where they were going to sit in relation to Mel when I gave them their seating assignments. If I followed the usual policy of seating them in alphabetical order the students mathematically calculated where their desks would be in relation to the stink of the century.

"If King Scobe seats me next to that stinker, I'll kill myself," said one boy, whom I later learned was named Phillip Peters.

I could see the mixture of terror and revulsion in their eyes as I lifted my computerized class list. What should I do? I had a choice. It was simple really. Do I seat them alphabetically or don't I? I quickly did a check of my list and realized that if I seated them that way; Mel would be in the very first seat – right in front of me – where he sat right now. He smiled at me when I looked at him, and I saw his yellow and black teeth. The only other time in my life that I saw black teeth was in the casinos of Mississippi and at the Horseshoe in Las Vegas when I became an advantage-player in the casinos – but that would be many, many years in the future.

"I figured where I would be sitting," he said.

"Very clever," I said, holding back the nausea that rocketed through me when I caught the stench of his breath. "Are all the windows opened?" I asked the students crammed in the back of the room.

"All the way," they chorused. They knew that I knew that they knew that this was going to be a rough period with such a stinker in the room.

The decision was made.

"Ladies and gentlemen," I said. "I don't think it's an educationally sound policy to seat kids in alphabetical order."

A huge cheer went up from the students whose lives and noses I'd saved by not following the standard policy. But I could also hear the loud groans that came from the kids who originally thought they wouldn't have to be near Mel and now their fates were up in the (stinking) air.

Now I had to come up with a foul-proof, I mean, fool-proof plan of seating in order to get Mel as far away from me as possible and simultaneously spare as many of the kids as I could from the horror. Letting the kids choose their own seats would be a disaster since all of them would struggle to get into the last seat of each row now that they saw Mel making himself comfortable in the first seat. The thought of five students squeezed per last desk of each row conjured images of fistfights and foreplay. *Think quickly, Scobe,* I thought.

I went to the window, stuck my head all the way out, took a deep breath and then went back to the lecturn next to my desk. I lifted the class list. Wonder of wonders – I placed Mel in the last seat of the last row over by the DO NOT OPEN: FIRE EXIT window, which I told Mel to open as wide as it would go. This was a window that opened wide enough for you to get out of the building in case of fire.

"But you're not supposed to open it," he said.

"That's not *this* year's fire exit window," I lied. "This year's is the one in the front of the room. They just haven't painted the sign for it yet."

"But it's so small, no one could get out of it," said Mel.

"Uh, they're going to expand it too," I said.

That mollified Mel. Actually, he wasn't a bad kid; he was just a bad-smelling innocuous kid. He even did all his homework but I never read any of it because I didn't want to touch something that he had touched. His homework also had a lingering scent to it, Mel's dead-animal scent. I just gave him straight B's, which was higher than the C average he ran in all his other classes. When he took a test, I'd have the kids mark each other's papers. But many kids did not want to touch his paper either, so finally I said to Mel, "You know Mel I trust you so much I am going to let you mark your own tests from now on." A cheer went up from the class. I had brilliantly handled the dilemma of how to handle something that Mel handled without having to handle it.

Now, on the second day of class I brought in a gigantic fan, placed it in the aisle blowing on Mel and out the DO NOT OPEN: FIRE EXIT window. In that way I saved the class. Mel's odor went sailing out the window – perhaps killing birds – but at least we humans were safe. I believe in being loyal to your species.

Of course, I hadn't really fully saved myself.

Perhaps I should have taken Mel aside and in an adult and sensitive and humane way addressed his particular problem. I should have used the finesse God gave me as a teacher to start a conversation on some trivial topic and slowly bring it around to his particular problem. "Hey, Mel, that was a very lively essay you wrote the other day. Your use of metaphor is quite unusual for a kid your age and oh, by the way, do you know you smell like hell?"

But I didn't do that. I couldn't. I just kept that fan blowing on him and prayed for Mel to set the all-time record for absences. He didn't. He was present every day, every stinking day. Maybe germs just died when they got close to his body.

And then came parents/teachers night.

My plan was well thought out. I would greet his parents as if nothing was untoward. I just prayed that his parents didn't stink too. I would tell them about a good composition he just wrote, which I hadn't read because I didn't want to touch it, and then I would subtly work in the fact that Mel smelled as if he were decomposing.

But the best laid plans of mice and lice often go astray.

It was a quick meeting.

"Mr. Scobe," said Mom as she and Mr. Odious entered my office.

"Hi, won't you sit down," I said cheerfully and sniffed subtly. *Thank you, God! Thank you! Thank you! They didn't stink!*

"We're a little concerned about Mel," said Mom.

"Really?" I figured they knew about his problem. Or maybe he told them about the huge fan blowing on him every day.

"Yes," said Dad. "He isn't participating in extra-curricular activities. Don't you think it's important that a child should?"

"Uh...yes...yes," I said flustered.

"What team do you think he should join?" asked Dad.

"How about the swim team?" I said.

"He hates the water, even as a baby he always hated taking baths," said Mom.

"No kidding?" I said, innocently.

"The school doesn't have a swim team does it?" asked Dad.

"Ah, no, but maybe we could start one for him," I said.

"The school doesn't have a pool, does it?" asked Dad.

"No, but he could use the pool at Meadow High – it's only about a mile away," I said.

"I think Mel needs something a little less strenuous," said Mom.

"How about a shower team?" I mumbled.

"What?" asked Dad.

"Nothing," I said.

"I think Mel would like to join your Science Fiction Club," said Mom. "He says he gets along with you. He wants a closer working relationship with you. Another student, Simon Michael, told Mel that your club is the best."

"I think he identifies with you," said Dad.

Aaaaaaaaaaarrrrrrrrggggggggghhhhhhhhhh!!!!!!!!! I thought. *Could it be I stink?* I started to smell myself. How could I stink? I showered every day.

"What are you doing?" asked Dad.

"What?" I looked up from under my armpit. "What?"

"What are you doing?" he repeated.

"Nothing, nothing," I said. Then I had an inspiration brought on by desperation. "Gee, I hate to tell you this, but I am quitting all my clubs this year."

"When?" asked Mom.

"Tonight," I said.

Just then my student monitor came in and told me their five minutes were up and my next appointment had arrived.

"Well, Mr. Scobe, it was nice meeting you," said Dad.

I stood up and shook his hand. "Same here," I said.

Then I shook Mrs. Odious's hand.

They started to leave. Then Mom turned around. "Oh, by the way, what classes are you teaching next year? Mel wants to sign up."

"What?"

"Yes, Mel wants to have you for English again next year," said Dad.

"Uh, ah, um, that might be...impossible...because – ah, I'm switching departments!"

"Really?" said Mom.

"Yes, I'll be teaching something Mel would find very boring next year," I said.

"What?" asked Dad.

"Hygiene," I muttered.

I don't think they heard that last remark as my student monitor again came in to say my next appointments were outside waiting for me. Mr. and Mrs. Odious were delighted that their darling had finally found a teacher that he liked and wanted to get closer to.

That year was interesting. In winter I couldn't use the fan or keep the DO NOT OPEN: FIRE EXIT window open, especially after the first snowfall covered Mel with an inch of white. Within a week of closing that window for winter, half the class dropped out – the half closest to Mel.

Of the kids that remained, most seemed to suffer from allergies because they were constantly holding handkerchiefs to their noses. As for me, I learned an important educational lesson from Mel – sometimes your class stinks through no fault of your own.

And Mel? I'll never forget him – that little stinker.

Wrong Way McKay

For the first year of my new teaching assignment my wife and I continued to live in Suffolk County on Long Island – in Sound Beach – which was about 65 miles from the school district. So each day I had a 130-mile commute. The second year – yes I made it to my second year – we moved into the Five Towns, where this school district was located.

Our rent was outrageous and my wife said to me, "We're going to find it hard to make ends meet so you better get a second job or work some clubs for extra money."

It so happened that the Cross Country track coach quit the job the year before and there was no one who wanted to attempt to coach this team – if there would be a team. Our high school put no stock in Cross Country track or any track for that matter (until Tony Sparandara, another great teacher, made the track team one of the best in the state – but that was in years to come); we were strictly a football and basketball school.

So I went into the principal's office and volunteered to coach the Cross Country team.

"Do you have any runners?" asked Mr. Krawitz, the principal. "Last year's coach said there wouldn't be any runners this year except Steve Beck and his brother Bryan – who's just a sophmore."

"Oh, I can get runners," I kind of lied there but I did have a clever plan. "We'll have a team – maybe not a championship team but a team nevertheless."

"Okay, you are the new Cross Country coach," said Mr. Krawitz shaking my hand. "Good luck. You have to have a team out on the field in one week though for us to keep the funding of the program."

In one week I had to field a team! There was one great Cross Country runner, Steven Beck, and his kid brother, Bryan. I needed at least seven kids to be on the team – or was that five? It didn't matter; I planned on having a full compliment of students.

Here was my brilliant plan. Most kids would love to have a varsity letter for sports – I mean athletes, even track athletes, are more respected than your normal run of the mill high school student. So I went into the halls of the high school and started to recruit kids that I knew would never have a chance to be on a varsity team because they – well, they weren't athletes in the traditional sense – oh, hell, they weren't athletes in any sense. I went up to fat kids and low-life greasers smoking behind the gym and my spiel was simple, "I am giving you a chance to get a varsity letter. There is no skill involved. All you have to do is run. You don't even have to run that fast. You just have to start the races and finish the races to get a letter – a real varsity letter that will be given out at a big dinner with all the pretty cheerleaders present."

Most of the kids looked at me as if I were nuts. But enough of them joined so that I did have a full team – 16 runners all together, including some who were actually pretty good. We practiced every day for two weeks – if you can call it that. Except for Beck, his brother Bryan, Craig Tischler and Richard Zaintz, my team really stunk. Most of the other runners were fat kids who could barely walk much less run – but they wanted to be varsity athletes and I gave them a golden opportunity.

Our first meet saw two things happen that you never saw happen in a Cross Country meet at our local park – called Sunken Meadow Park. The three-mile race ended and only eight of my runners finished somewhere in the pack. Seven of them came trotting in about 10 minutes after the next race started.

"What happened to you guys?" I asked.

"We stopped for a smoke," said one of them.

"You can't smoke in the middle of a race," I scolded. Then I realized I was missing one of the runners, Matt McKay. "Where's McKay?"

"He was behind us," said one of my smokers. "When we stopped for a smoke, he passed us but didn't follow the trail and went into the woods on another path."

"You mean he's out in the woods now?"

I looked at my team. "You mean one of our runners is still out there?"

I went to the officials running the meet and told them that one of my runners had gone the wrong way. He looked at me askance and said, "How the hell can anyone get lost on this course? I mean it's clearly marked!"

"I don't know how he got lost but he did get lost," I said. "I think we have to send people out to find him."

"Oh for Christ sakes," said the official. "I got a dinner engagement tonight and we could be here forever looking for this kid."

"Oh, okay, then let's just let him die, fine," I said.

"Why don't you send your kids into the woods to look for him?" said the official.

Before I could answer the next race was finishing. The top runners were coming in now and the official had to record their times. Then the second bunch of runners came in and finally the slowest runners struggled in, huffing and puffing, and behind those slowest of runners, running easily, and aimlessly with a beatific look on his face, was Matt McKay.

I went over to him. "What happened?" I asked.

"I just can't run as fast as everyone," he said.

"No, I mean, you got lost. How did you get lost?" I asked.

"I got lost?" he asked.

"You didn't realize you got lost?" I asked.

"I finished the race pretty good if I got lost. Those runners weren't too far ahead of me," he said.

"That was the race *after* your race," I said.

"The race after my race?"

"Yes, you went off into the woods and somehow got back into the race but it was the race after your race," I said.

"Oh," he said.

"You've got to stay with the pack and on the course," I said.

"Yes," he said.

Now reading this you might think that McKay was a stupid kid – far from it. He was extremely bright. I wouldn't be surprised if he were a doctor now or a scientist.

The next week in practice I watched McKay as he ran. He was slow moving as if he were fat, but he was quite skinny, but somewhere around the second mile or so, his face would take on that beatific look and he'd run with a look of pleasure on his face that I have never (or since) seen in an individual engaged in athletics.

Have you ever seen those television or magazine ads where they show people working out with big smiles on their faces? If you work out in a gym or run in races or with groups, you know what I know – no one works out with a smile on his or her face. Working out makes you feel good – when it's over – but during it, well it goes from terribly awful in the start to bearable by the finish.

I'm guessing that McKay got a jolt of whatever chemicals bathe the brain during the "second wind" time when suddenly you lose that initial fatigue and feel pretty good. I think he got a massive dose of those chemicals (I think they are endorphins) and he went off somewhere that few people have ever been. He went off in practice too – which was okay because it was just around the track – but he also went off in every race.

McKay got lost in the second race at Sunken Meadow too. He was well behind the smokers, who had again stopped halfway through the race to light up, and when he passed them he went off in a different direction than last time – but nevertheless the wrong direction. Once again he somehow found his way back to the finish line – again with the next race's runners.

First I had to scold the smokers for lighting up in the middle of the race. "Look you idiots, if some kid from another team sees you lighting up in the middle of a race and tells on you, the officials will tell Mr. Krawitz and I am sure he will kick your fat butts off the team." I called them "fat butts" because every smoker in that group was fat and I could play on the word "butt" as well – as in cigarette butt and backside butt. Also in those days, you could use words like fat and idiot because political correctness had not yet swept the land.

"So wait until the race is over and go somewhere off there," I pointed to the rest room building, "and smoke where no one can see you. Behind the rest rooms."

My fat butts listened to me and never stopped in the middle of the races the rest of the season to smoke. They were horrible runners, coughing and wheezing as they finished the races because they found it very difficult to make it through three miles without stopping for a cigarette break.

On the other hand, McKay could run all week. He was in terrific shape. He never got tired. He just couldn't run the races properly. He also couldn't run very fast. Of the 10 Cross Country meets at Sunken Meadow he got lost seven times. On one occasion, we had to finally get the team to head into the woods to look for him. We found him running around different paths.

So I started to call him Wrong Way McKay, a nickname that stuck. Our team was dismal. We lost every single meet we had – we finished last in all the group meets at Sunken Meadow where schools from all over Long Island competed and we lost every individual head-to-head competition we had with other schools at Eisenhower Park – even to a school for the slightly physically and mentally handicapped. That was a meet we all felt we could win and it crushed us that these kids were better runners than ours. "Man, some of them use crutches in real life," said one of my disappointed smokers.

Now it was the last race of the season and of my career as a Cross Country coach that Wrong Way McKay put himself into my all-time "I can't believe it" record book. We were running a race against a high school from the next town over from us. This was a head-to-head race at Eisenhower Park – an almost completely flat course. This other team stunk too so we thought we had a chance with them.

Even Wrong Way McKay had never gotten lost at Eisenhower Park – how could he when we could see him and he could see us from the start of the race to the finish of the race. Unfortunately, the officials had to change the meet's course on this occasion because some construction work was taking place in the area where our races were normally held.

The new course was flat but at the end there was a little hill, maybe 20 feet in height that you had to run down and then run a straight line of about 100 yards to the finish line. The officials went over the course with all the runners. All the kids nodded their heads when the official asked if they all understood where the race would be run. Yes, even Wrong Way McKay nodded his head.

Our neighboring school kicked our ass, which was to be expected, although Steven Beck, as he always did, finished in the top three (he finished high in every race he ran but all our other runners were so far back that it didn't matter for our team's overall scoring). Wrong Way McKay was last, also not unusual as he finished last in almost every race he ran.

At the finish line, we watched the kids come down the hill and head for us. You couldn't see them until they got to the top of the hill and then you'd see the top of a head, then the kid's whole head, then his body and down the hill he would run and head for us at the finish line.

Finally McKay's head appeared at the top of the hill and he ran down the hill, as had all the runners in the race before him. But then something happened. Instead of running towards the finish line, Wrong Way McKay headed right back up the hill. I started to scream, "No! No! This way! McKay, this way!" When Wrong Way McKay got to the top of the hill, he turned around and headed back down. I thought he had heard me.

He hadn't.

When he got to the bottom of the hill, he turned and headed back up the hill. Now all of us were screaming, even our runners who were smoking, "This way! This way!" We waved our hands; swung shirts and towels over our heads. The other team even started yelling.

Wrong Way McKay just kept running up and down the hill. Finally I sent some of our runners to escort him to the finish line. How could he have gotten lost when he could *see* the finish line from where he was? I don't know.

I retired from being the Cross Country coach, as I knew I wasn't cut out for it, and instead I concentrated on handling the Science Fiction club to which Wrong Way McKay belonged as well. What's interesting concerning my career as a coach is the fact that I didn't have one winning meet. Yet, many years before – in 1960 – I was on a basketball team that went undefeated in 55 games, even beating Lew Alcindor's (now known as Kareem Abdul Jabbar's) team in a New York City tournament. [You can read about this in my book *The Craps Underground: How Controlled Shooters are Winning Millions from the Casinos!*] I have experienced the height of success in athletics and the depths. I would have to say that I was probably the worst coach in the history of that high school.

This is no different than my advantage-play career in the casinos. Sometimes you are so good you go undefeated for weeks, months and years. I had about a 10-year streak in Las Vegas where I did not lose on any trip – although not all were spectacular wins. But I have had streaks where I couldn't do anything right and loss after loss after loss just kept coming. If you have the skill at these games, and you must play only games where skill can give you an edge, you still must expect that there will be good times and bad times. But overall and over enough time you should be ahead of the casinos. My athletic life was the same – I had good times and bad times but looking back I came out ahead.

One last thing to close out my coaching career: I did get a letter put in my "file" (all teachers had a file where good and bad letters and reviews of one's performance and behavior were saved – it was very originally called the "file") about allowing my students to smoke during races. Some skinny little creep from some other school had told on my fat butts who despite it all received their varsity letters in full view of the pretty cheerleaders.

Postscript: I finished writing this section on McKay on a Friday evening. I went to bed. I wrote all day Saturday since I write every day. Sunday morning I checked my emails and I had an email from Matt McKay. After 30 years of no letters, no calls, no emails, a student from my past, one I never thought I would be in contact with again wrote me. He had some nice things to say and, of course, he had been one of my favorite students of all time. The email arrived 24 hours after I finished this section.

God or fate works in mysterious ways.

The Disgusting Beast

I mentioned that I never had to write a disciplinary referral on a student in my classes, which is not the same thing as saying I had angels in every class I ever taught. In fact, if there were a kid who couldn't be handled by other English teachers, I often found that kid transferred to my class. "Give him to Scobe, he'll handle him."

Oh, thank you very much! It was nice to be so respected when the school needed me to handle some violent moron – except I never received more in salary or any other considerations for handling some of the dregs of society. Being good at something in public education was really no different than being bad at something in public education – tenure protected me from the pettiness of administrators, that is true and I was grateful for that because some administrators did not like my cavalier attitude, but it also protected many bad teachers from their just desserts – which was, to be blunt, being thrown out of the profession. How did they ever get tenure in the first place?

During my career, I had several murderers, some man slaughterers, many crooks, and a legion of drug addicts and criminals of lesser stripes in these "S" classes. I got along with all of them. They did their work, laughed at my jokes, and all was fine with the underbelly of the student world. I had more trouble with administrators than I did with the students over my career.

However, I did have some kids that I would have – if I could have – put a bullet in their heads on the front lawn of the school. Leading that small parade to my personal firing squad was Jeannie Muscovitz – the most disgusting beast I ever taught.

Jeannie came from an extremely wealthy family whose other children were quite nice. Talk about genetic roulette! The parents had two daughters and a son before they created Jeannie and all three were model children. They were all attractive, talented, intelligent, and personable – the type of kids all parents want.

Then along came Jeannie. It must have been a full moon when she was conceived and at her birth a werewolf may have bitten her. There must be some explanation for her grossness.

A bulkily built girl – big shoulders, big belly, big arms, and big thick legs and while noticeably fat, she looked incredibly strong – she dressed to show off the loathsomeness of her body – wearing skintight spandex which her belly fell out of and over. She had something of a mustache and beard which she unevenly shaved and she was, to be kind as I am kind of kind, a completely monstrous beast. Some of that was partly due to the constant scowl on her bulbous thick face. Most of it was due however to her decidedly ugly personality – loud, brassy, vulgar, foul, sexually charged, vile and what's worse, she wanted to control my class.

Sadly she had no respect for her fellow students, her teachers, her parents or for the people she ran down with her car. Here is one of the three car-hits Miss Muscovitz had by the time she was a senior in high school in her own words (as best as I can remember them) told to another student in the hall outside my classroom with me eavesdropping:

"These fucking Orthodox Jews, you can't even see them wearing all black those stupid morons, and they walk in the street and when it gets dark what do you think you can see them? Stupid morons. You can't see them, so I am making a left hand turn and they are right there in the middle of the street walking from one side to the other, the stupid morons, and they don't even look to see if a car is turning and screw them, so I hit the three of them. None of them died. So what's the big deal and why should I have to have my license suspended? The other two people I hit a couple of years ago when I first got my license shouldn't count."

One of her charming habits was to spit big wads of phlegm on the floor of the hallway or in the public drinking fountains throughout the school. You'd hear her take a big intake of air then hear the release, "Thew!" She also, as a testament to her delicate sense of humor, left wads of her phlegm on the banisters of the school's staircases. How much fun to slide your hand along the banister and get Muscovitz's gooey spit on your hand. When she had to go to the bathroom she'd say pleasantly to her teachers, "I have to take a shit." When they scolded her she would argue with them, "Well, what do you call it? You never have to shit?"

The first time she told me she had to "take a shit," I told her she could leave one but she wasn't to take one back to the class. That got a nice laugh from the students and a "that's stupid" from her.

It was a battle to keep this class contained because Jeannie wanted to run the show as she ran the show in all her other classes. The other students in the class were certainly not angels and their normal experiences in school could be chanted as follows: "Destroy the teacher! Destroy the teacher!"

Now when I taught a class I thought of it as an orchestra – one where I was titularly the conductor but a conductor that had to win over the musicians day after day. It didn't matter if that class were an advanced class or an "S" class. There could only be one rhythm in a class – *my rhythm* – and I had to get all the instruments (meaning all the students) in sync with me.

Here's a better analogy – all the students were guitars and I was also a guitar. They could all be strumming different tunes, different melodies – and the class would be chaotic. Or they could all be strumming the melody that my guitar was strumming – then the class was well behaved and teachable. I started playing my melody even before the first second of the first class by standing at my door and greeting each student personally as they came in. Getting the students to think you liked them – one on one – was a good start to keeping them playing the melody you desired. If they liked you they generally didn't want to destroy you.

Muscovitz wanted to be the guitar that strummed the tune for the whole class to follow. I had to deflect, dodge, duck, and use every ounce of my wit to keep the class with me and not with her. She always made comments during my lessons – trying to get the class to go berserk – and there were times when she had me on the ropes, where her guitar was as strong as my guitar. Keep this in mind – in a classroom you don't need every kid going crazy to have the class in total disarray, you just need a few and Muscovitz was trying to get those few to play her tune. However, I knew that if I sent a referral I lost; that she had beaten me, because that's what all her teachers had done since she was a brutish little hairy thick beast in elementary school. And it had done no good at all.

How would I defeat this ubber beast?

It occurred in February – yes, six months into the 10-month school year that I crushed her and gained complete control of the class.

I was teaching a lesson about something or other and, as I always did, I made some joke about this or that. The kids laughed. Humor is a great weapon in a teacher's arsenal. But Muscovitz the Beast screamed out, "That's not funny. That's stupid. You're a dick!"

There it was, a direct insult to the teacher. Muscovitz had stepped over the line. She could "take a shit" or leave her "spit" all over the school or run down black-clad Orthodox Jews going to temple on a Friday night, but those weren't a direct attack on the teacher – on me. This was. I think a normal teacher would have simply turned red, screamed back, and written a disciplinary referral. Muscovitz would have triumphed. She would have sat in the Dean of Students office saying, "That stupid moron King Scobe wrote me a referral. I didn't do nothing. That moron!" Then she would return to class the next day or the day after that if she got suspended and been a greater beast than she already had been because she had proven her point – even King Scobe couldn't control her. Her guitar was in control of the orchestra. She owned the class.

But the moment of decision came for me and when she said, "You're a dick," instead of getting all steamy and writing her a disciplinary referral I turned to her and said, "Call me by my first name – BIG!"

The class went into an uproar of laughter. Jeannie had been made to look like a fool. My one line, "Call me by my first name – BIG!" was enough to marginalize her for the rest of the year. In the next few months when she would attempt to disrupt, one or another of my dangerous felons (I had two man slaughterers in that class) would snarl at her and say something to the effect, "You leave BIG alone or I'll beat the shit out of you!"

It's nice to have the students playing your tune, isn't it?

Mr. Hussein
and the Bunsen Burner

His name: Hussein. His subject: biology. His hiring: a mid-year replacement. His first day: he came in, looked at the class, an average class with average kids of average intelligence, the majority of them Jewish, and he said, "I am not afraid of you people. I am totally unafraid."

The kids had no idea what the heck he meant. He eyed the class.

"This is a Bunsen burner," he said.

"I light my cigarettes with that," laughed one humorist.

"You will not speak until spoken to," said Hussein.

"What do ya mean?" said another kid.

All kids, even average kids, even nice kids, become sharks when it comes to weak or lunatic teachers. They can smell the blood in the water and they go for it. They thought that Hussein would be delicious meat for them – that decision had been made in the first 30 seconds as Hussein eyed the class balefully.

"I speak; you are silent," said Hussein.

One kid burped. The kids laughed. One kid made a fart noise. The kids laughed louder. Hussein would be dead meat now. He had lost control of the class in less than a minute.

Mr. Hussein lit the Bunsen burner. "I am unafraid of pain!" he screamed, and put his left forearm into the flames. "Aheeeeee-aheeeeee," he screamed. His skin started to bubble. He pulled his arm away from the flame.

"I am unafraid," he said, as the smell of burnt flesh filled the room. Oh, yes, the kids were quiet now. Hussein may be a lunatic, he may have left a bloody trail for the sharks to follow but he was the scary kind of lunatic, the kind that drank his own blood – the kind that might just put your head in the Bunsen burner.

The burner was still shooting out flame.

"This is a Bunsen burner. We use this to make chemical reactions in chemicals." At this point if Hussein had just been your average lunatic teacher, some kid would have made a smart-ass remark or a bodily function sound. The class stayed silent. "You all know what chemicals are don't you? Then what are they?" The kids just looked at their desks. "Heat causes chemical reactions. I want everyone to look at the Bunsen burner. Look at the burner now," he demanded.

The kids' heads shot up.

Hussein then stuck his right forearm into the burner, letting his skin bubble. One girl threw up in the back of the room. Hussein took his right forearm out of the flame.

"Girls should not be in school at this age with boys," he said. He looked over at another girl, "You, with the blonde hair, you take her away, out of my sight."

The two girls left the class and immediately headed down to the principal's office. The principal was in a conference, according to his secretary – actually the principal, a big, muscle-bound weight lifter with a heavier New York accent than I have, was committing adultery with the pretty but promiscuous PTA president at the very moment these two trembling girls wanted to tell him about the new teacher that was burning himself alive in their classroom.

"Please wait over there," said the secretary.

"You don't understand," said the escort.

"He will be with you when he is finished," said the secretary fully aware of the double meaning of her words.

The girls sat, defeated.

Hussein taught the class and then went into his second class and burned his hands in demonstration that he was not afraid of "you people." About one hour later the principal finished with the head of the PTA who had to rush out of the school to meet her incredibly wealthy husband for lunch at a local swanky restaurant. The girls were ushered in.

They told the principal everything that they had seen. The principal walked down the hall to Hussein's class and about a dozen students came up to him – as this was between periods – and told him what Hussein had done.

"He burned his arms!" said one student.

"He burned his hands!" said the second student.

"He's insane!" said a third student.

Hussein was getting ready to teach his third class – his arms and hands totally burned by his actions with the Bunsen burner in his first two classes. What would he burn in his third class? Too bad he never got to teach a third class.

The principal did not waste any time. He told Hussein he was fired and to go to a hospital to get his burns treated. Hussein started to scream, "I am not fired. You people cannot do this to me! I will not leave this building! You are discriminating!"

The kids who knew just how nuts this teacher was stayed way far back in the hallway. The other kids enjoyed the spectacle although the burns on Hussein's arms and hands nauseated some others. The principal had a teacher call the police and the police came within five minutes – in which time, according to some kids who told me, Hussein kept screaming and even started foaming at the mouth. But kids do exaggerate so I don't know if he really foamed at the mouth.

The police took Hussein out of the building and drove him to the local hospital where they dropped him off in the emergency room. He was not arrested but given a severe warning to never go on the school's property again or he would be arrested and jailed.

The next morning Hussein snuck into the building by entering the school through a side door. He was bundled up since it was February so he was able to scoot to his classroom, which was on the first floor, near the exit doors that he had entered. He made it to his classroom and then the students arrived for the first period. Hussein hid in the office in back, unseen by the students. The bell rang for the start of the class.

Hussein sprang into the room. His winter coat was off and his arms were wrapped in saran wrap, his flesh oozing puss and red with clotted blood under the saran wrap. He had left the emergency room when the cops left him and treated his wounds himself – or at least he wrapped them up like you would broiled beef.

"I am back!" he shouted at the class. "You cannot get rid of me. I am your worst nightmare!"

Luckily the boy by the door ran out of the room.

"Bring that boy back!" yelled Hussein. But no kid ran out after him. They just sat frozen in their seats staring at Hussein as Hussein glared at them. Then Hussein started to pull off the saran wrap. It must have hurt because he screamed as he did so, "Aheeeeee-aheeeeee!" One girl fainted as the puss clung to the saran wrap and made a string between his forearm and the wrap.

The principal came in about two minutes later with the security guards and they dragged the screaming, twisting, now foaming Hussein out of the classroom. This time the cops arrested him. He was never heard from again.

Forbidden Sex
The Old Man and the Girl

This male teacher, 56 years old and engaged in an affair with the parent of one of his female students, was a pot-smoking, hippie dressing, peace-medallion wearing horn dog who would always make pussycat sounds when female teachers passed by him, "Meow! Meow!" The female teachers hated him because he was always looking to rub himself against them while making pussycat sounds. If he got them alone, he would proposition them to have sex – he even propositioned them in the parking lot when everyone was going to their cars after a hard day's work. It didn't matter what the female teacher looked like either; it didn't matter if she had the personality of Attila the Hun, this horn-dog just wanted to do it. "It's a new generation in the 1970s," he said to me when I asked him why he kept making those stupid "meow" sounds to women. "Women need it these days and I am the man to do it."

So the fateful day arrived. The female student of the woman he was boffing sat in the front seat of the middle row in horn-dog's classroom. Horn dog was lecturing and in front of everyone he just reached out with both hands and grabbed the girl's ample breasts in his hands. "Mmmmm, these are nice," he said as the girl's eyes bugged out. "Can I suck on these?"

The girl jumped away. The other students stared in horror.

Then the girl ran out of the room, into the teachers' lounge, and shouted, "Mr. Saper just grabbed my breasts in class and said he wants to suck on them!" Our department chairman was there at the time and he ran across the hall to the classroom. Mr. Horn Dog was still lecturing as if nothing had happened. Most of the kids sat open-mouthed. Although he had tenure, horn dog was fired on the spot. We never saw him again. He ended his 30-year career in an unusual way.

"I think he must have been high," said Cathy Poe.

"Or stupid," said Barbara Aronowitz, another teacher.

"Or both," I said.

Little Miss Special Ed

She was pretty, sexy, a thirty-year old Special Education teacher and she knew how to dress provocatively. Any teenage boy would love to give her his time of day, that's for sure and in fact, many teenage boys discovered that they could give her the time of day too. She was available to the right teenagers – many of them.

What she liked to do was invite select boys to her classroom when she had a free period so they could watch her work out in her tight-fitting, skimpy workout clothes. She'd put a workout tape into the VCR and wiggle and squirm all over the room. If she had a pole she probably would have pole-danced for the boys. Then she would select one of them to arrange some after school special education lessons.

Teenage boys are not going to run to the principal to tell him that some gorgeous woman was giving them the best time of their young lives, so Little Miss Special Ed had a few years of unfettered carnal madness.

So it was sad for the last boy she doinked and sadder for Little Miss Special Ed, when she and he decided to do it in her classroom during one of her breaks. The principal was giving a new parent a tour of the building when he entered the room just as the boy was climaxing. "Aaaaaaaaaaaarrrrrgggggghhhhh!" the boy screamed. "Oooooooooooooo!" moaned the teacher. "Uhhh!" yelled the principal. "Oh, my," whispered the new parent during this unexpected aspect of the guided tour.

At first they tried to fire the teacher, but the boy would not file a complaint, nor would the parents. The boy and the teacher even denied they were having sex when the principal caught them. The parent on the tour did not want to get involved. The father of the boy said flat out, "That woman has been good for my son." The boy's mother said, "It's calmed him down a lot. He's much easier to get along with at home."

No other boy in the school came forward either. Although the sexual escapades of this teacher were now discussed in detail throughout the school, when the story hit the fan, no boy would publicly admit to having sex with her. However, every boy in the school admitted secretly to having sex with her. The ones who *really* had sex with her wanted more sex with her and the ones who really hadn't had sex with her wanted to have sex with her in the future, preferably the near future, too. By the end of the week, it was obvious that no charges would be filed against her.

Now what was the school to do with Little Miss Special Ed? Would the authorities let her return to indulge the fantasies of all the boys in the school? Or could they figure some way to make her harmless?

Since the public school system had to give special accommodations for the special education programs of the Orthodox Jewish private schools in the district, the district's superintendent Dr. Growmarten put Little Miss Special Ed in the Orthodox Special Education classes, which were segregated by gender and even conducted in different buildings – boys in one, girls in the other. She would only be teaching girls. What's more the Orthodox educators insisted that Little Miss Special Ed had to follow the dress code of their schools. So it was goodbye to the skimpy, sexy, revealing outfits and hello to ankle length dresses, and blouses buttoned to the neck. Ah, there is nothing like *tradition!* Sing it!

Boys Will Be Boys

Mr. Castrini, a good-looking social studies teacher, 35 years old with three children and a very nice wife given to anorexia and pimples, would give his female students extra points if they had sexual relations him. Now Mr. Castrini did have his set of standards. He didn't want ugly girls and he refused the attentions of several gay boys who felt they should be given extra credit too since they would be happy to service Mr. Castrini.

For several years, as the story goes, Mr. Castrini enjoyed his pastime and his female students enjoyed their high grades. I guess for these students it was easier to squirm than to study. Castrini had a large couch in his office, which would have allowed that activity in a comfortable fashion.

Mr. Castrini's undoing took place at the Senior Picnic in June. The Senior Picnic was the reward for seniors actually achieving seniorness. It usually took place at Jones Beach, a magnificent public beach on Long Island.

Castrini's cuties, as he called them, were all going to give him a mutual farewell sex romp – which meant he would give them an extra 10 points on the final exam. About five girls had agreed to give Mr. Castrini a good bye present. At the appointed time the girls and Mr. Castrini went into the eight-foot tall grass. Mr. Castrini had to tell the two gay boys that he was not interested in having sex with them. Those boys, Billy Jones and Darrell Washington, did not take kindly to being rebuffed a second time. Wasn't it discrimination that only girls could get more points because they had sex with the teacher?

"No," said Mr. Castrini, "I don't want you near me and that is final."

The two boys went right to the Assistant Principal, Mr. Romano, who hated Castrini, and they told him that some kids were in the grass taking drugs. Mr. Romano and Mrs. Reinhold, a sour old crow who hated to see anyone have any fun, stormed into the high grass just in time to see the activities.

Mr. Castrini was moaning and groaning and then he looked up and saw them staring at him.

He left the district and became an assistant principal in another district.

- Part Nine -
Adventures Growing Up in New York

As a kid I used to work summers for the New York City Housing Authority. My Uncle Nick got me the job; he was a supervisor – "a suit" as the workers disdainfully called them – so he pulled strings. Everything was patronage in New York City in those days. But what did I know about patronage? I didn't even know what the word patronage meant.

The job paid $60 per week, a fortune in those days. My father was having a tough time of it during these years so I would give over the whole check to my mother. But I could ask for $10 or $20 on the weekends to go out and I would get it.

I worked in a New York City housing project called Smith Houses, a collection of 17-story apartment buildings surrounding a giant grassy quad, and these projects could be seen to the right of the Brooklyn Bridge if you are looking at the Manhattan skyline driving or walking across to Manhattan. In the movie, *The Harder They Fall* (1956) it opens with a shot of these projects just after they were first built and later in the movie we discover that the lead characters, played by Humphrey Bogart and Jan Sterling, live there.

A large percentage of the people in these building when I worked there took welfare. The summers I worked there – 1964 (junior in high school), 1965 (senior in high school), 1966 (freshman in college), and 1967 (sophomore in college) – could be called the blooming of the welfare society in New York City. I think the welfare society peaked at 1.2 million welfare recipients for 7.8 million people – a staggering 15 percent of the citizens of New York City living off the other citizens of the City.

I didn't know any of this at the time. I was just happy I had a great summer job that I could travel to easily by train from my home in Bay Ridge, Brooklyn.

I wish I could say this job required extraordinary skills on my part – but it didn't. Over the four summers I did learn how to help a master gardener, I did assist a plumber and a woodworker; and I did assist in laying cobblestones on certain magnificent walkways in the projects. I was an assistant at all trades and a master of none.

My first day on the job was weird. I received my navy blue pants and navy blue button-down shirt – the uniform of a New York City Housing Authority worker. I felt proud to get these. Angelo, the foreman, said that my job was to sweep the benches in the little park by the pharmacy and the supermarket. The first shift went from 8AM to 9AM and then we had our morning coffee break before we went on a two-hour shift before lunchtime. I headed with my wheel basket, shovel, broom and ice pick on a stick to the area of park benches that I had to clean up.

I worked feverishly as this area was a small park used by a lot of people during the day and the nights. I swept up the litter from the cobblestone sidewalks; I ice-picked the litter with my stick from the grass, and by five minutes to nine I finished the area, my body sweating profusely.

When I got back to the workers' room, I put my equipment where it belonged, made myself a cup of ice coffee and then told Angelo that I had just barely finished the area. "Boy that was some job," I said.

"What do you mean, you just barely finished?" he asked.

"There was a lot to do. I worked like a maniac."

"You did the whole area in one hour?" asked Angelo.

"Yes," I said.

"That was your job for the whole day," explained Angelo.

"The whole day?"

"Yes," said Angelo, "the whole day."

"The boy doesn't know how things work in the City," said Alston Jackson, a man of about 45 years and a full-time City worker. "You work too fast and you make it not necessary to hire someone else to work. We don't want that. It cuts down the jobs; it also means we lose seniority."

"Yeah," said Big Willie, who fit his name and used to get all the jobs that required sitting on machinery so he wouldn't have to walk or stand. "The idea is for us to do as little as possible."

"Do you want me to go back to that area for the rest of the day?" I asked.

"Yeah," said Angelo. "But you have to always look like you're working, so that the suits don't catch you. They catch you then you get fired and I catch hell. I don't like to catch hell."

So after the coffee break I went back to my area for that day. I kept sweeping and ice picking up whatever blew over but sometime around 11 o'clock the residents started to come out in full force to spend their time sitting on the benches, drinking, smoking and talking to one another. Even close conversations, even face to face and inches apart encounters were shouted. No one knew how to whisper, but everyone knew how to litter. Despite the fact that the garbage cans were right there for their trash, most of the people out that day in the little park just threw their stuff on the ground.

I just kept sweeping my area, looking busy as I was supposed to, so workers wouldn't lose their seniority. One skinny, dissipated guy sitting next to another skinny even more dissipated guy on one of the benches shouted over at me, "Hey, blue boy, there's some paper here!" And he pointed to a piece of paper near his bench, which he had just thrown down. I went over and picked it up.

The next day I received another assignment. I swept up one of the parking lots. During part of this sweep I had to get fairly close to one of the buildings. As I swept along the side of the building something red and white hit my shoulder. The red turned out to be blood – I had a Kotex on my shoulder. I had never seen one of these *unused* before but now I saw my first one *used*. Who the hell would throw something like this out of a window at me? This was only a couple of years after my disastrous first kiss with Mary Sissallo and my second disastrous "clinger" with Jane. My image of womanhood did not include periods at that time in 1964, although I had some intellectual awareness that although women might be sugar and spice and everything nice – they also had these weird "spells," as my mother called them. This was all very vague in my mind – if it were weather it would be foggy in my head when it came to the biology of the fairer sex. Today, of course, with sex education in the schools, with television programs displaying and talking about all nature of sexual things and encounters, and with the looser moral framework, most boys who have passed their junior year of high school know everything, and probably tell their children about these things too!

The *thing* that landed on my shoulder, as God would have it, stayed there as if it were glued to me. I gingerly took it off, thankfully we wore gloves when we worked, and dumped it into my trash basket on wheels. When I went in for the coffee break I mentioned to the guys what had happened.

"Oh, man," said Alston, "she got you." He then laughed.

"Yeah," laughed Willie, "we forgot to tell you that over there that lady likes to hit you with her stuff."

"Stuff? What are you talking about?" I asked.

"Oh, boy, don't you know nothing?" asked Tony Martinez, who looked like a Greek god even though he wasn't Greek.

"So this sister throws her, you know, at me?" I asked. "You know I heard about this, you know."

"You know what? What's that you heard?" asked Tony.

"You know..." I trailed.

"Periods?" asked Tony.

I nodded. He shook his head in disbelief.

"You've got to stay away from the building," said Angelo who had overheard the conversation.

"She has pretty good aim," said Willie.

"Do the middle of the parking lot, at least twenty feet away from the building, then you should be safe," said Tony.

"Do you guys know who she is?" I asked.

"Yeah, Flow Washington. Flow is her nickname. She's a big nasty bitch who lost her boyfriend a couple of years ago and gained a hundred pounds," said Alston.

"Doesn't anybody complain about her?" I asked.

"Complain?" laughed Alston. "What for? What you think the cops care? There are murders everywhere in the City."

"It's unhygienic throwing that at someone isn't it?" asked Donnie DeAngelis another part-time worker, who lived in Staten Island and took the ferry into Manhattan every morning. I became pretty good friends with him during the years of our summer employment. He was my age but had skipped a couple of years of elementary school and was in Hunter College now.

"Hygienic? Man, what do you think, we should call the hygiene police?" asked Alston. "That won't sit well with the inmates."

"What inmates?" I asked. "What are you talking about?"

"Oh you got a lot to learn," said Big Willie.

"The boy doesn't know nothing," laughed Alston.

"I know I got hit with…you know; I know that."

"You see, the people around here, they are very excitable, because a lot of them have nothing to do all day and they are looking for something to get upset about," said Alston. "So you don't want to give them too much to get excited about. We call them the inmates because a lot of them came from prison or are going to go to prison in the future. Arresting one of them for what she did to you would be a little too much and might cause an increase in the excitement level. Do you understand that?"

"No," I said. "But I'll take it on faith."

"All right, coffee break's over," shouted Angelo, who was the strongest man I have ever met. He used to lift this giant anvil over his head. I couldn't even raise it an inch. Strangely, Angelo used to wear a jacket and tie on his way to and from work when he rode the subways and then change into his navy blue uniform in the workers' station.

"We got the whole summer to educate you," said Alston. "You got a lot to learn about the nature of things in the City and in the US of A."

"We'll teach you about life," said Big Willie, mounting the mechanical grass cutter and driving down the ramp.

I went back to the parking lot and stayed away from the building where Flow hunted the workers during certain times of the month.

I passed an uneventful week after that attack. I worked hard, Angelo complimented me on my "work ethic" and old Gallagher, an Irishman who drank a lot (sorry about him aptly fitting the stereotype but it was what it was) took me aside and explained I should tone down that work ethic a little because I was making everyone look bad. Donnie De (our nickname for Donnie DeAngelis) also had a good work ethic and Gallagher told him to tone it down too.

"You never want to make anyone look bad," said Gallagher. "We all try to work about the same, you got that lad?"

"I think so," I said.

The guy with no work ethic at all was Bobby Blaine, another summer worker who had only three teeth left in his mouth at the advanced age of 19. Bobby was so white he looked like an albino but he had sunken black eyeballs. He did have a somewhat pink coloration too. He never went out in the sun – even though our job was mostly outdoors. He just stayed in the shade or hid somewhere until his assignment time was over and he could rush back into the workers' station. Bobby did almost no work and would look for places where he could guzzle undisturbed whatever booze he had brought that day. Although both Gallagher and Blaine drank all day long, neither was stumbling drunk. I guess they spaced out their drinks in such a way that they stayed comfortably blitzed but were still able to function. Gallagher, being a regular worker, actually did some work during the day; Blaine didn't.

Our lunch times were spent eating quickly and then playing stickball. The very first day we all went out to play stickball, which took place in a usually deserted playground, except at night when the drug addicts took it over. Part of the 8AM to 9AM shift was clearing out the needles and other garbage left in the playground by the druggies overnight. This job required hosing down the vomit, urine and feces left by the area's inmates.

Once a month, meaning three times a summer, Donnie De and I had to clean out the incinerators that burned the garbage. It took about three days to do all the buildings. In those days tenants could dump their garbage down their floor's garbage shoot and these huge incinerators burned everything to a crisp. The tenants were not allowed to throw aerosol cans down the shoots or paint or turpentine or anything that could explode and kill a worker such as myself. The tenants never obeyed that ruling, of course, and when we went down to clean out the incinerators you'd occasionally hear the pop of aerosol cans exploding – despite the fact that the incinerator had been cooling down.

The most horrible cleaning experience we had happened in the summer of my second year at the projects. I was putting in the long shovel we used to take out the ashes and I lifted something heavy.

"Crap, what's this?" I said.

"What's wrong?" asked Donnie De.

"I think I got a big rat or a cat or a brick or something," I said as I struggled to lift the shovel. Although what I picked up couldn't have weighted more than five or six pounds when it was at the end of a nine-foot pole it was awkward trying to lift it out.

Now I wished I hadn't lifted it out.

"Oh, no," said Donnie De, looking at the shovel's contents when I finally got it out of the incinerator. "Oh, God."

"What?" I asked.

"Look," he said.

I looked.

"Oh, man," I said.

We went to the service phone in the basement and called Angelo. "Angelo," I said. "We found a dead baby in the incinerator. It's badly burned but it's a baby though. I think it was thrown in when the incinerator was cooling down."

The police came with their body bags and took the baby. They asked Donnie De and me some questions and left.

At lunch, before our daily stickball game, I was still a little shook. Who would throw a baby down the shoot into the incinerator?

"Get over it," said Alston. "It happens sometimes. It might have been born dead or the mother is a druggie and doesn't want to spend money on a baby or it's some girl who hid the pregnancy. The quickest way to get rid of the problem is to dump it down the shoot into the incinerator. If they had dumped the baby just a few days ago you'd have lifted the bones and probably wouldn't even have noticed them."

"Won't the police find the mother?" I asked.

"She'll go to prison for murder," said Donnie De.

"I'm guessing that corpse gets planted in potter's field and the police don't do nothing," said Alston.

"The police ain't going to care," said Big Willie.

"Get off it. You guys are nuts, murder is murder," I said.

"You got a lot of learning to do," said Alston.

"How come Donnie De and I are always doing the learning?" I asked.

"Because you don't know anything about the real world, that's why," said Alston.

The dead baby was a topic of conversation for a few days. Whenever Donnie De and I saw a girl coming out of the building where the baby had been we'd ask each other, "Do you think that's her?"

The baby issue was laid aside as the July 4th weekend approached. Gallagher was in charge of making a giant flowerbed in the center of the quad, which could be seen from all the windows facing that direction. The City had evidently given special money "to pretty up the place," according to Gallagher. I was his assistant.

It took us a good week to complete the job and we actually worked whole days doing it. Gallagher took special pride in our accomplishment and we all went up to the roof of one of the 17-story buildings to have a look at the design we created.

"Hey, Gallagher, you are some fine gardener," said Alston.

"That is beautiful," said Tony.

"I'll drink to that," said Bobby Blaine.

Big Willie did not make the trip up to the roof because he didn't like being on his feet too long and he also didn't like the stench in some of the elevators because some of the tenants used them as toilets. "These people don't have no manners," he would say. "You should go in a toilet not in an elevator." Although the elevators were cleaned every morning by the indoor maintenance staff a lot of crap (literally) could happen in the 24 hours after that.

I just held my nose when the doors opened. If the elevator were dirty I just tried to make it to the top without breathing. If it were clean I breathed. These were New York City housing project survival skills. Many of the normal tenants, people stuck living in these buildings, just took the stairs if they could make it to their floors without dying from exhaustion.

Big Willie drove to the middle of the quad and waved at us – giving what looked like a thumbs up approval of Gallagher's Garden, as it became known. Many of the residents, particularly the old ones (today called *senior citizens* – which I am fast becoming) were gracious and told us how much they appreciated the garden. Needless to say, Gallagher was ecstatic.

A week after the 4th of July holiday I was coming into work on a Monday and passing Gallagher's Garden. It looked really messed up – like someone had thrashed around in it, destroying most of the plants that we had carefully planted. I walked across the broad lawn to take a look at the damage. Inside the middle of the garden rested a dead body, of a skeletal woman whose skin looked like wrinkled tanned leather, obviously dead of an overdose, since the needle was lying right next to her. She was really stiff so she probably died a couple of days ago. She must have gone into Gallagher's Garden to do her drugs, overdosed, thrashed around, and died. Didn't people see her from their windows? How come no one called the police? How come no weekend worker called the police?

"They don't care that someone died first of all," said Alston. "And they don't trust the police."

So I called the police; they and the emergency medical team tramped through Gallagher's Garden with the body bag and stretcher, took the dead woman out and away. The garden was a mess and it took Gallagher and me another couple of weeks to straighten it all out – since we had to ask the City for more flowers and money. Luckily they had it and we got it but we got it piecemeal, which made fixing the garden take longer than making the garden in the first place. Unfortunately, in future years the City stopped funding this particular "prettying-up" and the garden died, not to be replaced. When I left the housing project after my last summer, Gallagher's Garden had become nothing but weeds.

I learned a little about sex in my very first year working at Smith Houses – just before becoming a senior in high school. I learned that women liked sex too. Tony taught me by explaining his experiences with the ladies – which were many, the experiences *and* the ladies. In fact, Tony had women stopping by to make appointments with him for sexual relations. As I said, Tony looked like a Greek god and the women went bananas over him.

The scariest few days I ever spent at the housing project occurred in my third summer. Some nut threw coke bottles from what turned out to be the 17th floor but only at the white workers as they came to the workers' station during breaks or lunch. The first time it happened, I was coming up the ramp with my cart and something exploded behind me. I turned around and I saw green shards of glass – some of which looked like sand.

I went into the workers' station. Then Alston came in. I told him I thought someone had thrown a bottle down at me. No one had thrown anything at him. Then Donnie De came in – white as a ghost.

"Someone threw a coke bottle at me," he said.

Then Bobby Blaine came in – but he was always white as a ghost. "Fucking coke bottle was thrown at me. I could feel the fucking wind as it passed my head."

For several days this maniac kept hurling coke bottles at us. But he wasn't stupid. If we were looking up, no coke bottle came down. Then he had to change his tactics as we always looked up when we came to the workers' station. He went to other buildings and hurled the bottles at us when we were pretty far from the workers' station.

"What the hell's the matter with this guy?" asked Donnie De.

"He doesn't like us," said Alston.

"The cops better catch him," I said.

"You see many cops staking out the place?" asked Alston.

"Every once in awhile," I said, and then I gave a second thought to the topic. "Actually not too much. It's the regular Housing Authority cop that walks the beat. I haven't seen any others."

"Why does this guy want to kill us?" I asked.

"Why isn't this guy working a job instead of trying to hit us with bottles?" asked Donnie De.

"I hope he falls off the fucking roof," said Bobby Blaine.

"He has nothing else to do," said Alston.

"I'll bet he's some dopey dropout," said Donnie De.

"That could be," said Alston.

"And what about that guy last year who was pissing out his window at me?" I said

"That fuck hit me in the head with his piss," said Bobby Blaine.

"Then a few weeks ago I had a bag of shit land on my shoulder and when this guy was caught because I saw what apartment he was in he said he did it to teach me a lesson. What lesson was that? What was I supposed to learn?" I asked.

"Yeah, what lesson was that?" chimed in a boozy Bobbie Blaine.

"Look," said Alston, "I am not saying that the shit guy and this coke bottle guy aren't idiots but they do what they do because they are bored. They hate you because you work and have a life. That's all."

The police caught the coke bottle thrower several days later and arrested him in the act of trying to heave one off the roof. The cops had been smart and made it seem that they weren't watching for this creep but they were. They had some police on the rooftops with binoculars and cameras and they saw him pick up a bottle and actually took a picture of him. He didn't explain why he was throwing those coke bottles at us – but Alston was probably right. At least he had an explanation, anyway.

Donnie De and I became the permanent cobble-stoners in our last summer at the projects. Donnie De was a perfectionist, I was his assistant, and we laid cobblestones all summer. It was tedious work but like Gallagher's Garden when a job was completed you had something to show for it. Unlike Gallagher's Garden once those cobblestones were cemented in it would take a supreme effort to dislodge them, whereas one thrashing, dying druggie had destroyed Gallagher's Garden.

One day while on my knees putting in the layer of sand for the cobblestones, I heard the "pop, pop, pop" of firecrackers. I looked up and this guy with a Bible in his hands ran like a maniac down the sidewalk with another guy shooting at him. I could actually read the words "Holy Bible" on the book as the guy ran past me. The next "pop, pop, pop" hit the runner in the back and also in the back of the head. He went down with a thud, and scrapped a short distance along the sidewalk as his running momentum continued even after he died, with the blood from his head slowly moving onto the sidewalk, then onto the cobblestones we had laid yesterday which ran alongside the sidewalk.

The shooter ran in the opposite direction but we heard that he actually ran right into the Housing Authority cop who walked the project as his beat – and I mean smack into him so that both fell to the ground. It was some drug thing between these two guys. The runner kept his drugs in the Bible; the shooter wanted the Bible but panicked after he blew away his prey.

One of the saddest and most sickening moments happened while I swept in front of one of the buildings at mid-afternoon, just after lunch, and a bunch of kids suddenly looked up and a few screamed. I turned around just in time to see a little kid hit the pavement and splatter. He had fallen from the 14th floor. Window guards were not mandatory in those days and this child's parents never bothered to protect their windows from such accidents. Seeing a kid hit the pavement became a strong memory – I used to have nightmares about it.

A curious event occurred during each of these summers – there was a little girl with dark hair who would say hello to me every once in a while. She would say hello as if she knew me. I was once working with Donnie De clearing out some dumpsters of residual garbage and the young girl came over and said, "Hi."

I said, "Hi," back to her.

Donnie De looked up. "Who are you talking to?" he asked.

"Some little girl I've seen occasionally around. She always says hi to me."

Donnie De looked where I pointed. "There's nobody there," he said. I looked over. "She must have walked away," I said. No one else saw this little girl as she had an uncanny knack of disappearing when I tried to point her out.

I never found out who she was – at that point. I once asked her what her name was but she just smiled. I once asked why she said "hi," as if she knew me, and she said something very odd, "Oh, I don't know you yet."

I titled this part "The New York Experience" because working that job in the projects opened my eyes to a lifestyle I had never encountered before. When I hit the projects I was not emotionally prepared to have people throw stuff at me, or to meet up with people who hated me and threw bottles at me trying to kill me, or bags of feces, or have some idiot piss out the window trying to hit me or have Flow take aim at me. I had never seen a drug addict before. I had never heard of welfare even.

Obviously most of the people I met in the projects were just regular people. But still by way of analogy, if you were a teacher and had a class of 30 kids and a few were really nasty, you would be more aware of the nasties than of the good kids because the nasties impinged more on your classroom life.

As to the New York experience as a whole, I am a New Yorker through and through – born in Brooklyn Hospital (which doesn't exist any more) in Bay Ridge, a section of Brooklyn where I lived for the first 22 years of my life, where I gained my easily distinguishable New *Yawk* accent, which makes you sound stupid even if you have a high IQ. I went to college in New York State, three different New York colleges for graduate degrees, and I have lived in various parts of Long Island, New York from 22 years of age until this moment writing this sentence.

I loved my upbringing in Brooklyn because it allowed me to go into the City whenever I wanted. When you live in one of the boroughs of New York City (Manhattan, Brooklyn, Queens, the Bronx and Staten Island) when you say "the City" you are referring to Manhattan. The other boroughs you refer to by their regular names but Manhattan you just call "the City."

Where I grew up in Brooklyn I could see the skyline of Manhattan, a truly impressive sight that I never got tired of or used to. I saw the World Trade Center being built (I also saw it being destroyed from a viewpoint not far from where I live now on Long Island); I also saw the Verazano Bridge being built – its entrance ramp going right through the area that used to belong to my Nana Rose's house on 92nd Street. The government used Eminent Domain to take her house from her to build that awesome bridge.

I had a great childhood – loving parents, a few good friends, and a great neighborhood to enjoy. As a teenager I used to go into the City and enjoy museums and plays (you could see a Broadway play for $3 to $8) and first-run movies. In those days the big-budget movies such as *West Side Story* only opened at one theatre in the City, so if you wanted to see it without having to wait months for it to come to your neighborhood theater, you took the train into the City. These movies were reserved seat engagements in luscious theaters. The popcorn was good in these theaters too, because they used real butter. Maybe that's why my cholesterol is so high today.

One of my favorite things to do was take the train to the Brooklyn Bridge exit in Brooklyn, then walk across the bridge, looking at a most amazing sight – the entire skyline of the City. Once in the City I would head uptown to the shows or the museums or Madison Square Garden, where I attended New York Knicks games. The City was a walker's paradise in the 1960s.

In 1961 I attended 23 Yankee home games – the season Roger Maris hit 61 home runs and Mickey Mantle hit 54 home runs. I remember Ebbets Field where the Brooklyn Dodgers played and where I caught a ball hit by Gil Hodges on Gil Hodges night. As a really little kid, my father introduced me to Joe DiMaggio when he took me to a game at Yankee Stadium. I remember what my father said to me when he introduced me, "Frankie, you are shaking the hand of the greatest baseball player who ever lived." I just remember DiMaggio looking down at me, shaking my little hand, and nodding. In DiMaggio's 13 seasons with the Yankees, the team went to the World Series 10 times and won nine of them. Today, as I wrote in another chapter, I know the DiMaggio of craps, the Captain.

I've had a wonderful life and it continues to this day.

- Part Ten -
Adventures of Today

I Don't Wear an Earring

Here's a letter I received from a television viewer: "I was watching *Hit the Jackpot* on the Discovery channel and I noticed that you were wearing an earring. I thought you were a conservative kind of fellow. That doesn't go with earrings."

I have nothing against men or women who wear earrings but I do not now, nor have I ever worn an earring. What this viewer actually saw on this television show was a bead of sweat hanging off my ear. That's right, on a national television show, on a channel that seems well financed, that shiny thing hanging off my ear was my own sweat.

You see that show, about slot machines and slot jackpots, was not filmed in the airy precincts of a casino. Indeed, not. It was filmed in the basement of the producer's home – the low-ceilinged basement. Yes, the show looks really good on television and I did a commendable job (in my unbiased opinion) of appearing to be comfortable and relaxed.

But here's the inside story. The producer needed to finish this project quickly. Since she lives in New York and I live in New York, it seemed stupid to fly out to Vegas to film my segment, which was one-half hour of the hour-long show. She decided to film at her house, which was in a ritzy part of upstate New York.

I arrived on time and the producer and I talked a little bit about what I would talk about on the television show. She had been impressed with my book *Break the One-Armed Bandits!* and wanted to focus on many of the ideas that I wrote about.

That was fine with me. That would give my book some good publicity.

"Where are we filming?" I asked, noticing that it was just she and I in the house.

"Downstairs, the basement, we've decorated it to look like a casino backdrop," she said.

Her dog ambled over, a smelly thing, a hairball with spittle, holding a disgustingly ratty yellowish tennis ball in his wet mouth.

"That's Dracula," said the producer. "He's friendly."

Dracula rubbed up against my leg, leaving some shiny spit on my suit pants.

We went downstairs to the basement. A cameraman and a sound technician were down there already, putting the finishing touches on the "set."

"We're just about ready," said the cameraman.

The producer made the introductions.

"Okay," said the soundman. "We're ready."

The lights came on. Now with about a seven-foot ceiling, the basement heated up to frying proportions in about a third of a second, maybe even less.

"Are you hot?" asked the producer.

"Yes," I said.

"Here's some water," she said. "I have a wet towel and we'll wipe you off when we see you sweating."

I couldn't tell her that my underarms were already sweating, as were other lower parts of me.

"Now, Frank, just to get a sound test, state your name, spell it, and state the name of the book we're basing this interview on," she said.

"My name is Frank Scoblete, F-R-A-N-K-S-C-O...."

From upstairs came the loudest howling I ever heard, "Roooffawwwwyeooooow! Roooffawwwwyeooooow!"

"...B-L-E-T-E..."

"Roooffawwwwyeooooow! Roooffawwwwyeooooow!"

"Hold up," said the producer, "I was afraid this would happen. Dracula doesn't like to be alone. We'll have to bring him down here. You don't have any problem with the dog being here do you, Frank?"

"No," I said.

"Roooffawwwwyeoooow! Roooffawwwwyeoooow!"

"I'm coming Dracula!" yelled the producer.

She zipped up the stairs. I heard her open the door and I heard the dog scramble down the stairs, and then he appeared, the nauseatingly drool-soaked tennis ball still in his mouth. I wondered if he was able to do that terrible howling with that putrid thing in his mouth?

Dracula ran around the basement like a madman … mad dog, actually.

"He has to calm down; he gets so excited," said the producer.

Finally Dracula quieted.

"Okay, Frank, give us the title of the book," said the producer.

"The title of the book…"

I noticed Dracula walking right towards me into the hot lights.

"Sorry, the title of the book is…"

Dracula shoved his head into my crotch.

"Owwww!" I yelled.

Dracula dug in even deeper.

The producer got up and dragged him back to her chair.

"He likes you," she said.

The basement was now a thousand degrees.

"Frank's head is sweating a little. Where's the towel?" said the cameraman.

We all looked around. Dracula's tennis ball was on the floor by the producer's chair and Dracula was a little ways from it with the towel secured in his wet mouth.

"Dracula, we need that towel," said the producer.

It looked to me like Dracula made the towel go into his wet mouth another few inches. The producer grabbed the towel and Dracula started shaking his head like a mad dog again.

"I'm fine," I said, "I don't need the towel." Inside my suit I was soaking wet. The dog still shook his head like a maniac with the towel in his mouth.

"I'm fine," I repeated.

The producer stopped grabbing the towel and Dracula stopped shaking his head. When Dracula saw that we were not interested in the towel anymore, he dropped it on the basement floor and sauntered over to get his tennis ball.

"Okay, Frank, I'll ask you the questions. You kind of repeat the questions and then answer them," said the producer. "I'm sure you've done this a lot."

"Yes, no problem, I'm ready," I said and thought, *Let's do this before I melt away!*

The producer asked me a question and I rephrased the question and answered it. I could see that Dracula was eyeing me.

"Frank, in your book *Beat the One-Armed Bandits*," said the producer.

"It's *Break* the One-Armed Bandits," I said.

Dracula moved towards me.

"What?" asked the producer, distracted by Dracula.

"I…uh!" and the dog dug his head, with gooey tennis ball in his dripping mouth, into my crotch again.

There was absolute silence in the basement.

"You know," said the producer, "He might just stay quiet if we let him stay there. He's under the camera's range."

"Let him stay," said the cameraman, "Or we'll never finish this interview."

"Do you mind, Frank?"

Now, my gentle readers please hear me out and understand. It is important for writers to be on television. Book sales usually soar after a television appearance, especially when they print the title of your book under you as you are answering questions; your publishers and editors are happy to see one of "theirs" on the tube which allows you to ask for more money for your next book; it makes you appear important. You understand all this, I hope?

Because I said, "Yes" to the producer, "I don't mind"

(*The dog's head shoved into my you know what.*)

"I can do this interview"

(*Even if this smelly beast neuters me.*)

"There's no problem."

(*Although the basement is hotter than hell itself.*)

And I did the interview with Dracula digging into me as if he were attempting to reach China.

But I looked okay when they broadcast the show, even with my "earring," although the book sales for *Break the One-Armed Bandits!* did not go up because the book was titled *Beat the Bandits!* when it appeared on screen under my sweaty head.

You can't win them all.

But one thing I know for sure – Dracula had a great time during that television interview.

Eat? Me?

By the time you read this I will be skinny. Okay, maybe not skinny as in "My God! Frank Scoblete is so skinny now!"

but more like, "You dropped a lot of weight and you look good."

You see I have a bone to pick with casino gambling – and it's not a bone with juicy steak on it or fried chicken on it, or pork with delicious barbeque dressing dripping all over it, or…uh, excuse me, I've been dieting and I am thinking about food a lot.

My bone has to do with the fact that when I started my casino eating career, I mean, sorry, my casino *gambling* career, over 20 years ago, I was 5'7" tall and weighed a mere 145 pounds. Yes, having just come from my life in the theatre, as a leading man who always got the girl, I could also run 10 mile races at 6 minutes a mile, I could do 100 pushups and 100 pull ups and 1,000 sit ups, I could now see that my wife, the beautiful AP is eating this delicious apple crumble that she makes….Ohhhh! There I go again.

I am not good on a diet. These past 24 hours have been hell on my nerves. And by my calculation I have another 4,800 hours to go on this darned thing. If my local pizzeria took so long to deliver their incredible scrumptious pepperoni pizza just dripping with grease and cheese and….

Sorry. I am now 5'6.5" tall and I weigh in at 215. I am a huge Chunky candy bar. Yes, I have gained an unsightly 70 pounds and somehow lost half an inch in height as my weight drags me to the ground. When I went to my doctor, a nice attractive woman of about 50 years old, skinny, a yoga teacher too, and really no casino is offering her free booze, free food, free shows, and…uh, sorry, she told me that right now all my blood work is okay and my prostate is "perfect" (that's her quote! My quote was, "Can you stop *that* now!")

"Get control of your weight. I want to see you lose forty pounds in the next year," she said.

That is so easy for a 50-year old, skinny woman to say. If I told her to lose 40 pounds, she would disappear and cease to exist. But I don't tell her to do that. I am too nice a guy.

Okay, now some of you are guffawing, "Yo, Scoblete goes to a woman doctor, ha! ha!"

Okay, fella, who is smarter, you or me? I say me, and you know why? Because when I hit 50 years old I did have a male doctor. He was six feet four inches tall and he said to me, "It's time for you to have *that* exam," and *that* exam is the one mentioned above, where I am "perfect" mind you, and he held up his hand with the latex glove on it and his hand looked just like those GIANT HANDS they sell at sporting events with the one finger pointing and I knew an absolute truth then – THAT THING is not going into me.

So I switched to a woman doctor who is maybe five feet tall and has very small, delicate, feminine fingers. I figure with so little meat on those bones, even as she ages, the finger she uses for *that* exam, will always be thin.

Bones, yes, I forgot, my bone to pick with the casinos. The casinos thought they could get me to forget that, but I remembered. I am like a lion that remembers where his food is buried. Do lions remember that? Or maybe it is jackals that remember their food stores?

The casinos made me fat because they *forced* me to eat all those comped buffets, all those comped gourmet meals, and drink all those comped drinks and they *forced* me to play those table games for endless hours instead of going to the gym where the treadmill awaited to torture me with the loss of about 100 calories a mile. My word! Only one hundred crummy calories a mile! You eat a brownie and there are maybe three or four hundred calories in it. You have to run three or four miles just to get rid of the damn brownie. And what if you like to put some vanilla ice cream on the brownie? That's another three or four hundred calories. Then I love nuts when I have ice cream and those are loaded with calories. I also prefer brownies that have nuts in them because I like the crunchiness of them.

So let's see, just for a stinking brownie I have to run maybe a dozen miles. The main meal at a buffet is composed of many important elements – like seven or eight different meals. How can you go to a buffet that is comped, that is totally free and not eat everything in sight?

You can't. It's against God, and nature, and a modern-day appetite.

So you have to figure that I would have to run for several days without sleep just to work off my lunch. So, okay, when would I play the casino games that got me the buffet comp in the first place? I wouldn't. Without playing the games I would not get the comps! You see the dilemma I am in? I'd be in the damn gym all the time working off brownies and ice cream and steak and chicken and pork and rice of different varieties and Chinese food, and pizza and the occasional salad my wife forced me to eat so it looks as if I had a balanced meal.

Forget about it, working out for 72 straight hours is not fun and I refuse to do that. Why would I fly to Vegas or drive to Atlantic City to just work out endlessly in the gyms? You'd have to be nuts to do that – like a pecan nut, or a walnut or a peanut slathered with fudge.

I *want* those comps! I mean I *deserve* those comps, after all, for my play. I am only getting what I deserve.

Also, come on let's be *honest* here, those people who do nothing but work out in the gyms all the time, there is something seriously wrong with their buff selves. Their minds are gone. All they do is look in the mirrors to see how good they look. I never look in the mirror, not since I transcended the 180-pound mark a few years back. I am not vain!

What the heck am I talking about here? You see how confused I am? The casinos have done this to me. Wanting to force me to work out for days straight in the gyms without eating anything. How crazy are those casino people? They should ban the gyms from the casino hotels. There should be a law. Yes, I want a new law that no casino properties are allowed to have gyms because gyms are inhuman!

And they should loosen their comps even more so that we can eat for 24-hours straight if we want to.

That's my bone to pick with the casinos! There I said it.

I could use a brownie.

- Part Eleven -
Epilogue

I've had some of the greatest adventures – my teaching career, producing, acting and directing; my Weird World astral experiences; the joy of beating the casinos at their own games; knowing the Captain and the Arm; enjoying the friendship of wonderful people such as my advantage-play buddies Dominator (whose editorial advice on this book was excellent), Howard "Rock 'n Roller," Jerry "Stickman," Mr. Finesse, and my best man Satch (an original member of the Captain's crew) and his wife Annette (A.P.'s matron of honor), also best-selling authors Bill Burton, Henry Tamburin, Jean Scott, John Robison, John Grochowski, John Brokopp, Don Catlin, Fred Renzey and Walter Thomason, along with blackjack brain Dan Pronovost, among others.

I had good times with my teaching friends such as Barry Kissane, Cathy Poe, Tony Sparandara, Larry O'Neill, Lenore Israel, Gabe Uhlar, Jim Duffy (who cast me in my first play for an amateur group – I played Dr. Einstein in *Arsenic and Old Lace*), Louis Valente, Louis Rotondo and, of course, Greg Monahan, my department chairman, and Edwin Krawitz, my second principal who put up with me and helped me get tenure – and for your information, I never punched him.

I did have friends on the "outside," apart from teaching and advantage-play in the casinos – Lucy and George, Dom DeAngelis, Alston Jackson, Big Willie Wesley, Joe Dunne, Pete Casales, and Bob Joe. And to the members of the greatest basketball team in the history of the universe, Our Lady of Angels which was 55-0 and New York City Champions, the team I wrote about in my book *The Craps Underground* – wherever you guys are, I will never forget you – Patrick Heelan, Steven Gardell, Douglas Bernhardt, Billy Bell, Ken Peterson, Tammie Cronin, Louie Dotrina, and James Gallagher. And to the best teachers I ever had in my life: Sister Patricia Michael, Brother Barnabus and Brother Jonathan.

I now enjoy the friendship, company and the excellence of performance of my Golden Touch Craps instructors: Daryl "No Field Five," Billy "the Kid," "Street Dog," Arman "Pit Boss," Jake from Pitt, Randy "Tenor," Nick "T-Lefty," "Randman," Doc Holliday, Fred "Chip," and "Missouri Rick." And to the Atlantic City Boardwalk Rollers who have helped out tremendously when I go to the Queen of Resorts: Marilyn "the Goddess," Charlie "Sandtrap," and John "Skinny."

I've said this before and I will say it again – I had the best parents in the world, a great sister Susan and brother-in-law Tony, a wonderful niece Melanie, a great nephew Jason. I have great parents-in-law in Don and Peg.

And I count my in-laws Charlie and Donna among my friends as well.

I hope you enjoyed this book. Without readers there would be few writers. I have had many more adventures but I didn't want to make this book as large as New York's phone book.

I really don't know what it has been all about. If you have a theory, you can write to me at: _contactus@goldentouchcraps.com_.

For more about Frank Scoblete, go to:
www.GoldenTouchCraps.com/frankbio.shtml